BCG

Carl Stern

George Stalk Jr.

THE BOSTON CONSULTING GROUP

PERSPECTIVES ON STRATEGY

FROM
THE BOSTON CONSULTING GROUP

PERSPECTIVES ON STRATEGY

FROM
THE BOSTON CONSULTING GROUP

EDITED BY
CARL W. STERN AND
GEORGE STALK, JR.

John Wiley & Sons, Inc.

NEW YORK • CHICHESTER • WEINHEIM • BRISBANE • SINGAPORE • TORONTO

This book is printed on acid-free paper. ∞

Copyright © 1998 by The Boston Consulting Group, Inc. All rights reserved.

Published by John Wiley & Sons, Inc.
Published simultaneously in Canada.

This publication is designed to provide accurate and authoritative information in regard to the subject matter covered. It is sold with the understanding that the publisher is not engaged in rendering professional services. If professional advice or other expert assistance is required, the services of a competent professional person should be sought.

Library of Congress Cataloging-in-Publication Data:
Perspectives on Strategy from the Boston Consulting Group
/ edited by Carl W. Stern and George Stalk, Jr.
      p.   cm.
    Includes index.
    ISBN 0-471-24833-9 (cloth : alk. paper)
    1. Strategic planning. 2. Competition. 3. Boston Consulting
Group. I. Stern, Carl W. II. Stalk, George, 1951–
III. Boston Consulting Group.
HD30.28.P373 1998   97-43063
658.4'012—dc21   CIP

Printed in the United States of America.

10 9 8 7 6 5 4 3 2 1

Contents

Foreword

Looking back, it's hard to imagine that a few short essays could have had so much impact on business thinking. Addressed to the chief executives of large enterprises, *Perspectives* developed a devoted following, even circulating in bootleg copies in some companies. *Perspectives* challenged executives to think about their businesses strategically rather than simply operationally. They combined economic insight with an understanding of how management decisions can be distorted by organizational compromise. Their radically simple logic was unsettling. *Perspectives* helped many people understand for the first time that:

- Being number one or number two in a business is a *necessity*.

- The prevailing management practices in diversified companies had to be scrapped and replaced with real *portfolio* management.

- Japan's competitive strength came from *strategic intent* as much as from macroeconomics or culture.

- Beating the *competition* is more important than beating the last quarter.

- *Cash flow* is pivotal in determining a business's real rate of return.

- Regulation can have a *devastating* effect on market mechanisms.

Few if any of these insights were wholly original. They owed much to a wide assortment of executives, economists, thinkers, and academics in many fields, as well as BCG's learning from work on real problems for farsighted corporations. But these notions had seldom been crafted into such coherent prescriptions, or argued as provocatively.

And they were prescient. Most of the forces driving the evolution of business strategy in the last several decades can be found in these essays: technology's declining costs and increasing power, the rise of Japan and then Asia in manufacturing, the restructuring of American industry to enhance shareholder value, and organizational learning and knowledge management, to name only a few.

In creating these *Perspectives,* Bruce Henderson, BCG's founder, invented a demanding form. He said each took six to ten drafts, with relentless self-editing. The results forced the reader to think and rewarded repeated reading.

Although most *Perspectives* credited one or two authors, these writers were in fact the tip of a much larger iceberg: unconstrained give and take among members of the firm and its clients. In the early 1960s, when BCG was small, the entire firm gathered every Monday morning in the library (with its still empty shelves) to debate a current issue. Even the newest associate might be called on to defend a point of view. The goal was clear: to penetrate beneath the surface to the real determinants of competitive success. This drive to transcend the conventional carried over to our work for clients. Best practice is fine, but there is always something better.

The best ideas have many parents, and are but the forerunners of what's to come. In this spirit, we publish this selection of *Perspectives* as both a memorial to Bruce Henderson and a tribute to the clients, employees, and friends, past and present, of The Boston Consulting Group.

John S. Clarkeson
President and Chief Executive Officer, 1985–1997

Preface

Bruce Henderson and Perspectives

"Few people have had as much impact on international business in the second half of the twentieth century as the founder of The Boston Consulting Group" is how the *Financial Times* characterized the legacy of Bruce Henderson just after his death on July 20, 1992. Bruce would have been pleased with the epitaph: Impact was what Bruce's life was all about.

From his earliest days, Bruce was obsessed with making a difference, with leaving something behind. An engineer by training, he never tired of quoting Archimedes to aspiring staff: "Give me a lever and a place to stand, and I'll move the world."

Bruce was at once a relentless contrarian and a passionate proselytizer, a combination that can only be explained by his unique background. Born on a Tennessee farm on April 30, 1915, he began his business life early and auspiciously, as a Bible salesman for his father's publishing company. He earned his undergraduate engineering degree from Vanderbilt University. He attended Harvard Business School, but opted to leave in 1941—ninety days before graduation—to join Westinghouse Corporation, where he became one of the youngest vice presidents in the company's history. In 1953, President Eisenhower chose him to serve on a five-member team charged with evaluating the foreign aid program to Germany under the Marshall Plan. In 1959, Bruce left Westinghouse to head Arthur D. Little's management services unit, and in 1963 he accepted the improbable challenge from the CEO of the Boston Safe Deposit and Trust Company to start a consulting arm of the bank. This was to become The Boston Consulting Group.

Bruce—and The Boston Consulting Group under his leadership—aspired to nothing less than changing the way the business world thought about competition. The vehicle was strategy. Although some of the fundamental precepts had been well developed and well accepted in the military sphere, they were astonishingly absent from business thinking when Bruce founded BCG in 1963. Developing the discipline of business strategy secured a place of honor for Bruce in the business pantheon and propelled BCG from a one-man operation to the 3,000-professional, worldwide organization it is today.

Bruce was an intense, curious, argumentative man with a voracious appetite for experience and ideas. He had an astonishing ability to borrow from a wide range of disciplines, synthesize and integrate disparate concepts, and then explore their implications for business. He drew enormous energy and excitement from pushing ideas to their logical limits. He was fond of quoting Jay Forrester: "While most people understand first-order effects, few deal well with second- and third-order effects. Unfortunately, virtually everything interesting in business lies in fourth-order effects and beyond."

His medium of choice was *Perspectives:* concise pieces designed to stimulate senior management thinking on a range of business issues. Bruce liked to refer to them as "a punch between the eyes." In *Henderson on Corporate Strategy* (HarperBusiness, 1984), he described their stylistic intent as follows:

> Statements that senior business managers would find believable are not supported. Only provocative material is argued. The subject matter is chosen to be deliberately provocative, significant in implication, and relevant to the policy decisions of corporate competition.

To date, over 400 *Perspectives* have been published. They have been translated into at least six languages and circulated to senior executives around the globe.

This book comprises 75 *Perspectives* written by various members of The Boston Consulting Group between 1968 and 1997. It traces the evolution of BCG's thinking on strategy and documents the many significant contributions BCG has made to the field. But more than just a historical record, this collection represents a reference for business concepts that stand on their own. It demonstrates how timeless truly insightful ideas are. A fitting tribute, we hope, to the memory of Bruce Henderson—a great thinker and an inspirational leader.

Carl W. Stern
George Stalk, Jr.

Acknowledgments

Our deepest debt is to the many clients of The Boston Consulting Group. Virtually every idea expressed in these pages had its genesis in client work. We are gratified that so many outstanding executives have found it fruitful to work through some of their toughest management issues with us, and we are honored by the abiding trust that these enduring relationships represent.

This book is a tribute to Bruce D. Henderson, founder of The Boston Consulting Group, and to all BCG authors, past and present. BCG has a highly self-critical culture. The healthy debate that greets and hones new ideas can occur only if a few intrepid individuals are willing to hang themselves out a bit, to hold their ideas—and inevitably themselves—up for scrutiny. We salute their intellectual curiosity and their courage.

It is also a tribute to the many generations of BCG staff and alumni. Behind every author is an engaged group of professionals who helped develop and burnish the ideas-in-process in the best Hendersonian tradition.

A few of our colleagues deserve specific acknowledgment. Bolko von Oetinger, David Hall, and Linda Bilmes played central roles in motivating and initiating this project. Susan Crowe and Ted Buswick provided invaluable writing and editorial support. John Clarkeson offered unstinting encouragement and backing. We also thank Renana Meyers at John Wiley for superbly guiding us through the editorial process, and Nancy Macmillan and Christine Furry for copyediting excellence.

Finally, we thank our families—for their love and for their forbearance.

Carl W. Stern
George Stalk, Jr

PART ONE

The Nature of Business Strategy

WHAT IS STRATEGY? Today, we must concede, it is probably the business world's most used and abused word. We have strategies for everything: from advertising to logistics to human resources to custodian engineering. This is a shame, for the concept of strategy is both profound and useful.

Bruce Henderson captured it classically: "All competitors who persist over time must maintain a unique advantage by differentiation over all others. Managing that differentiation is the essence of long-term business strategy."

Bruce never stopped searching for a grand, unified theory of strategy. His quest took him far afield—ultimately into the realm of modern biology and evolution. *Strategic and Natural Competition*, one of Bruce's last *Perspectives*, represents the culmination of his thinking on the nature of strategy.

STRATEGIC AND NATURAL COMPETITION

BRUCE D. HENDERSON, 1980

Strategic competition leads to time compression. Competitive shifts as a result of strategy can take place in a few short years. The same evolution by natural competition might require generations.

Strategic competition is a relatively new phenomenon in business. It may well have the same impact upon business productivity that the industrial revolution had upon individual productivity.

The basic elements of strategic competition are:

- The ability to understand competitive interaction as a complete dynamic system that includes the interaction of competitors, customers, money, people, and resources.

- The ability to use this understanding to predict the consequences of a given intervention in that system and how that intervention will result in new patterns of stable dynamic equilibrium.

- The availability of uncommitted resources that can be dedicated to different uses and purposes in the present even though the dedication is permanent and the benefits will be deferred.

- The ability to predict the risk and return with sufficient accuracy and confidence to justify the commitment of such resources.

- The willingness to deliberately act to make the commitment.

This description of strategy sounds like the basic requirements for making any ordinary investment. It is that. But it is far more. Strategy is all-encompassing in its commitment. Strategy by definition involves the commitment and dedication of the whole firm. Failure of any competitor to react and then deploy and commit his own resources against the strategic competition of another competitor can result in a complete inversion of the competitive relationships and a major shift in the equilibrium between them. That is why strategic competition leads to time compression. Natural competition has none of these characteristics.

Natural competition is wildly expedient in its moment-to-moment interaction. However, it is inherently extremely conservative in its change in characteristic behavior. By contrast, strategic competition is deliberate, carefully considered, and tightly reasoned in its commitments, but the consequences may well be radical change in a relatively short time.

Natural competition is evolutionary.

Strategic competition is revolutionary.

Natural competition is really low-risk incremental trial and error. Small changes that seem to be beneficial are gradually adopted and maintained. Other small changes are tried and added. It is learning by trial and error without the need for either commitment or foresight. It is the adaptation now to the way that things are now. It is the basic pattern of evolution. It is Darwinian natural selection. It functions even if controlled by pure chance or pure expediency. For these very reasons it is inevitably very conservative, gradual, and produces nearly imperceptible change near term regardless of the ultimate consequences long term.

Strategic competition by its very commitments seeks to make a very large change in competitive relationships. Its revolutionary character is moderated only by two fundamental inhibitions. Strategic failure can be as sweeping in its consequences as strategic success. And characteristically an alert defense has a major competitive advantage over the attacker. Strategic success usually depends upon the culture, perceptions, attitudes, and characteristic behavior of competitors and their mutual awareness of each other.

This is why in geopolitics and in military strategy as well as in business strategy the pattern of competition contains long periods of natural competition punctuated by relatively sudden and major shifts in relationships as a result of strategy. It is the age-old pattern of war and peace even though competition continues during peace.

Currently, normal modern business behavior seems to fall between the extremes of these two modes. However, a shift toward strategic competition seems to be the secular trend. The successful use of strategic competition by the most aggressive direct competitor can make the same foresight and dedication of resources the prerequisite for survival of others. Eventually, the mastery of strategic competition will be a requirement for adapting to that kind of environment in which most of the change is the result of strategic commitments.

Natural competition should be respected. It is the process that produced the infinite and exquisite complexity, variety, and interaction of all the forms of life on planet Earth. This was accomplished by pure chance, with no plan, foresight, or objectives. The starting point was the equivalent of sterile chemical soup. However, it took millions of years of nearly infinitesimal changes and adaptations.

Natural competition must be completely understood. It is the foundation. It is the system and pattern of interaction upon which any form of strategic competition must build and modify. Understanding of natural competition is required in order to predict the effect on those relationships as the result of intervention in the feedback loops of that system.

Differences between competitors is the prerequisite for survival in natural competition. Those differences may not be obvious. But competitors who make their living in exactly the same way in the same place at the same time are highly unlikely to remain in a stable equilibrium. However, any differences may give one competitor or the other an advantage over all others in some part of the common competitive environment. The value of that difference becomes a measure of the survival prospects as well as the future prosperity of that competitor.

There is nearly an infinite number of combinations of competitive factors in an environment that has a large number of variables. It should not be surprising that the world is filled with a vast variety of competitors, all different, which seem to exist in a moving but stable equilibrium. The range of size, behavior, and characteristics is not accidental; it is inevitable. It is also stable even though ever changing in detail. Those differences are the a priori requirement for the survival of each and every one of them in their particular subsection of the environment. That is natural competition as it always has been.

Strategic competition is not new. The elements of it have been recognized and used in warfare since the human race became able to combine intelligence, imagination, accumulated resources, and deliberately coordinated behavior. The distilled wisdom of many centuries has been expressed in many maxims such as "concentrate strength against weakness."

But most military strategy has been focused on the battle itself or the war rather than on the equilibrium of the relationship that continued through both peace and war. Geopolitics is this larger perspective of the continued competition of this dynamic equilibrium over time. Yet there is still a very limited general theory about geopolitical dynamic equilibrium.

The general theory of business competition is almost certainly in its infancy. But the elements of a general theory that integrates all of the elements seem to be developing. The integration itself is the critical development.

The classic economic theories of business competition seem to be so simplistic and sterile that they are obstacles to progress and understanding rather than contributions. They seem to be based on views of competition as a static equilibrium in a static economy rather than a dynamic equilibrium. They are based on theoretical concepts of cost behavior that have never been observed in reality and that directly contradict observable and quantifiable evidence. They make assumptions about competitive behavior that are neither observable nor useful in predicting competitive behavior. The frame of reference of "perfect competition" is a theoretical concept that has never existed and probably could not exist. Unfortunately, these classical theories have been used to develop public policy that is equally unrealistic.

Development of a general theory of business competition will permit the prediction of the consequences of any kind of business competition. It can be the base of both strategic competition and constructive public policy. The general public would benefit on both counts. The development of a general theory of business competition will require the testing and revision of many interlocking hypotheses.

We would now hypothesize that:

- Effective competition will result in a range of sizes of competitors from very large to very small. This spectrum of sizes will be stable over time.

- Competitors who survive and prosper will have unique advantages over any and all other competitors in specific combinations of time, place, products, and customers.

- For any given competitor, there will be different competitors who will provide the constraints for almost every combination of relevant factors. Therefore the frontiers or boundaries of competitive parity will be constantly changing as any one of the competitors changes, adapts, grows, or redeploys.

- Perpetual conflict will exist along those frontiers where competitive ability is at parity.

- Very little conflict will exist where clear superiority is visible. The military analogy of the battlefront is useful in visualizing this.

- Business competition inherently has multiple fronts with a different competitor on each front.

- Any redeployment of resources will change the balance of competitive parity on at least two fronts. If one is strengthened, others will be weakened.

- Whenever a front or zone of competitive parity becomes stable or static, then "bourgeois" competition will develop. Such bourgeois competition exists when the defense always acts as a hawk and the offense always acts as a dove. This is a mutual recognition of mutually predictable behavior.

- The fewer the number of competitive variables that are critical, the fewer will be the number of competitors. If only one factor is critical, then no more than two or three competitors are likely to co-exist. Only one will survive if the available market shrinks. This is the "Rule of Three and Four."

- The greater the number of potentially important variables, the larger will be the number of coexisting competitors but the smaller will be their absolute size.

- The more variable the environment, the fewer the number of surviving competitors. In this case, the ability to cope with the greater change in environment becomes the overriding and controlling factor.

- The entry of a new competitor depends on the ability of that competitor to develop and identify a clear superiority compared to all existing competitors in some subsection of the total market. Sequence of entry is important.

These and other hypotheses are direct derivatives from the observable facts and generally accepted theories of evolution in the biological and ecological sense. They are the pattern of natural competition.

The earlier work of The Boston Consulting Group attempted to develop a general theory of competition based on the following:

- Observable patterns of cost behavior

- Considerations of the dynamics of sustainable growth and capital use

- The role of the capital markets in permitting these effects to be leveraged or discounted

- The relationship between these in a system of competition

We recognized early the inappropriateness of accounting theories developed for other purposes as a model of economic behavior. We then developed the concepts that can be summarized as "cash in and out is all that counts."

From this start, the concepts of the experience curve, the growth share tradeoff, and the product portfolio were developed. This was further extended by analysis of shared experience, business risk versus financial risk tradeoffs, the cost of proliferation, and cultural and behavioral extrapolation for competitors.

Many of these ideas are now commonly accepted assumptions and part of the business language.

This conceptual framework of business competition is far from complete. The knowledge and insight into competitive systems is expanding at an exponential rate. It is parallel to the expansion of our knowledge and insight into the physical sciences in the last century.

We believe that insight into strategic competition has the promise of a quantum increase in our productivity and our ability to both control and expand the potential of our own future.

The Development of Business Strategy

Foundations

IN THE MID-1960s, Bruce Henderson and a team from his fledgling firm were retained by a leading semiconductor fabricator. Their brief: Find out what was driving the industry's chaotic pricing behavior. The team discovered that prices were not in fact behaving chaotically at all—they were paralleling costs in a systematic decline of 25 percent each time accumulated volume doubled. The experience curve was born, and the development of business strategy began.

It was not the experience curve itself that was noteworthy—an analogous phenomenon, learning curve reductions in direct labor costs, had been documented during World War II. It was the implications that were truly revolutionary. If total value-added costs fell predictably with accumulated experience—and relative accumulated experience was in most circumstances very close to relative market share—it meant that systematic cost differences, proportional to relative market share, should arise between competitors. At the time, neither business doctrine nor economic theory recognized such a possibility.

The ramifications were far-reaching. Competitive advantage mattered, and it could be gained and managed in a deliberate way. Market share was an extraordinarily valuable asset that should not be liquidated casually.

This notion put pricing and capacity decisions in a new light. Pricing to recover product development costs and optimizing capacity utilization in a growing business, both well-established business practices, amounted to selling off the future for a transitory gain. On the other hand, preemptive pricing and capacity addition could be used to buy market share, lowering relative costs while making a business seem less attractive to competitors.

The same was true of financial policies. Most thought of debt as a way to lever a given ROA up into a higher ROE—with attendant financial risk. Experience curve thinking turned that around, pointing out that, at a given ROE, debt would permit a lower ROA. Employed aggressively, debt could fund preemptive pricing and capacity additions, and thereby buy market share and ultimately lower business risk. Similarly, dividends were exposed as potentially costly in competitive terms, as they lower the sustainable growth rate and hence market-share gains.

But perhaps the most powerful implication of the value of market share was for resource allocation. Most large companies, then as now, comprised a portfolio of businesses that varied in competitive position and growth potential. Experience curve logic suggested that the common practice—for each business to fund its own growth—was suicidal. High-growth businesses were unable to generate enough cash to keep pace with the market and were forced to liquidate share, while mature businesses generated more than they could invest productively. Better to use the excess cash flow of these mature cash cows to fund a play for dominance by the "stars" and "question marks" while growth in their markets remained high. If these businesses could establish and hold leadership positions, they would become cash cows themselves when growth in their markets slowed. The growth-share matrix provided a framework for implementing such a virtuous cash-flow cycle.

Bruce Henderson wrote prolifically on the experience curve and its implications in the 1960s and 1970s. A selection of the best of these *Perspectives* follows. In assessing them, a question we must ask is: Their historical value aside, how do they hold up in today's more complex competitive world?

Clearly, accumulated experience is not the only route to cost advantage. Indeed, it seems irrelevant to the economics of many industries today (although, in its purest form, it has enjoyed something of a renaissance in recent years as a basis for advantage under time- and capability-based strategies). Further, cost differentials and relative market shares cannot be viewed as the sole source and measure of competitive advantage—innovation, customer franchises, and brand value are equally important.

But if "competitive advantage, whatever its source" is substituted for "accumulated experience" and "relative market share," then most of the concepts introduced in these classic *Perspectives* remain sound. The portfolio, in particular, although admittedly widely misperceived and misused as a generic business-categorization tool, remains sound as a framework for resource allocation.

The fundamental insight—that competitive advantage can be gained and must, therefore, be managed, both in fact and in the minds of competitors—remains fresh and valid. That it is an asset of great value certainly remains true, although advantage seems harder to sustain in today's fluid markets than it did 30 years ago.

THE EXPERIENCE CURVE REVIEWED: HISTORY

Bruce D. Henderson, 1973

Experience curve is the name applied in 1966 to overall cost behavior by The Boston Consulting Group. The name was selected to distinguish this phenomenon from the well-known and well-documented learning curve effect. The two are related, but quite different.

It has been known for many years that labor hours per unit decline on repetitive tasks. This effect was particularly easy to observe in such things as aircraft production in wartime. The rate of labor decrease was characteristically approximately 10 to 15 percent per doubling of experience. This expectation has long been a part of military contracting.

The so-called learning curve effect apparently had somewhat limited application, however. It applied only to direct labor. Unless the job changed, this meant *the time required* to obtain a given cost decline tended to double each cycle of experience. This masked the far-reaching implication of the possibilities of job element management with volume changes.

The Boston Consulting Group's first effort to formulate the experience curve concept was an attempt to explain cost behavior over time in a process industry. Long-continued, successful cost reduction by the client had resulted only in the company's survival as a marginal competitor. The correlation between competitive profitability and market share was strikingly apparent. The pattern of the learning curve was an attractive initial hypothesis to explain this. The company was chasing its larger competitors down the cost curve.

Later, a study of the cost of television components showed striking differences in the rate of cost improvement between monochrome parts and color parts. This was difficult to explain, since the same factory, the same labor, and the same processes were involved at the same time. Again, the idea of progress down a cost curve provided a plausible hypothesis.

Semiconductors provided the evidence on which to build the experience curve concept itself. The wide variety of semiconductors offered a chance to compare differing growth rates and price decline rates in a similar environment. Price data supplied by the Electronic Industries Association was compared with accumulated industry volume. Two distinct patterns emerged.

In one pattern, prices in current dollars remained constant for long periods and then began a relatively steep and long-continued decline in constant dollars. In the other pattern, prices in constant dollars declined steadily at a constant rate of about 25 percent each time accumulated experience doubled. That was the experience curve in 1966.

Work with clients since 1966 has proven the universality of the experience curve relationships. A real understanding, however, required many, many client assignments.

Application of the experience curve to problem solving and policy determination discloses many technical questions.

- What is an appropriate unit of experience where the product itself changes, too? The transport airplane is an example.

- What is the relationship between experience effects on similar but different products such as semiconductors?

- How are technological changes integrated into experience effects?

- What effect does capital investment intensity have?

- Does the same effect appear in overhead and marketing functions?

Accounting data is frequently misleading for cost analysis. The choice of treatment as expense versus capital can distort apparent cost change.

Over time, the experience curve has become recognized as essentially a pattern of cash flow. The average cost is by definition the total expenditure divided by the total output. The unit cost is the rate of change in that ratio. Projection of this relationship is frequently both simpler and more accurate for cost forecasting than even the most elaborate conventional accounting analysis.

Understanding of the underlying causes of the experience curve is still imperfect. The effect itself is beyond question. It is so universal that its absence is almost a warning of mismanagement or misunderstanding. Yet the basic mechanism that produces the experience curve effect is still to be adequately explained. (The same thing is true of gravitation.)

It can be observed that if high return on investment thresholds are used to limit capital investment, then costs do not decline as expected.

It can also be observed that extensive substitution of cost elements and exchange of labor for capital is characteristic of progress down a cost experience curve.

Direct Costs per Megawatt, Steam Turbine Generators, 1946–1963. Each Dot Corresponds to a Year. The Horizontal Scale Is the Total Cumulative Output of the Specific Firm Involved to That Year. SOURCE: Confidential information from General Electric, Westinghouse, and Allis-Chalmers was made available in public records as the result of antitrust litigation

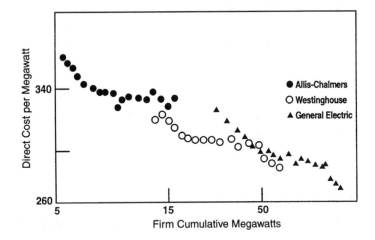

The experience curve is a contradiction of some of the most basic assumptions of classic economic theory. All economics assumes that there is a finite minimum cost that is a function of scale. This is usually stated in terms of all cost/volume curves being either L-shaped or U-shaped. It is not true except for a moment in time.

The whole concept of a free enterprise competitive equilibrium assumes that all competitors can achieve comparable costs at volumes much less than pro rata shares of market. That is not true either.

Our entire concept of competition, antitrust, and nonmonopolistic free enterprise is based on a fallacy if the experience curve effect is true.

The experience curve effect can be observed and measured in any business, in any industry, for any cost element, anywhere.

Most of the history of insight into the experience curve effect and its significance is still to be written.

THE EXPERIENCE CURVE REVIEWED: WHY DOES IT WORK?

BRUCE D. HENDERSON, 1974

"Cost of value added declines approximately 20 to 30 percent each time accumulated experience is doubled."

This is an observable phenomenon. Whatever the reason, it happens. Explanations are rationalizations.

The whole history of increased productivity and industrialization is based on specialization of effort and investment in tools. So is the experience curve. It is a measure of the potential effect of specialization and investment.

Learning

Workers learn. If they learn to do a task better, they can do it in less time. This is equivalent to producing more in the same time. Characteristically, output can increase 10 to 15 percent each time total output is doubled. This is the well-known learning curve measure of man-hour productivity increase.

Based on the learning curve, labor costs should decline only 10 to 15 percent each time accumulated experience doubles.

Specialization

When scale of activity increases so that numbers of people are involved, then it becomes possible to specialize.

If two people are doing the same thing, it becomes possible to break the task into two parts. One person does all of one half. The other person does all of the other half. Each will therefore do his respective task twice as often for a given total output.

The learning curve just described predicts that with twice the experience the labor time should be reduced 10 to 15 percent.

Increase in scale permits such specialization. Consequently, each worker will approach a total experience at any point in time that would be twice as much as the worker could have achieved without specialization. Doing half as much but twice as often equals the same amount of effort but twice the experience with the task. Consequently, specialization permits 10 to 15 percent less time per unit or 10 to 15 percent more output in a given time.

If the scale doubles simultaneously with total experience, then these two effects should occur simultaneously. Costs decline 10 to 15 percent because of learning plus 10 to 15 percent because of specialization. The sum of 20 to 30 percent cost decline is alone an approximation of the total experience curve effect.

Where growth in output increases at any constant rate, then change in scale and change in total experience can and often do occur in parallel.

Investment

By definition, a profitable investment is one where money spent now results in a future payout that is larger than the original investment. All the return on investment comes in more output for the same total cost, but deferred.

If the cost of money is extremely high, then virtually no investment can be justified. If the cost of money were zero, then any investment that would recover the investment and something more by eternity could be justified.

The cost decline in experience curves is a partial function of rate of investment. The control on this element is the cutoff rate on added investment. If the cutoff rate is high, costs decline slowly. If the cutoff rate is low, costs decline rapidly.

Return on investment does result in cost reduction. Without investment, capacity increase cannot occur and neither can cost reduction at constant capacity.

A significant part of the experience curve cost reduction is the result of return on investment.

Scale

The experience curve effect is the result in part of increased scale. Yet there is no justification for increased scale unless there is growth. There is no need to add capacity at all.

With growth there is constant addition of capacity. Each added increment of unit capacity becomes a smaller percent of the total capacity unless size of the increment is increased also. Both capacity utilization and scale effect are affected by growth.

The effect of scale is well known, though very difficult to measure precisely. There is, however, a formula that is known to approximate scale effect in the process industries:

"Capital cost increases by the six-tenths power of the increase in capacity."

This exponential change is equivalent to an increase of 52 percent in capital cost to provide a 100 percent increase in capacity. The total capital cost became 152 percent instead of 100. The total output became 200 instead of 100. The average became $^{152}/_{200}$ = 76 percent of 100 percent. That is a very common and typical experience curve cost decline rate.

Average production unit size normally increases in proportion to rate of total output or even faster. If it does, then capital cost should go down as fast or even faster than in proportion to a 76 percent experience curve.

Since capital tends to displace labor over time, this scale effect becomes increasingly important with growth in volume and experience.

There are limits on scale due to load factors and logistics provided there is a finite total market. But if the total market grows, then scale can be expected to grow too.

Scale effect applies to all operations, not just to process plants. Marketing, accounting, and all the overhead functions have scale effects also.

Scale effect alone is sufficient to approximate the experience curve effect where growth is constant and scale grows with volume.

For most products, a 70 to 80 percent slope is normal, with the steeper slope for those where the maximum value is added and where shared experience with slower growth areas is least. However, it is probable that few products decline in cost as fast as they could if optimized.

It is known that costs are more likely to decline if it is generally expected that they should and will.

It must be remembered that experience curve costs are not accounting conventions. They are cash-flow rates divided by output rates. Accounting data is an approximation of this but generally tends to show lower average costs since assets are deferred recognition of cash expenditures.

This means that cost of capital and return on capital from value added are both included in experience curve costs. Trading profits or losses from price levels are excluded from this cost calculation.

Experience curve costs on the foregoing basis are probably more accurate representations of cost than any accounting convention, since they are based on cash flow only, not projections, and because such costs include the cost of capital.

The reasons for the experience curve effect are not particularly important. The important fact is that the experience curve is a universally observable phenomenon. If costs do not go down in a predictable fashion, then and only then do the underlying reasons become important. Analysis will usually show the reasons to be inadequate investment, improper value-added definitions, or occasionally just mismanagement.

Summary

The experience curve is the result of the combined effect of learning, specialization, investment, and scale. The effect of each of these is an approximation, and so the experience curve effect itself is also an approximation.

The combination of these factors should permit a considerably steeper experience cost curve than is actually observed. However, some additional overhead cost is introduced by the need to coordinate and plan these changes.

All elements of cost do not have the same experience base. Also, some cost elements share experience with other products.

Consequently, only new and unique products with completely new cost elements can be expected to go down the cost experience curve with the maximum slope.

THE EXPERIENCE CURVE REVIEWED: PRICE STABILITY

BRUCE D. HENDERSON, 1974

Whenever real (deflated) prices fail to parallel real (deflated) cost trends, then market shares will shift. When market share shifts, then relative costs of competitors will shift also. The market leader with the largest share will lose share eventually if prices do not go down as fast as costs.

When prices decline faster than the leader's costs on trend, then there is always some competitor who is growing faster than the industry average. That competitor's margin will usually stay constant while all other competitors' margins shrink.

Price and market share are stable only when prices are declining in parallel to costs and prices are low enough to prevent gain in share by high-cost competitors.

Crushed and Broken Limestone. SOURCE: U.S. Bureau of Mines

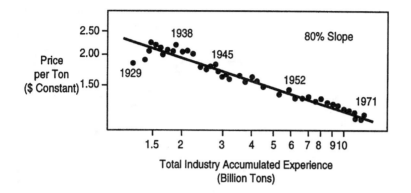

Total Industry Accumulated Experience
(Billion Tons)

Costs characteristically decline 20 to 30 percent in real terms each time accumulated experience doubles. This means that when inflation is factored out, costs should always decline. The decline is fast if growth is fast and slow if growth is slow.

It is obvious that prices must approximately parallel costs over time. Otherwise, margins would constantly widen on trend, or conversely, they would continually narrow and then become negative. But costs net of inflation do continually decline as a function of experience. This experience curve effect can be observed in all manner of products and services.

Two characteristic patterns can be observed in almost all kinds of prices. In one, the prices parallel costs after removing inflation. Examples are crushed rock and integrated circuits.

Integrated Circuits. SOURCE: Published Data of Electronics Industry Association

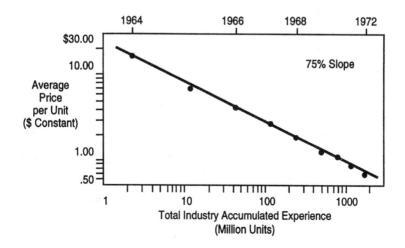

Total Industry Accumulated Experience
(Million Units)

Freestanding Gas Ranges

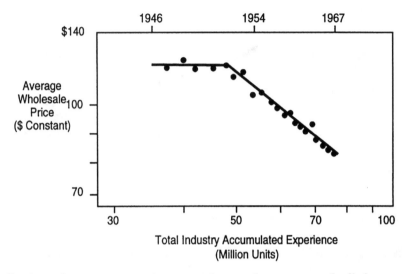

Total Industry Accumulated Experience
(Million Units)

In the other pattern, prices remain nearly constant, declining very slowly. Then at some point in time, prices begin to decline much more sharply than in the previous pattern. Examples are gas ranges and polyvinylchloride.

Characteristically, the price during the initial flat portion of the curve is a constant price in the "then current" value. But if inflation is removed, the real price declines slowly in "constant" money value.

Polyvinylchloride

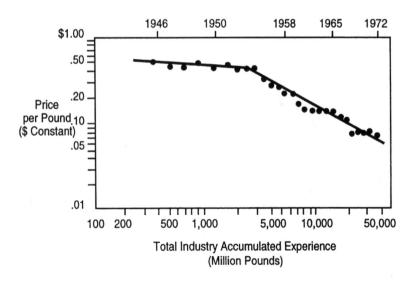

Total Industry Accumulated Experience
(Million Pounds)

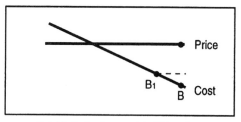

Total Industry Accumulated Experience

B₁ : loses share
B : holds share

A constant price is a strategic target. The increasing margin of the leader is an attractive inducement to enter and to grow even faster. Yet any reduction in share of the leader also reduces his rate of accumulation of experience and slows his rate of cost reduction. The new entry starts at high costs but reduces those costs rapidly because of the faster rate of growth.

Competitors are racing each other down the cost curve by accumulating experience. If X grows enough faster than Y, the relative costs can be reversed. The interaction between the competitors produces a continuing shift in their relative margins.

Differences in growth rate determine the potential rate of shift in margin between two competitors. For practical purposes there can be only one price or "price equivalent" at equilibrium between vendors of equivalent products. If any competitor is willing to sell at a lower price, he will tend to gain share and grow faster and thereafter improve his relative margin unless all others match the price change.

Prices are stable only when three conditions are met:

• The growth rate for all competitors is approximately the same.

• Prices are paralleling costs.

• Prices of all competitors are roughly equal for equal value.

A change in price will not change price stability, except temporarily, unless it changes relative growth rate of competitors. Temporary price changes matched by competitors have essentially no effect on relative cost or on stability.

However, a price change that affects competitors' relative growth rates will affect price stability eventually. Paradoxically, long-term effects tend to be the reverse of short-term effects. An increase in price tends to encourage growth in capacity as well as to affect financial

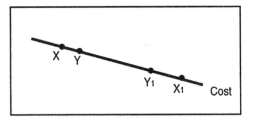

Total Experience for Each Competitor

resources. Rarely will all competitors be affected equally by any price change. If any competitor changes growth rate, prices will be destabilized if any competitor tries to maintain previous profit margins. The competitor who loses share will eventually have to charge relatively more and vice versa.

Characteristically in the United States, a majority of new or fast-growing products go through a two-phase cycle. The first phase has steady prices or very slowly declining prices in constant dollars. This phase is followed by another phase of a long period of steeply declining prices. Usually, only one competitor will be able to preserve profit margins. It is always the fastest-growing competitor.

The break in price is characteristically triggered by some combination of the following:

- A very successful and aggressive new entry willing and able to maintain a modest profit margin

- Growth of new entries at a rate that eventually preempts all growth from the original leader

Two-phase Pattern

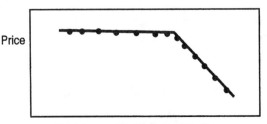

Total Accumulated Industry Experience

Characteristic Pattern if B Is Allowed an Initial Price Advantage and if B Gains Market Share Rapidly while Holding Constant Margin

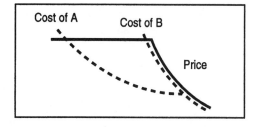

* An economic recession that produces temporary significant overcapacity

The fastest-growing competitor has the fastest decrease in costs. As soon as costs are below the current price he has an option. He can maintain constant margins and convert decreasing costs into lower prices. The alternative is to hold prices and let the margin widen. The first option tends to perpetuate the cost decline in addition to perpetuating the high growth rate. The other alternative stabilizes prices but stops shifts in cost and market share.

If the fastest-growing competitor maintains a constant margin, he can then lower prices faster than anyone else's costs can decline. The strong probability is created that competition with shrinking margins will not invest to maintain margin. Small competitors are often conceded a price differential until they become large and low-cost competitors.

By contrast almost all prices in Japan follow a pattern in which prices steadily decline in parallel to costs. Market share tends to be more stable in Japan than in the United States. In Japan the efficient producer tends to grow faster than the higher-cost competitor. In the United States the reverse is often true.

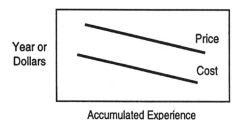

Price stability is determined by the willingness of the leader and low-cost competitor to set prices low enough to keep any competitor from growing faster than the market. Price stability is maintained by the low-cost competitor maintaining prices parallel to his costs. Any other policies will destabilize prices and shift market share.

THE PRICING PARADOX

Bruce D. Henderson, 1970

The profit equation has three variables—price, volume, and cost. Of these, price is the most common candidate for manipulation since nothing else need change to produce profits for everyone, provided everyone changes prices together. That togetherness is what gives birth to dreams of "industry statesmanship," as a way to better profits through higher prices.

In fact, both volume and cost are easier to change than industry price levels. Efforts to change industry prices can cause them to ebb and flow like the tide, with equal net effect on mean sea level. Above-normal prices inevitably attract additional capacity until prices become depressed. Depressed prices inhibit capacity replacement or additions until prices rise. This is a corollary of the economic truism that competition will force prices down to approach costs or it will cause costs to rise to approach prices.

The consequences of a price advance are predictable. At best, other producers will follow the leader and there will be a substantial price rise. But this in turn sets up a ready-made umbrella for the new capacity of these other competitors who must force their way into the market to fill their added capacity.

The usual result is an artificial list price that hides real price cuts at the expense of the market leader. Because of the price leader's price rise, his profit erosion is obscured temporarily until he decides at some later date that he must retain his share of market. In the meantime, he has subsidized the invasion of his market share by competitors and justified their investment in more capacity.

Short term, the others may not follow his price leadership. Consequently, he must not only retract the price increase, but suffer some market-volume loss also.

Over the longer term, the consequences are quite different. Long term, share of the market is determined by who has the capacity and who can use it fully. Long term, the maintenance or addition of capacity is nearly always a function of profits in the past and their effect on profit expectations in the future.

Over the long term, profit and profit expectations are based upon anticipated relative costs and operating rates. As a consequence, short-term higher prices for the industry tend to encourage capacity additions and to provide the cash flow to justify that expansion.

All of this is simple classic economics, but the strategic implications are not immediately obvious:

- If you have the lowest cost at nominal capacity, then it is to your advantage to keep prices down at all times sufficiently to dissuade competition from making additional-capacity investments, unless, of course, you can raise them and still stay at nominal capacity.

- Also, it is to your advantage to invest in added capacity yourself as long as you can do so and maintain your cost advantage. This requires that the added capacity be operated at a load factor high enough to provide cost levels no higher than competitors' average costs. In fact, in an active technology you must make capacity additions to maintain a cost advantage.

- If your fixed costs are higher but your operating costs are lower than competitors', then you are more sensitive to changes in operating rate. It is to your advantage to accept any kind of price depression short term that provides a high operating rate. Only under these conditions can you maintain a relative cost advantage. For the same reason, you can accept a lower price level than can your competitors without out-of-pocket loss. This situation is usually true of the new facility.

If you are the low-cost producer with the newest facilities, then any price that is required to operate your facility at nominal capacity is not only justified but a prerequisite for maintaining your relative cost advantage. Any higher price is relatively disadvantageous. Conversely, the interests of high-cost producers must be to keep prices high or to obtain a higher operating rate.

Competitive strategy comes into play in the efforts to induce competitors to accept practices that shift *relative* costs.

The producer with the new low-cost facility must induce competitors to believe that he can and will depress prices indefinitely—until prices are below their cost, if need be—to the point that his new facilities are operating at average industry capacity. In fact, he has the power to do this. He benefits most, however, if he does not need to depress prices to fill his new capacity.

The producer with the higher-cost facilities but in possession of the market must attempt to convince competitors that high prices for the industry are to everyone's advantage. In this way, he can offset his relative cost disadvantage. He may also find it necessary to convince competitors that it will be too costly to wrest away his existing market share by price action. If he can induce competitors to use nonprice means of competing, then their added costs may defer for a long time their realization of the inherent advantage of newer and more efficient capacity.

Short term, the really critical elements of strategy are those that induce a competitor, for whatever reason, to accept a lower operating rate. This imposes a relative cost handicap that has no offsetting virtues.

Long term, the critical elements are those that determine the willingness of competitors to make further capital investment in capacity. Any uncertainty, risk, or competitive policy that can delay this kind of decision produces a higher profit level on average for those who are already in production.

Viewed in this light, the following conclusions can be drawn:

- Short-term price increases tend to depress industry profits long term by accelerating the introduction of new capacity and depressing market demand.

- Short-term price increases favor the high-cost producer relatively more than the low-cost producer.

- The lower-cost producer has everything to gain and little to lose by depressing prices until he is operating at nominal capacity.

- The perfect strategy for the lowest-cost producer is one that persuades others to permit him to obtain maximum capacity use with minimum price depression—at the others' expense in terms of operating rate and profit.

- The perfect strategy for the high-cost producer is one that persuades others that market shares cannot be shifted except over long periods of time and, therefore, that the highest practical industry prices are to everyone's advantage.

Paradoxically, it is often the strongest and lowest-cost producer who leads the way in establishing higher prices, even though he himself may be operating below his optimum capacity. When this happens, it must be considered a strategic victory for the higher-cost producer in the market.

If all of this seems obvious, it is difficult to explain the concern of businessmen, security analysts, and others regarding industry price levels. It would appear that the factor of vital concern should be relative costs—or rather, relative profit margins. The concentration of attention on short-term profits, which are often transient profits, frequently produces the very opposite long-term effect on performance from that desired.

THE MARKET-SHARE PARADOX

BRUCE D. HENDERSON, 1970

Market share is very valuable. It leads to lower relative cost and therefore higher profits. Unfortunately, most efforts to improve market share depress profits, at least short term.

There are two principal reasons for a shift in market share between competitors. The most common is lack of capacity. The other reason is a willingness to lose share to maintain price.

Lack of capacity is a common occurrence. It must be. It is expensive to maintain unused capacity for very long. Even in the face of projected *industry* growth, it is not surprising that not all *individual* producers feel they can justify the incremental investment in added capacity. On the other hand, nothing is more obvious than the fact that your capacity limits your market share. If the market grows and your capacity does not, then whoever has the capacity takes the growth and increases their share of the market—at your expense.

The decision to add capacity is a fateful one. Add too soon, and extra costs are incurred with no benefits. Add too late, and market share is lost. Added capacity means more than bricks and machines. It also means capable personnel in the proper proportions in the proper place. The lead time required is long. The decision must anticipate the need.

The competitive implications of all this are made more complex by the cost differentials among competitors. Simple arithmetic shows that the high-cost producer must add capacity in direct proportion to the low-cost firm if relative market shares are to remain constant. But the high-cost producer's return on the capacity investment is lower than that of the more efficient firm because of the differential in profit margins.

The market-share paradox is that, if the low-cost firm would accept the high-cost producer's return on assets, the low-cost firm would preempt all market growth. And the resulting increase in his accumulated experience would further improve his costs and steadily increase the cost differential between the competitors thereafter. In short, *if the same investment criteria were used by all firms, then the low-cost firm would always expand capacity first and other firms never would.*

All firms do not use the same investment criteria. The fact that market share is stable proves this. However, this also means that shares are unstable if there is vigorous competition.

The low-cost producer can take market share, but only if he is willing to sacrifice near-term profit. The high-cost producer can obtain a significant return only because he is allowed to do so in order to maintain current prices.

The tradeoff is inviting. Since the low-cost firm typically has the largest market share, his higher-return expectations often lead him to sacrifice share to maintain near-term margins. The loss of a modest amount of the market may seem far less costly short term than meeting a price concession of a minor competitor or spreading the price reduction necessary to fill proposed new capacity over his entire sales volume.

Unfortunately, the tradeoff is cumulative. More and more share must be given up over time to maintain price. Costs are a function of market share because of the experience effect. Lost market share leads to loss of cost advantage. Eventually, there is no way to maintain profitability.

The rate of growth is the critical variable in resolving the market-share paradox and the tradeoff between share and near-term profits.

- Without growth, it is virtually impossible to shift market share. No one can justify adding capacity. Neither can anyone afford to lose share at the price of idle capacity. Under such constraints, since prices will tend to be very stable, the appropriate strategy is to maximize profits within existing market shares.

- With only very little growth, a higher near-term profit now may be worth considerably more than continued modest profit. Those who should hold share into the no-growth period are only those with enough share—and the resulting cost position—to anticipate satisfactory profits.

- With rapid growth, market share is both very valuable and very easy to lose. On the one hand, any improvement in share will be compounded by growth of the market itself and then again by improved margins as cost improvement accrues from increased volume, and hence experience. On the other hand, growth means that capacity must be added rapidly, in advance of the growth, or share will be lost automatically; to gain share, capacity addition must be based on preempting the growth component.

Any shift in market share should be regarded as either investment or disinvestment. The rate of return can and should be evaluated just as it would be in any other business situation. *Change in market share should be an investment decision.*

MORE DEBT OR NONE?

BRUCE D. HENDERSON, 1972

Use more debt than your competition or get out of the business. Any other policy is either self-limiting, no-win, or a bet that the competition will go bankrupt before they displace you.

If you are the low-cost competitor, you can carry more debt with less risk than your competition. That debt could be converted into more profit by leverage. But it can also be converted into lower prices at the same profit, while both decreasing the risk from competitors and maintaining a lower overall risk level than the competition.

Failure of the low-cost competitor to use more debt than the competition is self-limiting. It is failure to compete. It is also a failure to maximize shareholder profits at risk levels below competition's risk.

A high-cost competitor must use more debt to survive and grow, unless his more efficient or fortunate competitors unwittingly hold a price umbrella. A higher permanent debt level is the only way for the high-cost competitor to compensate for higher costs while still maintaining competitive prices and growth rates.

Without higher debt, the high-cost competitor is in a no-win position. *The higher-cost competitor must lose market share if he maintains the same debt/equity ratio and uses the same dividend payout ratio as his lower-cost competition. It is inevitable.* Relative growth must inevitably be in proportion to return on equity under these conditions.

The varying product margins of multiproduct companies often obscure these basic relationships. Failure to focus on the specific financial policies of specific lead competitors and react accordingly compounds the lost opportunity.

Properly used, debt can increase debt capacity faster than it increases the assets in which the debt is invested. Properly used, debt can decrease risk, decrease price, and increase shareholder profit simultaneously.

Proper use of debt will usually require that each product support more debt than any competitor chooses to use. Failure to do so on average is either self-defeating restraint on competition or a no-win position justifying no further investment.

Proper use of debt will inevitably mean that the low-cost competitor drives out all competition, unless antitrust laws force prices to be held up to protect higher-cost competition.

Few companies minimize their risk by using debt properly.

THE RULE OF THREE AND FOUR

BRUCE D. HENDERSON, 1976

A stable competitive market never has more than three significant competitors, the largest of which has no more than four times the market share of the smallest.

The following conditions create this rule:

- A ratio of 2 to 1 in market share between any two competitors seems to be the equilibrium point at which it is neither practical nor advantageous for either competitor to increase or decrease share. This is an empirical observation.

- Any competitor with less than one-quarter the share of the largest competitor cannot be an effective competitor. This, too, is empirical but is predictable from experience curve relationships.

Characteristically, this should eventually lead to a market-share ranking of each competitor one-half that of the next larger competitor, with the smallest no less than one-quarter the largest. Mathematically, it is impossible to meet both conditions with more than three competitors.

The Rule of Three and Four is a hypothesis. It is not subject to rigorous proof. It does seem to match well observable facts in fields as diverse as steam turbines, automobiles, baby food, soft drinks, and airplanes. If even approximately true, the implications are important.

The underlying logic is straightforward. Cost is a function of market share as a result of the experience curve effect.

If two competitors have nearly equal shares, the one who increases relative share gains both volume and cost differential. The potential gain is high compared to the cost. For the leader, the opportunity diminishes as the share difference widens. A price reduction costs more and the potential gain is less. The 2 to 1 limit is approximate, but it seems to fit.

Yet when any two competitors actively compete, the most probable casualty is likely to be the weakest competitor in the arena. That, logically and typically, is the low-share competitor.

The limiting share ratio of 4 to 1 is also approximate but seems to fit. If it is exceeded, then the probable cost differential produces very large profits for the leader at break-even prices for the low-share competitor. That differential, predicted by the experience curve, is enough to discourage further reinvestment and efforts to compete by the low-share competitor unless the leader is willing to lose share by holding a price umbrella.

There are two exceptions to this result:

- A low-share competitor can achieve a leadership position in a given market sector and dominate it costwise if there is enough shared experience between that sector and the rest of the market and he is a leader in the rest of the market.

- An otherwise prosperous company is willing for some reason to continually add more investment to a marginal minor product. This can be caused by accounting averaging, full-line policy, or mismanagement.

Whatever the reason, it appears that the Rule of Three and Four is a good prediction of the results of effective competition.

There are strategy implications:

- If there are large numbers of competitors, a shakeout is nearly inevitable in the absence of some external constraint or control on competition.

- All competitors who are to survive will have to grow faster than the market in order to even maintain their relative market shares with fewer competitors.

- The eventual losers will have increasingly large negative cash flows if they try to grow at all.

- All except the two largest-share competitors will either be losers and eventually eliminated or be marginal cash traps reporting profits periodically and reinvesting forever.

- Anything less than 30 percent of the relevant market or at least half the share of the leader is a high-risk position if maintained.

- The quicker any investment is cashed out or a market position second only to the leader gained, then the lower the risk and the higher the probable return on investment.

- Definition of the relevant market and its boundary barriers becomes a major strategy evaluation.

- Knowledge and familiarity with the investment policies and market-share attitudes of the market leader are very important since his policies control the rate of the inevitable shakeout.

- Shifts in market share at equivalent prices for equivalent products depend upon the relative willingness of each competitor to invest at rates higher than the sum of both physical market growth and the inflation rate. Anyone who is not willing to do so loses share. If everyone is willing to do so, then prices and margins will be forced down by overcapacity until someone begins to stop investing.

There are tactical implications that are equally important:

- If the low-cost leader holds the price too high, the shakeout will be postponed, but he will lose market share until he is no longer the leader.

- The faster the industry growth, the faster the shakeout occurs.

- Near equality in share of the two market leaders tends to produce a shakeout of everyone else unless they jointly try to maintain the price level and lose share together.

- The price/experience curve is an excellent indicator of whether the shakeout has started. If the price curve slope is 90 percent or flatter, the leader is probably losing share and still holding up the price. If the curve has a sharp break from 90 percent or above to 80 percent or less, then the shakeout will continue until the Rule of Three and Four is satisfied.

The market leader controls the initiative. If he prices to hold share, there is no way to displace him unless he runs out of the money required to maintain his capacity share. However, many market leaders unwittingly sell off market share to maintain short-term operating profit.

A challenger who expects to displace an entrenched leader must do it indirectly by capturing independent sectors or by investing far more than the leader will need to invest to defend himself.

There are public policy implications:

- The lowest possible price will occur if there is only one competitor, provided that monopoly achieves full cost potential even without competition and passes it on to the customer.

- The next-lowest potential price to the customer is with two competitors, one of which has one-third and the other two-thirds of the market. Then cost and price would probably be about 5 percent higher than the monopoly would require.

- The most probable, and perhaps the optimal, relationship would exist when there are three competitors and the largest has no more than 60 percent of the market and the smallest no less than 15 percent.

A rigorous application of the Rule of Three and Four would require identification of discrete homogeneous market sectors in which all competitors are congruent in their competition. More typically, competitors' areas of competition overlap but are not identical. The barriers between sectors are sometimes surmountable, particularly if there are joint cost elements with scale effects. Yet it is a commonly observable fact that most companies have only two or three significant competitors on any product that is producing a net positive cash flow. Other competitors are unimportant factors.

The Rule of Three and Four is not easy to apply. It depends on an accurate definition of relevant market. It requires many years to reach equilibrium unless the leader chooses to hold his share during the high-growth phase of product life. However, the rule appears to be inexorable.

If the Rule of Three and Four is inexorable, then common sense says: if you cannot be a leader in a product market sector, cash out as soon as practical. Take your writeoff. Take your tax loss. Take your cash value. Reinvest in products and markets where you can be a successful leader. Concentrate.

THE PRODUCT PORTFOLIO

Bruce D. Henderson, 1970

To be successful, a company should have a portfolio of products with different growth rates and different market shares. The portfolio composition is a function of the balance between cash flows. High-growth products require cash inputs to grow. Low-growth products should generate excess cash. Both kinds are needed simultaneously.

Four rules determine the cash flow of a product.

- Margins and cash generated are a function of market share. High margins and high market share go together. This is a matter of common observation, explained by the experience curve effect.

- Growth requires cash input to finance added assets. The added cash required to hold share is a function of growth rates.

- High market share must be earned or bought. Buying market share requires an additional increment of investment.

- No product market can grow indefinitely. The payoff from growth must come when the growth slows, or it never will. The payoff is cash that cannot be reinvested in that product.

Products with high market share and slow growth are *cash cows*. Characteristically, they generate large amounts of cash, in excess of the reinvestment required to maintain share. This excess need not, and should not, be reinvested in those products. In fact, if the rate of return exceeds the growth rate, the cash *cannot* be reinvested indefinitely, except by depressing returns.

Products with low market share and slow growth are *pets*. They may show an accounting profit, but the profit must be reinvested to maintain share, leaving no cash throw-off. The product is essentially worthless, except in liquidation.

All products eventually become either cash cows or pets. The value of a product is completely dependent upon obtaining a leading share of its market before the growth slows.

Low-market-share, high-growth products are the *question marks*. They almost always require far more cash than they can generate. If cash is not supplied, they fall behind and die. Even when the cash is supplied,

The Matrix

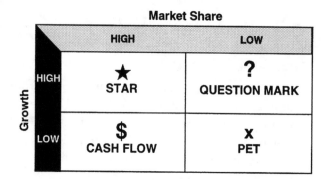

if they only hold their share, they are still pets when the growth stops. The question marks require large added cash investment for market share to be purchased. The low-market-share, high-growth product is a liability unless it becomes a leader. It requires very large cash inputs that it cannot generate itself.

The high-share, high-growth product is the *star*. It nearly always shows reported profits, but it may or may not generate all of its own cash. If it stays a leader, however, it will become a large cash generator when growth slows and its reinvestment requirements diminish. The star eventually becomes the cash cow, providing high volume, high margin, high stability, security, and cash throw-off for reinvestment elsewhere.

The payoff for leadership is very high indeed if it is achieved early and maintained until growth slows. Investment in market share during the growth phase can be very attractive if you have the cash. Growth in market is compounded by growth in share. Increases in share increase the margin. High margin permits higher leverage with equal safety.

Optimum Cash Flow

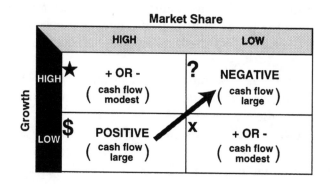

Success Sequence

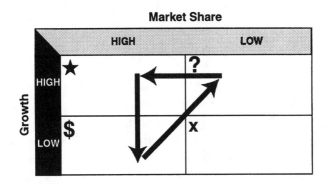

The resulting profitability permits higher payment of earnings after financing normal growth. The return on investment is enormous.

The need for a portfolio of businesses becomes obvious. Every company needs products in which to invest cash. Every company needs products that generate cash. And every product should eventually be a cash generator; otherwise it is worthless.

Only a diversified company with a balanced portfolio can use its strengths to truly capitalize on its growth opportunities. The balanced portfolio has:

- Stars whose high share and high growth assure the future
- Cash cows that supply funds for that future growth
- Question marks to be converted into stars with the added funds

Pets are not necessary. They are evidence of failure either to obtain a leadership position during the growth phase or to get out and cut the losses.

Disaster Sequence

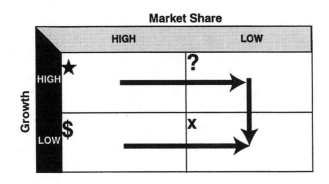

THE REAL OBJECTIVES

BRUCE D. HENDERSON, 1976

Investors want their money compounded with safety. Managers want opportunity and defendable security. Business growth seeks to provide both. It may not be so. Business growth has some characteristics that may defeat both investors and management expectations and hopes.

Growth requires added cash in proportion. Growth is an investment opportunity. But the opportunity from growth is real only if it provides a means of returning the invested cash after it has been compounded. This can begin to happen only when the growth has stopped, or substantially so. Growth can indeed lead to business security and stability. But this will be true only if the competitive advantage can be achieved and maintained before maturity and competitive equilibrium have set in.

Business success cannot be measured until the direct investor's cash input has been returned with his profit. Until then, all profit and all apparent success is merely a promise. Reported profit is only a signal. It is a misleading signal unless it represents the probable ultimate competitive position. Cash is all that counts. But cash really counts only when it is no longer needed to defend the competitive position. Competitors are the control on the ability to convert paper profits into real profit for investors.

The nature of competition changes drastically with continued growth. Cost elements shift dramatically in relative weight even though all may decline in real terms. Production costs shift from labor to raw materials and capital costs. Marketing costs shift from selling, education, and service to logistics. Distribution costs begin to overshadow production costs in some kinds of businesses, and the opposite happens in other kinds.

Competitive economics do shift with change in scale, growth rate, and product maturity. Early leaders may have quite different characteristics from those who are merely able to grow with the market until it matures. They in turn may be quite different from the ultimate real winners.

The ultimate success depends upon the ability to achieve and maintain superiority in the most heavily weighted cost components before product maturity and competitive equilibrium have been reached.

While this is the end objective, the means of reaching it may require several quite different kinds of competitive capabilities in the interim periods.

- Early success is no forecast of eventual superiority.
- Current reported profitability is no proof of success. It is only a forecast.
- Growth is evidence only of a compounding investment level in the hope of achieving eventual superiority.

In the final analysis, all true profit payable to the original investor must be represented by the cost superiority differential over the higher-cost marginal competitor who must reinvest his net cash generation just to hold his position.

Effective strategy analysis requires that you find a way to proceed and progress from wherever you start to a dependable competitive advantage at maturity and equilibrium. This in turn requires that you foresee both the shifting economics and the changing behavior of your competitors. If you succeed, then you must translate that insight into the action required now and at each stage as the market matures. Strategy success is action now consistent with a required sequence of actions until a defensible competitive superiority is achieved.

That is what competitive strategy is all about.

Milestones

"TO ADVANCE THE state of thinking about business strategy"—this aspiration, inspired by Bruce Henderson, became the soul of The Boston Consulting Group. In the 25 years since Bruce's breakthrough work on competitive advantage, BCG has continued to innovate. This section highlights *Perspectives* and other publications that represent milestone contributions to the field.

As BCG and its clients began to apply principles of competitive advantage, they learned that the world was not as monolithic as the experience curve implied. In particular, market leaders were not always able to achieve and maintain the kind of success their positions appeared to warrant. Indeed, we frequently saw smaller, more focused players outcompete the leader for the most attractive pieces of business, first becoming more profitable, then growing faster, and ultimately threatening the leader's position.

We observed that industry leaders tend suffer a life cycle as pronounced as the industries they lead. As markets mature, they fragment into segments with distinct product and service needs, and price elasticities to match. For the producer, these needs translate into different costs to serve each segment. It seems particularly difficult for industry leaders, with their time-honed excellence across their markets as a whole, to spot the segments as they emerge, and to "deaverage" their costs, their product/service offering, and their prices accordingly. This opens an opportunity for competitors to establish a position, generally in the low-cost-to-serve segments.

BCG's focus on market segments and their unique economics led to an exploration of the fundamental trade-off between scale and complexity. Beyond the risks of average costing and average pricing, broad-line producers often find it difficult to achieve the economies of scale implied by their overall size. Lot sizes shrink, and the costs of managing variety mount. Competitors need to be alert to the relative advantages of broad market coverage and focus.

By the late 1970s, businesses clearly varied in inherent reward potential. Where slowing demand and increasingly global competition came together with limits to scale, competitive advantage became an elusive goal for many companies. In particular, mature industrial sectors in which products were largely undifferentiated and technology was no longer proprietary appeared to have reached stalemate. Their flat supply curves demonstrated the difficulty of any competitor achieving a sustainable competitive cost advantage. The only way to escape from stalemate was to transform the business—either by finding a way to reintroduce scale or, more commonly, by injecting a note of innovation and differentiation—to create a more promising competitive environment.

By the early 1980s, a solution to the scale/complexity dilemma began to emerge. Toyota innovated a production process that reduced setup times, work-in-process inventories, and indirect labor by a factor to 5 to 10. Flexible manufacturing allowed broad-line competitors to reduce dramatically the costs associated with handling product proliferation, breaking the compromise between scale and complexity.

But flexible manufacturing was about more than lower manufacturing costs and higher asset turns. The real payoff was in marketing. Producers could offer unprecedented variety in increasingly short cycle times. As a result, distributors could carry broad lines with lower inventories. And customers could get precisely what they wanted, precisely when they wanted it. Time-based competition, as we called it, was a marketer's dream come true.

Flexible manufacturing and time-based competition inspired a general concern with process excellence in all aspects of business operations in the late 1980s and early 1990s. One outgrowth was the recognition that transformational strategies could be built around horizontal capabilities, as Wal-Mart and others had done. Another was reengineering for cost reduction alone, which became the reigning management fad of the early 1990s, but without changes in marketing led to only short-lived gains in competitive advantage.

Reengineering lowered general cost levels and, in the best companies, rationalized core processes and increased organizational nimbleness. But its very ubiquity underlined its limits: A tool that every player uses may become essential for staying in the game, but it is unlikely to confer competitive advantage. Some industries even suffered a sort of reengineering stalemate, as general cost reductions were bid away in the form of lower prices. It was inevitable that attention would turn to how to *use* reengineered capability. The mid-1990s have seen a reinvigorated search for growth and, accordingly, a renewed focus on strategy.

What's next? All evidence suggests we are entering a truly revolutionary era. Artificial barriers, trade and regulatory, have been falling steadily; global markets are becoming the rule. A quantum leap in the economics of information is catalyzing an acceleration of this already fast pace of change. It is relaxing the information-based ties that bind functions, departments, suppliers, and customers in a company's value chain. Affected industries will deconstruct into horizontal layers, each with its unique economics and scope for competitive action. New competitors will emerge. Existing competitors will transform themselves or wither away.

It should be an exciting era for the strategist. Layers will add a new dimension to the concept of strategy, and the instability of industry boundaries will lend the search for sustainable competitive advantage new urgency.

LIFE CYCLE OF THE INDUSTRY LEADER

BRUCE D. HENDERSON, 1972

Companies who are pioneers develop great technical expertise. This is very valuable to their customers, particularly in the early stages of the development of the customer's own expertise. This is a source of great pride. It is considered to be proof of leadership. This reinforces emphasis on technical development. Technical pride leads to tailoring each order to the optimum specification.

This in turn leads to the evolution of a manufacturing organization that is geared to produce a very wide variety. Likewise, the marketing organization seeks out the unusual and the technically difficult orders where this kind of flexibility and excellence offers the greatest competitive advantage. This is where the wide profit margins are.

These things reinforce each other. The company's leadership and success reinforce the corporate culture. They preserve and strengthen this pattern of competition.

Almost all original leaders developed this way. They became leaders and prospered because they did. It is necessary. In the early stages of every product and every industry, customers must have this kind of service and resource. The leader is rewarded handsomely because his greater experience and scale result in proportionately lower costs (i.e., the experience curve effect).

However, as the market becomes very large, the leader comes under price pressure from much smaller and less well equipped competitors. The problem usually appears first with the largest and most knowledgeable customers. They have become expert themselves. They buy product, not service. Such sophisticated customers do not need the full range of technical services and manufacturing variety that are available. They begin to find smaller, less competent suppliers who can give them an acceptable product at a lower price. At this stage, such competitors are rarely profitable. However, since they are able to concentrate their experience in a particular sector, their costs come down rapidly in that sector and their competence in that sector increases rapidly.

This competition poses a serious problem for the original leader. Large markets always have a number of sectors that differ materially in their needs and characteristics. The costs of serving these sectors differ widely. It is often very difficult to set prices in a fashion that reflects the differences in services actually rendered or available.

If prices are high enough to cover the cost of the most expensive services available, then large portions of the total market will be lost to the specialized competitors who provide limited services and price accordingly. These prices are too low to cover costs for those customers who need and use the specialized service. A price midway between the two is worse than either, since it has the handicaps of both.

Under these conditions, market leaders usually try to price to preserve their average margin. This accelerates their margin shrinkage, because they tend to lose their volume base on price while increasing their proportion of high service, high cost, technical output.

This trend, if continued, changes the whole character of the leader with respect to costs, product characteristics, price policy, growth rates, and kinds of market sectors served. He becomes a high-price, high-cost, low-volume specialist. If the problem is not recognized and dealt with explicitly, it leads first to unprofitable business and then to inability to compete except in low-volume, high-margin specialties. By then, survival requires specialization in certain sectors and abandonment of the balance.

If the problem and its roots are recognized early enough, however, the leadership, the volume, and the profitability can be protected and preserved. But for this to happen, major changes in policy are required. These changes are to policies that are fundamentally different from those that brought early success. This is where most pioneers lose their leadership.

Price policy, product scope, marketing focus, manufacturing method, and production system must be fundamentally altered. This is a complex problem.

- Identifying market segment costs is very difficult. Many of these costs are joint costs. If one segment is served, the cost is often incurred in all segments. There is an infinite number of possible combinations of services and customer characteristics.

- Prices cannot always reflect different costs for those who do and those who do not need a service. If prices are not parallel to costs in all sectors, then a competitor can concentrate on a sector in which he has either a price advantage or a cost advantage.

- Competitors' costs in different sectors are never equivalent, even if average costs are the same. Since expected profit margins control investment, these differences will tend to produce differential growth rates. But cost differences are increased by shift in market share caused by differing growth rates.

- Changing marketing focus is of little help unless manufacturing facilities and production methods are modified to take advantage of the change. Yet optimization of one is often incompatible with optimization of the other.

- Modification of manufacturing to obtain the optimum cost in any segment may curtail or restrict the product line or the service capability and therefore shrink the volume and experience base overall.

- Marketing advantage, manufacturing costs, and volume potential are mutually dependent variables.

Overall optimization depends on competitors' characteristics, sector by sector.

It is a rare pioneer or industry leader that successfully makes the transition from generalized excellence across the board to focused competition segment by segment against specific competitors. There are too many forces that work against this adjustment.

- Marketing, engineering, and manufacturing all tend to take the policies and current character of the other two as a given and permanent constraint.

- The competitive success in concentration on certain sectors tends to continually concentrate the remaining business in those sectors that are the most complex, the most specialized, the least repetitive and, therefore, the least likely to permit future cost reduction based on experience. The more successful the company has been in the past, the more the entire structure and company tradition will tend to inhibit a change in style or concept of competition.

- In cyclical business, a few good years make everything seem all right. In the down cycle, the problems are blamed on business conditions.

- The management of such businesses, particularly publicly owned businesses, tends to be measured on near-term results. Major change in policy takes time, costs money, and does not demonstrate its value until long after the cost and effort are incurred. Management has a disincentive to change.

It is easy to understand why many pioneers and early leaders are displaced by lesser competitors.

The health and life cycle of the pioneer are determined by two factors. The first is his ability to recognize significant differences in customer segments and optimize his cost of serving each segment separately. The second is his appreciation of the cost value of experience that is common to more than one segment.

THE EVILS OF AVERAGE COSTING

RICHARD K. LOCHRIDGE, 1975

Average costing leads to the loss of market share. Given the normal accounting procedures of any business, some costs are assigned directly to particular products sold to specific customers. All others are averaged, that is, divided among all products and customers. This leads to a misstatement of real costs and a potential competitive threat.

Costs are a function of market share. The leading competitor in any business should have the lowest costs. This low-cost position allows the leader to make the most profit, charge the lowest prices, or add the most value to his product. He may do all three. In any case, there seems little reason to expect a low-share competitor to be able to compete effectively, let alone to gain share on the market leader.

In business after business, however, new entrants gain share on the leader and displace him. In some cases, this is because the return expectations of the leader are so high that a price umbrella is held over the competition. A competitor with a lower return expectation can enter the business and grow to a leadership position. In other cases, the new entrant practices an aggressive financial policy relative to the leader. With greater use of debt and higher retention, the new entrant, despite lower initial returns, can add capacity at a greater rate than the leader.

In many cases, however, the displacement of the leader is the result of average costing. Although costs are averaged across the entire business, overhead and other costs often differ greatly from one product to another. A focused factory can produce high-volume products much more cheaply than a plant designed for flexibility. As a result, broad product lines tend to raise the manufacturing cost of all products. Cost averaging ignores this and therefore overstates the real and potential cost of the high-volume products to a much greater extent than the cost of the low-volume products.

The broader the product line and the larger the number and variety of the customers, the greater the use of overhead cost averaging. Since the leader typically has the largest product line and the biggest customer base, he tends to do the most cost averaging.

The costs to serve different sets of customers are also averaged. Usually, all sales and marketing expenses are averaged across products in such a way that they are averaged across sets of customers as well. Yet different groups of customers have different needs. Large buyers tend to be sophisticated users of the products. They therefore place greater emphasis on price and delivery than on education, service, and support. The result is that it costs less to serve the larger customers than the smaller. This is intuitively obvious. However, costs are rarely classified by customer group; the real differences in cost of service are hidden by cost averaging.

Average costing leads to average pricing. Average pricing means that some customers are being overcharged while others are being subsidized. This is particularly true if the overcharged customers concentrate their purchases on higher-volume products. The problem is compounded when the leader institutes across-the-board price increases in times of inflation. Across-the-board increases, by their very nature, ignore the changes in product and customer mix that occur as markets mature.

The new entrant in the business is forced to focus because of his basic cost disadvantage. If he hopes to be successful, he focuses on those sectors of the market that are being overcharged. He will probably charge less than the leader to penetrate the market. It is only in these sectors that he can deliver product profitably because of the average pricing umbrella. It may be a strategy born of necessity rather than insight, but it still works.

The overcharged customers tend to be the largest and most price-sensitive sector of the market. The leader abandons them to the new entrant because his average costing reports them as less profitable accounts at the lower price levels. These customers also tend to be the fastest-growing sector of the business. The new entrant not only establishes a base-load business upon which to improve his relative cost position, he also grows faster than the leader.

Continued averaging by the leader produces a new set of customers who are being overcharged. The new entrant grows rapidly, improves his costs, and expands into these sectors as well. Eventually, the original leader is displaced. Despite a basic cost advantage to start with, average costing and average pricing lead to a loss in share. The strategic implications for the new entrant are clear:

- Focus on sectors in which the leader is negating his underlying cost advantage through averaging.
- Tailor your offering specifically to that sector's needs. Price to penetrate.
- Broaden the offering only as you improve your relative cost position and as the leader's continued averaging opens other sectors to attack.

The strategic implications for the market leader are also clear:

- Analyze your costs by groups of customers as well as by products.
- When you do have to allocate costs, intentionally bias the assignment of costs away from the rapidly growing, vulnerable segments.
- Differentiate your service to each sector of the market as required, and price accordingly.
- Avoid the evils of average costing.

SPECIALIZATION OR THE FULL PRODUCT LINE

MICHAEL C. GOOLD, 1979

Larger scale lowers costs. Product proliferation raises them. Proliferation can offset scale and more. Yet product families can have lower costs because of their scale than any individual product standing alone. This is true both in the factory and in the marketplace. Every company must choose between the benefits of breadth and those of focus.

In production, two factors are critical in this tradeoff. Every common component provides scale and cost improvement potential. Every deviation from identical cost elements adds overhead cost for coordination.

This proliferation of cost elements adds to both the cost of the variation and to the cost of the elements that are not varied.

If two products are completely unrelated, then they share no scale effect advantage. But neither do they create an overhead cost for coordination. This results in a tradeoff. A focused factory for each of two independent products can be very cost-effective. Combined production offers some increase in scale and shared experience but has inherently higher costs otherwise.

The same cost tradeoff exists in the marketing function. Each customer would prefer a product exactly tailored for him in its characteristics and service support. Every salesman would like to be able to offer this at no added cost. But there is an added cost for every variation both in the factory and in the marketplace. Only certain customers will find that the added value exceeds the added cost and be prepared to pay the higher price needed to maintain profit margins. This means that either demand will be low or profits will be reduced.

The infinite richness of possible tradeoffs and combinations of both product characteristics and customer preferences produces an apparently insuperable degree of complexity. The possibility of analysis and solution would indeed be remote if it were not for the characteristic Pareto (lognormal) distribution of the principal elements.

A limited number of customers usually provide the vast majority of the volume. A limited number of products usually provide the vast majority of the revenue. These combinations of products and customers are the core of the business. This is where analysis should start. This is the frame of reference that can be used to determine the added value and the added cost of extensions to either product line or customer base.

Other varieties of product and other customer classifications are characteristically marginal in their contribution to the firm. Far worse than this, they may create added cost that will be hidden by an average allocation to all products and customers. As a consequence, the essential core business may be deemphasized or overpriced, while the marginal extensions of the product line and customers served may be underpriced or overemphasized in their importance. This may be true even though a real competitive advantage exists in the core business while there is no comparable advantage in the extension coverage.

All the logic of cost effectiveness and competitive advantage favors the focused competitor who avoids product and customer proliferation of this type. That is why it so often seems to happen that a relatively modest sized competitor who is focused can sell at a lower price and still make better profits than his larger and seemingly more formidable competitor.

There is both a paradox and an opportunity here. Focus can result in superior costs. But if this superior cost position can be used as a basis for low costs in extensions to the product/customer range, profitable new opportunities may exist. Focus comes first on the core business areas, but it can still be the basis for a broad product line by building on shared experience and scale.

The basic rule is that you should never expand a product line or a customer base into a segment in which you do not expect to be able to obtain a competitive advantage over any other competitor in that segment. The practical definition of a segment is that combination of customers and products for which a given competitor does have such an advantage.

It is not enough to be able to sell into someone else's segment temporarily because your marginal revenue exceeds your out-of-pocket costs. Such raids and skirmishes are inevitable and endemic on the boundaries of nearly all segments of the market. For continued success, the fundamentals must be observed.

The fundamental rule has two parts. The first is that you should never attempt to serve a market segment (except on an opportunistic basis), unless you can reasonably expect to establish a true competitive advantage in the segment, as you define it, when compared to any other competitor. The other part of the fundamental rule says that when your competitive ability is based upon a relationship to an existing segment that you already dominate, then all marginal costs created by the added segment must be fully (or more than) compensated for by the marginal increase in revenue for the added products or services that represent the added segment.

These determinations cannot be made with reference to products and customers alone. The critical differences are between you and your competitor, and these differences affect your comparative ability to serve any given classification of product/customer pairing. Competitors define the market segments by their differences.

As competitors adjust to the facts of the marketplace and the behavior of each other, the definitions of the relevant segments change, too. Product lines, services, features, and customer characteristics and preferences, as well as the adaptations of competitors, all change. With all this change there must be a continuing reference point. That reference is the existing core of your business in which you have a clear competitive advantage over any competitor. If you cannot preserve that, you cannot protect and extend any of your business with advantage.

Focus of both production and marketing for the core business is essential. No costs are relevant to the core business except those that are in fact unavoidable for its own health. From that point, extension of the product line depends upon the ability to establish a true competitive advantage in new products or customer groups, without at the same time damaging the core business.

STALEMATE: THE PROBLEM

JOHN S. CLARKESON, 1984

Business competition does not always produce a winner. If the differences between competitors are minimal, their struggle may produce only losers. And conventional strategies may only make things worse.

The basis for profitability in a competitive system is competitive advantage. If no competitor can gain a significant and sustainable advantage over the rest, the result may be stalemate.

Under condition of stalemate, the profits of the participants are cyclical but low on average and few participants do much better or worse than the rest. And yet most competitors caught in a stalemate are slow to recognize the fact and reluctant to rethink their strategies. Many prefer to wait for demand to catch up with supply, for prices to return to "realistic levels," or for excess capacity to be shut. Others try to rationalize the industry by gaining a dominant share. In stalemate, both patience and determination usually go unrewarded.

Recognizing stalemate for what it is, however, can open up whole new avenues leading to superior returns.

Stalemate can occur wherever two or more enterprises compete on equal terms across the board and no one achieves that upper hand. This most often occurs where technology is not proprietary and the product is relatively undifferentiated. Further, if the capacity of a low-cost facility represents a small portion of the total needed to satisfy demand, then there are likely to be numerous competitors, each with a low-cost facility, and stalemate may be inevitable.

The industry conditions that result from stalemate are usually beyond the control of any of the participants. Prices are truly determined by the laws of supply and demand. They will tend to settle at or near the marginal cash costs of the highest-cost facility needed to supply demand. Unless you can offer an economically differentiated product that commands a higher price, you can be profitable only by achieving lower costs than the marginal producer.

The way to visualize this phenomenon is to develop an industry supply curve by arraying all the producing units in order of increasing cost (see figure). The difference between the costs of the highest- and lowest-cost producers is an indicator of the overall return potential of the industry. All other things being equal, a large difference, if it is stable, will be more profitable than a smaller difference. Careful data gathering and analysis of cost determinants can create remarkably accurate pictures of competitors' cost positions.

In stalemate, the difference between the highest- and the lowest-cost facility is too small; as a result, the profitability of the lowest-cost facility—and everyone else—is mediocre.

Large sectors of American industry have experienced sustained periods of stalemate over the past ten years, including segments of steel, basic chemicals, forest products, tires, electrical equipment, construction materials, and synthetic fibers and textiles. These industries have all earned less than the average of U.S. industry over the business cycle.

Increasingly, each of these industries has also faced significant international competition. The same characteristics that permit ease of entry for domestic competitors—available technology and know-how,

An Industry Supply Curve. Each Bar Represents a Producing Facility. Its Vertical Dimension Is the Facility's Cash Cost per Unit; Its Width Is the Plant's Capacity

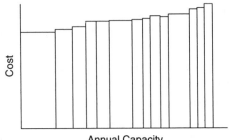

minimal marketing barriers—have attracted investment by offshore competitors with access to low-cost resources, including energy, labor, capital, or all three. Other industries are vulnerable to similar competition if the forces leading to stalemate are not avoided.

Stalemate is not confined to manufacturing. Any service where the customers' cost to switch is low can stalemate, as has happened in bank lending to large corporate accounts, in high-traffic transportation routes, and in nonspecialty retailing.

What is responsible for the shallow supply curves that characterize stalemate? One factor is the rate of technological progress and experience. As a technology matures, the difference in cost between successive generations of facilities or delivery systems will become smaller, especially when capital costs are included.

The other factor is the rate of investment. As an industry adds capacity—almost always at a rate faster than demand is growing—the oldest facilities are displaced.

Such investment behavior produces a steady decline in real costs and real prices. This is the practical basis of the experience effect: real costs are reduced by the substitution of more productive for less productive capacity. But in a stalemate situation, the improvements produced by experience do not result in significant differences among competitors.

This misunderstanding of the experience effect has led some competitors to pursue costly strategies to gain market share. In stalemate, market share is of little value. A new entrant with a new facility or delivery system will often have lower costs than a higher-share older competitor with a collection of production units of various ages.

Yet investment continues at a rapid rate. This testifies to weaknesses in the resource-allocation systems of many companies. These errors are due in part to inadequacies in the capital budgeting process, especially in long-term price forecasting.

Corporate management should identify where stalemate is present or likely to evolve in its current business portfolio. Strategies that exacerbate the competitive conditions should be avoided. The rules and procedures for allocating resources to stalemate businesses are different from the rules for other businesses; the nature of a winning strategy is different. Breaking stalemate requires a new approach to the business and a sharp departure from conventional patterns of competition.

What is the appropriate response to stalemate in your industry?

Acknowledging stalemate can be difficult. It requires confronting some deeply rooted patterns in the organization's behavior. Despite low historical returns, stalemated businesses are used to receiving significant investment, in part to try to improve returns.

It is necessary, therefore, to identify how these projects clear the hurdles intended to discourage low-return investments. The answer may lie in future price forecasts, which are often decisive in the calculated return. Prices do rise periodically to the level required to justify new investment, but seldom remain there long enough to produce the expected return. Forecasts can be made significantly more realistic by using analysis based on supply curves.

There are other pressures as well. One is the natural desire of operating management to close the book on marginal operations, including difficult labor relations, operating headaches, and other legacies. A greenfield investment often promises a fresh start. Yet some of the best investments during a period of rising real capital costs are available to those willing to rebuild and refocus older facilities.

One way not to break a stalemate is by a strategy of preemptive capacity addition, unless it alters the basic nature of the business. Other low-cost preemptive capacity moves are unlikely to change the slope of the supply curve. If you later try to harvest your investment with higher prices, no barrier exists to prevent competitors from entering and lowering prices again.

Finally, it is necessary to overcome the inertia that dictates reinvestment in a business simply because you can't think of an attractive alternative. Recognizing a stalemate for what it is often becomes the first step in committing to explore new avenues for corporate direction.

A stalemated business can be made more profitable once it is agreed that heavy future investment is neither necessary nor appropriate. Overheads maintained in anticipation of future growth can be pared back. Similarly, make-or-buy decisions can be reviewed. This is true especially of process engineering and systems development, where licensing and joint venture may appear more attractive when the business is viewed from a new perspective.

The second response to stalemate is to use supply-curve analysis to identify higher-return alternatives. A production system that is a middling performer in a large segment may be reconfigured into a low-cost producer when retargeted on a smaller segment. By examining competitors' options in supply-curve terms, you may be better able to anticipate competitive reactions.

The third response should be to reexamine a stalemated business for opportunities to restore competitive advantage. It usually requires a willingness to innovate. The starting point is to challenge each of the conditions that produced stalemate.

- *Restore competitive advantage.* While you may compete on equal terms in most of the activities that constitute your value added, there may be specific steps in which you have or can develop a significant edge over your competition. Developing a strategy around that activity—manufacture of a component, a distribution system, or a service—may create a new business opportunity. Union Carbide recently broke with tradition to promote the licensing of its new Unipol process for polyolefins rather than restrict its availability. Banc One sells its processing capabilities.

- *Differentiate.* Although many commodity products are not stalemated, the hallmark of most stalemates is the inability of any competitor to command a price premium. The requirement to load fully a world-scale facility at minimum cost naturally focuses many competitors on the large-volume, standard-product segments. Yet a few companies consistently find ways to uncover special needs of their customers, tailor the product or its delivery, and improve price realization. International Paper has upgraded a classic commodity, linerboard, by giving it barrier properties.

- *Develop proprietary technology.* While every competitor in a stalemate has learned a few tricks to produce his product more cheaply, the differences are marginal. An alternative open to some companies may be to attempt a breakthrough development, alone or in a venture with the leading third-party process equipment supplier, especially in the early stages of a next-generation technology. Michelin and Pilkington, in tires and flat glass, upset stalemates this way. The worst course is a halfway one—to spend enough to keep up with what outside suppliers will do anyway buy not enough to create a breakthrough.

When you do achieve a breakthrough, your decision on whether to license should be influenced by how long you believe it will be before a new stalemate results.

The best time to escape stalemate is before it happens. Early in the life cycle of any industry, the absence of industry standards, the high rate of growth, and the early profits available from developing new applications all obscure the fact that at maturity there may be no sustainable advantage. Seeing a stalemate coming can tell you when to take your profits and withdraw and when to show determination to win in the end. In stalemate, a shakeout will result only in survivors, not winners.

Stalemate is an ever more common fact of life. Finding new ways to create competitive advantage will be the measure of success for much of American business.

STRATEGY IN THE 1980s

RICHARD K. LOCHRIDGE, 1981

The economic environment and competitive dynamics of each era produce dramatic change in the requirements for strategic success. This is true despite the presence of fundamental strategy principles and laws of economics.

In the 1950s, dramatic growth and the postwar requirements for reindustrialization made a company's success depend on its ability to meet demand and to respond to changing market requirements. In the 1960s, increased competition and the internationalization of many industries made cost efficiency and market share critical determinants of success. The 1970s brought high inflation coupled with low growth, increased competition in traditional fields, added regulation, and dramatic growth in international trade, which again changed the rules of the game. Strategies in pursuit of market share and low-cost position alone met unexpected difficulty as segment specialists arose and multiple competitors reached economies of scale. The most successful companies achieved success by anticipating market evolution and creating unique and defensible advantage over their competitors in the new environment.

These external changes have led to a complex and sometimes confusing variety of competitive environments. In some cases, only the largest competitor makes adequate returns. In others, all competitors make low returns and there is little variance from best to worst. In still others, some of the most profitable are the smallest, focused competitors. No simple, monolithic set of rules or strategy imperatives will point automatically to the right course. No planning system guarantees the development of successful strategies. Nor does any technique. The business portfolio (the growth/share matrix) made a major contribution to strategic thought. Today it is misused and overexposed. It can be a helpful tool, but it can also be misleading, or worse, a straitjacket.

The strategy requirements of any business are ruled by the competitive environment and the potential for change in that environment. Two factors in particular give one a sense of the nature of that environment. The first is the size of the advantage that can be created over other competitors. The second is the number of unique ways in which that advantage can be created. The combination of these two factors gives a sense of the long-term value of a business and dictates the strategy requirements.

There is a fundamental difference between businesses in which the size of the potential advantage that can be created by a competitor over all other competitors is large and those in which it is small. The reward potential for a successful strategy is only large where the size of the advantage that can be created is also large. The long-term value of any business is determined by the size of its advantage over the marginal, but viable, competitor. When all or most competitors can achieve equal costs without price differentiation, then returns of the whole industry will be depressed to a level sufficient only to fund capacity additions to meet market growth requirements. Regardless of the reported returns, cash available to shareholders will be small or negative for all competitors in such industries. Only when real advantage exists can real returns accrue.

There is also a fundamental difference between businesses that offer only one or a few ways to achieve advantage and those that present several ways. When differentiation is costly and not valued by customers, low price and relative cost position determine success. This sort of environment has relatively straightforward strategy requirements. When a variety of approaches is possible, however, then so is a variety of strategies. Competitors can succeed by tuning their offering and costs exactly to meet a specific segment's demand. If advantage can be created by doing this, a small competitor can thrive as an industry specialist. When advantage cannot be created, or is dissipated with increased size, then the industry remains fragmented.

These two factors—the size of the advantage and the number of ways it can be achieved—can be combined into a simple matrix to help guide more creative strategy development. The specific requirements for success are different in each quadrant.

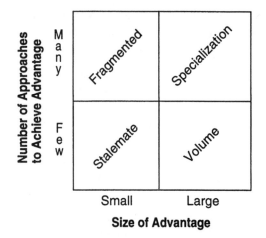

Corporate success requires that most of a company's businesses retain advantaged positions in volume and specialization businesses. Even high market share or relatively low cost position in stalemate and fragmented industries may not be exceptionally valuable. In fact, the value of success in businesses that best fit on the right side of this matrix is always higher than in those that fit best on the left. The market performance of stocks also reflects this reality.

Too many companies pursued strategies during the 1970s that were inappropriate to their specific competitive environments. Market share, for example, often lacks value in stalemated and fragmented businesses. In specialization businesses, focus and superior brand image may be more rewarding than mere size. This matrix is not a solution to all strategy. Most businesses, of course, present elements of each type of competitive environment. In any case, simple rules and models cannot substitute for creative, well-thought-through strategies.

Over time, the nature of the competitive environment can change. Businesses that start out as fragmented industries can evolve toward specialization and even on to the volume category. McDonald's did this in away-from-home eating. Businesses that start out as volume businesses can migrate toward stalemate. This has happened to much of the world's paper industry. Others that were clearly volume have moved toward specialization, as both the Japanese auto producers and a few European companies have proved to the large U.S. auto companies. Some have remained volume businesses by going toward world-scale economics, as Caterpillar has shown in construction equipment.

The challenge of the 1980s will be for companies to anticipate, or even cause, these major evolutions toward a new basis of competition. Those who are slow to react or fail to see the potential will be bypassed. New leaders will emerge. Returns for those who fail to adapt quickly will erode. The extraordinary performers of the coming decade will be those companies that can develop strategies to transform the basis of competition, to create advantaged positions in the new environment, and to preserve those positions from attack.

In a diversified company, the challenge is immense. A portfolio that is disadvantaged in specialized and volume businesses and has assets tied up in stalemate and fragmented industries will result in failure. The successful companies will be those with advantaged positions in volume and specialized businesses. Extraordinary success will accrue to those few strategists willing and able to create sustainable advantage, especially to those able to change the basis of competition.

REVOLUTION ON THE FACTORY FLOOR *

THOMAS M. HOUT AND GEORGE STALK, JR., 1982

A revolution in manufacturing is completely transforming the economics of production. It is doing so by reducing the cost penalty of product diversity. The change is shaking up the rules of competition in industries ranging from automobiles to earthmoving equipment to housewares. Within companies, the traditional conflict between marketing, which wants to offer customers more models, and the factory, which has wanted to limit product line variety for the sake of production efficiency, is becoming a thing of the past.

A broad product line services a wider range of customers, but it inherently costs more than a narrow, high-volume-per-model line. More models mean more machine setups, hence more downtime. Work-in-process (WIP) inventories have to increase to keep assembly areas supplied to produce a changing mix of final products and to avoid even more costly setups from low-volume lots. Also, the more

* This article originally appeared in *The Wall Street Journal,* July 12, 1982.

diverse the product mix, the longer any given volume takes to get through a plant and the more scheduling and handling overhead it requires.

Today, however, the cost penalty for diversity is being sharply cut, thanks to a dramatic shortening of setup times in the factory. All plant operations—machining, welding, assembling, and so forth—require equipment setups. Setups that used to take hours can now take minutes as a result of new, sophisticated machine tools and microprocessor control and sensory technologies. With the aid of computer controls, machines can now switch rapidly from one preset tool-and-die configuration to another, without the need for trips to the toolroom or the trial runs and adjustments usually necessary after manual handling. The faster setups are the key to collapsing the structure of downtime, inventory and overhead cost that plagues the conventional factory.

Toyota pioneered these developments in the 1970s, largely to avoid the cost penalties it began to see as it doubled its model range. But there is nothing uniquely Japanese about radically cutting setup time. Global competitors on both sides of the Pacific—such as Komatsu and Caterpillar in construction equipment and Matsushita and General Electric in home appliances—are adopting essentially the same practices.

One large engine manufacturer, over a five-year period, roughly tripled its number of models while reducing WIP inventory by half, doubled the output per factory worker and cut material waste and rework by 40%. Across a broad range of products, reducing factory cost added after purchased materials by 15% to 35% from earlier levels is well within reach.

The marketing and competitive implications of these new plant economics are powerful. Because product variety costs less now, there will be more of it. Truck builders, for example, will pay less for the unusual engine their customers often want. Before, more product variety tended to increase finished goods inventories, causing carrying costs to rise. Now, however, shorter setups increase effective plant capacity and reduce the cycle time it takes for the complete model mix to move through the factory. This allows the manufacturers to increase their model range in finished goods stock and keep their delivery lead time constant without raising their inventory costs. Black-and-white television sets are a case in point. The model variety has risen, while prices have continued to fall.

A manufacturer may find other uses for his WIP inventory savings. He could, for instance, use them by placing more finished goods inventories at more field stocking points to widen his market presence. This is exactly how Toyota gained U.S. market share in forklift trucks in the 1970s. Toyota was the last to run out of stock in cyclical expansions.

The economies of scale which larger competitors in broad-line businesses have enjoyed are changing. The new setup economics will tend to reduce the cost benefits of size between two competitors with similar product mix. Traditionally, plant scale economies have been of two kinds—plantwide savings from greater automation and fixed overheads spread over more volume, and the benefits of more dedicated machines and assembly lines that never need setups. Shorter setups will have little effect on the first advantage but will significantly dilute the second. Full-line producers with smaller market shares may suffer less manufacturing disadvantage than before.

As with any change in the rules, the competitor who exploits more swiftly and completely will gain the advantage. Industry leaders typically have greater engineering resources and more opportunities for high-markup, low-volume specialty products which shorter setups would favor. (General Motors over Ford in cars and DuPont over Monsanto in synthetic fibers are examples.) But industry leaders may resist change. Engineering and production managers, for instance, may be heavily committed to their current systems. But the new setup economics is a powerful lever, and it's unlikely that a leader will be able to hold its lead without making these new investments.

This set of economic relationships is fairly straightforward, but making it work for you is not. It requires both capital and imagination—typically a doubling or tripling of equipment investment and a thorough rethinking of plant flows, layout, and line-balancing logic. The role of workers is also important. Greater flexibility and intelligence are demanded of both people and machines. Machine tools and material-handling devices must be redesigned. Experimentation is necessary: radical systems that work take time to develop.

Developing the actual working system will most likely demand some proprietary engineering advances. Off-the-shelf technology will go only so far. Unusual savings will often come only from an original, unique machine-tool configuration or a component redesigned to accommodate automatic handling. Companies whose cultures have devalued manufacturing will have trouble.

In addition, component suppliers have to make comparable changes in production operations if their deliveries are to match the manufacturer's shorter runs, lower inventories, and greater variety. More frequent and rigorously scheduled deliveries are critical. Usually the manufacturer must educate the supplier, specify a tighter set of dimensional tolerances, and may even help underwrite his investment. In general, more supplier coordination and discipline are needed.

The payoffs from these investments, however, can be enormous. First, shorter setup time increases the use of machines and direct labor. It also reduces foreman and indirect labor time spent during setup. Second, shorter setups lower work-in-process inventory. They cut down on stock orders and the buffer inventory one needs ahead of and behind any operation. Third, simplifying traditionally long and complex setups reduces maintenance costs, raises production yields, and cuts down time spent solving problems. It's usually the difficulty, not the frequency, of setups that causes broken tools, high machine wear, and work rejected for being out-of-tolerance.

Reducing setup times by a factor of 5 or 10—quite common now for able manufacturers—dramatically increases the effective capacity of machines and plants. Each unit of output spends less time in the factory, reducing normal burden rates. Lower inventories eliminate not only their carrying costs but also the number of material handlers and schedulers who manage them.

Inventory turns go up by multiples, not mere percentages. Higher yields and lower maintenance reduce the cost per usable unit of output. The higher effective capacity allows slower machine running speeds with no loss of output, thus improving product quality by reducing machine wear.

Changing Will Be Better

Once the heavy investment is made by one competitor, the high interest rates associated with inventory carrying costs and uncertain, shifting demand patterns will differentiate him from the competitor who did not invest. Both will want to reduce inventories and change product mix quickly. The producer with a short setup time can achieve these without cost penalty; the other cannot. The latter can increase inventory turns via more setups only at the expense of more machine downtime and considerably more indirect labor time spent in setup.

The strategic payoff from the investment lies in marketing, and in better control of competitors. Shorter setup times enable a company to serve distribution channels better and to capture, at acceptable cost, higher-price, low-volume products. Broad-line producers everywhere will have to reckon with these new economics of diversity.

TIME—THE NEXT SOURCE OF COMPETITIVE ADVANTAGE*

GEORGE STALK, JR., 1988

Like competition itself, competitive advantage is a constantly moving target. For any company in any industry, the key is not to get stuck with a single simple notion of its source of advantage. The best competitors, the most successful ones, know how to keep moving and always stay on the cutting edge.

Today, time is on the cutting edge. The ways leading companies manage time—in production, in new product development and introduction, in sales and distribution—represent the most powerful new sources of competitive advantage. Though certain Western companies are pursuing these advantages, Japanese experience and practice provide the most instructive examples—not because they are necessarily unique but because they best illustrate the evolutionary stages through which leading companies have advanced.

In the period immediately following World War II, Japanese companies used their low labor costs to gain entry to various industries. As wage rates rose and technology became more significant, the Japanese shifted first to scale-based strategies and then to focused factories to achieve advantage. The advent of just-in-time production brought with it a move to flexible factories, as leading Japanese companies sought both low cost and great variety in the market. Cutting-edge Japanese companies today are capitalizing on time as a critical source of competitive advantage: shortening the planning loop in the product development cycle and trimming process time in the factory—managing time the way most companies manage costs, quality, or inventory.

In fact, as a strategic weapon, time is the equivalent of money, productivity, quality, even innovation. Managing time has enabled top Japanese companies not only to reduce their costs but also to offer broad product lines, cover more market segments, and upgrade the technological sophistication of their products. These companies are time-based competitors.

From Low Wages to Variety Wars

Since 1945, Japanese competitors have shifted their strategic focus at least four times. These early adaptations were straightforward; the shift to time-based competitive advantage is not nearly so obvious. It does, however, represent a logical evolution from the earlier stages.

In the immediate aftermath of World War II, with their economy devastated and the world around them in a shambles, the Japanese concentrated on achieving competitive advantage through low labor costs. Since Japan's workers were still productive and the yen was devalued by 98.8% against the dollar, its labor costs were extraordinarily competitive with those of the West's developed economies.

Hungry for foreign exchange, the Japanese government encouraged companies to make the most of their one edge by targeting industries with high labor content: textiles, shipbuilding, and steel—businesses where the low labor rates more than offset low productivity rates. As a result, Japanese companies took market share from their Western competition.

But this situation did not last long. Rising wages, caused by high inflation, combined with fixed exchange rates to erode the advantage. In many industries, manufacturers could not improve their productivity fast enough to offset escalating labor costs. By the early 1960s, for instance, the textile companies—comprising Japan's largest industry—were hard-pressed. Having lost their competitive edge in world markets, they spiraled downward, first losing share, then volume, then profits, and finally position and prestige. While the problem was most severe for the textile business, the rest of Japanese industry suffered as well.

The only course was adaptation: in the early 1960s, the Japanese shifted their strategy, using capital investment to boost workforce productivity. They inaugurated the era of scale-based strategies, achieving high productivity and low costs by building the largest and most capital-intensive facilities that were technologically feasible. Japanese shipbuilders, for example, revolutionized the industry in their effort to raise labor productivity. Adapting fabrication techniques from mass production processes and using automatic and semiautomatic equipment, they constructed vessels in modules. The approach produced two advantages for the Japanese. It drove up their own productivity and simultaneously erected a high capital-investment barrier to others looking to compete in the business.

The search for ways to achieve even higher productivity and lower costs continued, however. And in the mid-1960s, it led top Japanese companies to a new source of competitive advantage—the focused factory. Focused competitors manufactured products either made nowhere else in the world or located in the high-volume segment of a market, often in the heart of their Western competitors' product lines. Focusing of production allowed the Japanese to remain smaller than established broad-line producers, while still achieving higher productivity and lower costs—giving them great competitive power.

Factory costs are very sensitive to the variety of goods a plant produces. Reduction of the product-line variety by half, for example, raises productivity by 30%, cuts costs 17%, and substantially lowers the break-even point. Cutting the product line in half again boosts productivity by 75%, slashes costs 30%, and diminishes the break-even point to below 50%. (See "The Benefits of Focus.")

In industries like bearings, where competition was fierce in the late 1960s, the Japanese fielded product lines with one-half to one-quarter the variety of their Western competitors. Targeting the high-volume segments of the bearing business—bearings for automobile applications was one—the Japanese used the low costs of their highly productive focused factories to undercut the prices of Western competitors.

SKF was one victim. With factories scattered throughout Europe, each geared to a broad product line for the local market, the Swedish company was a big target for the Japanese. SKF reacted by trying to avoid direct competition with the Japanese: it added higher margin products to serve specialized applications. But SKF did not simultaneously drop any low-margin products, thereby complicating its plant operations and adding to production costs. In effect, SKF provided a cost umbrella for the Japanese. As long as they operated beneath it, the Japanese could expand their product line and move into more varied applications.

Avoiding price competition by moving into higher-margin products is called *margin retreat*—a common response to stepped-up competition that eventually leads to corporate suicide. As a company retreats, its costs rise as do its prices, thus "subsidizing" an aggressive competitor's expansion into the vacated position. The retreating company's revenue base stops growing and may eventually shrink to the point where it can no longer support the fixed cost of the operation. Retrenchment, restructuring, and further shrinkage follow in a cycle that leads to inevitable extinction.

Cutting Variety Yields Higher Productivity, Lower Costs, and Reduced Break-even Points

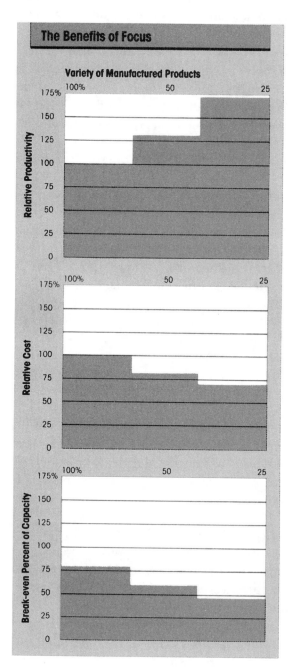

SKF avoided this fate by adopting the Japanese strategy. After a review of its factories, the company focused each on those products it was best suited to manufacture. If a product did not fit a particular factory, it was either placed in another, more suitable plant or dropped altogether. This strategy not only halted SKF's retreat but also beat back the Japanese advance.

At the same time, however, leading Japanese manufacturers began to move toward a new source of competitive advantage—the flexible factory. Two developments drove this move. First, as they expanded and penetrated more markets, their narrow product lines began to pinch, limiting their ability to grow. Second, with growth limited, the economics of the focus strategy presented them with an unattractive choice: either reduce variety further or accept the higher costs of broader product lines.

In manufacturing, costs fall into two categories: those that respond to volume or scale and those that are driven by variety. Scale-related costs decline as volume increases, usually falling 15% to 25% per unit each time volume doubles. Variety-related costs, on the other hand, reflect the costs of complexity in manufacturing: setup, materials handling, inventory, and many of the overhead costs of a factory. In most cases, as variety increases, costs increase, usually at a rate of 20% to 35% per unit each time variety doubles.

The sum of the scale- and variety-related costs represents the total cost of manufacturing. With effort, managers can determine the optimum cost point for their factories—the point where the combination of volume and variety yields the lowest total manufacturing cost for a particular plant. When markets are good, companies tend to edge toward increased variety in search of higher volumes, even though this will mean increased costs. When times are tough, companies pare their product lines, cutting variety to reduce costs.

In a flexible factory system, variety-driven costs start lower and increase more slowly as variety grows. Scale costs remain unchanged. Thus the optimum cost point for a flexible factory occurs at a higher volume and with greater variety than for a traditional factory. A gap emerges between the costs of the flexible and the traditional factory—a cost/variety gap that represents the competitive advantage of flexible production. Very simply, a flexible factory enjoys more variety with lower total costs than traditional factories, which are still forced to make the trade-off between scale and variety. (See "The Advantage of Flexible Manufacturing.")

For Flexible Factories, the Optimum Cost Points Occur at a Higher Volume and with Higher Variety than for Traditional Factories

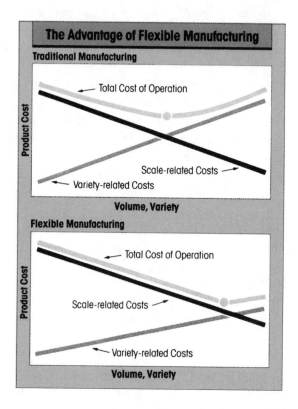

Yanmar Diesel illustrates how this process works. In 1973, with the Japanese economy in recession, Yanmar Diesel was mired in red ink. Worse, there was no promise that once the recession had passed, the existing strategy and program would guarantee real improvement in the company's condition.

As a Toyota supplier, Yanmar was familiar with the automaker's flexible manufacturing system. Moreover, Yanmar was impressed with the automaker's ability to weather the recession without losing money. Yanmar decided to install the Toyota procedure in its own two factories. The changeover took less than five years and produced dramatic results: manufacturing costs declined 40% to 60%, depending on the product; factory break-even points dropped 80% to 50%; total manufacturing labor productivity improved by more than 100%.

But it was Yanmar's newfound capability in product variety that signaled the arrival of a unique strategic edge: during the restructuring

Yanmar more than quadrupled its product line. With focused factories, Yanmar could have doubled productivity in such a short time only by reducing the breadth of the product line by 75%. The Toyota system made Yanmar's factories more flexible, reducing costs and producing a greater variety of products.

As its inventor, Taiichi Ohno, said, the Toyota production system was "born of the need to make many types of automobiles, in small quantities with the same manufacturing process." With its emphasis on just-in-time production, total quality control, employee decision making on the factory floor, and close supplier relations, the Toyota system gave the many Japanese manufacturers who adopted it in the mid-1970s a distinct competitive advantage.

A comparison of a U.S. company with a Japanese competitor in the manufacture of a particular automotive suspension component illustrates the nature and extent of the Japanese advantage. The U.S. company bases its strategy on scale and focus: it produces 10 million units per year—making it the world's largest producer—and offers only 11 types of finished parts. The Japanese company's strategy, on the other hand, is to exploit flexibility. It is both smaller and less focused: it manufactures only 3.5 million units per year but has 38 types of finished parts.

With one-third the scale and more than three times the product variety, the Japanese company also boasts total labor productivity that is half again that of its American competitor. Moreover, the unit cost of the Japanese manufacturer is less than half that of the U.S. company. But interestingly, the productivity of the Japanese direct laborers is not as high as that of the U.S. workers, a reflection of the difference in scale. The Japanese advantage comes from the productivity of the overhead employees: with one-third the volume and three times the variety, the Japanese company has only one-eighteenth the overhead employees.

In the late 1970s, Japanese companies exploited flexible manufacturing to the point that a new competitive thrust emerged—the variety war. A classic example of a variety war was the battle that erupted between Honda and Yamaha for supremacy in the motorcycle market, a struggle popularly known in Japanese business circles as the H-Y War. Yamaha ignited the H-Y War in 1981 when it announced the opening of a new factory which would make it the world's largest motorcycle manufacturer, a prestigious position held by Honda. But Honda had been concentrating its corporate resources on the automobile business and away from its motorcycle operation. Now, faced with Yamaha's overt and public challenge, Honda chose to counterattack.

Honda launched its response with the war cry, *"Yamaha wo tsubusu!"* ("We will crush, squash, slaughter Yamaha!") In the no-holds-barred battle that ensued, Honda cut prices, flooded distribution channels, and boosted advertising expenditures. Most important—and most impressive to consumers—Honda also rapidly increased the rate of change in its product line, using variety to bury Yamaha. At the start of the war, Honda had 60 models of motorcycles. Over the next 18 months, Honda introduced or replaced 113 models, effectively turning over its entire product line twice. Yamaha also began the war with 60 models; it was able to manage only 37 changes in its product line during those 18 months.

Honda's new product introductions devastated Yamaha. First, Honda succeeded in making motorcycle design a matter of fashion, where newness and freshness were important attributes for consumers. Second, Honda raised the technological sophistication of its products, introducing four-valve engines, composites, direct drive, and other new features. Next to a Honda, Yamaha products looked old, unattractive, and out of date. Demand for Yamaha products dried up; in a desperate effort to move them, dealers were forced to price them below cost. But even that didn't work. At the most intense point in the H-Y War, Yamaha had more than 12 months of inventory in its dealers' showrooms. Finally Yamaha surrendered. In a public statement, Yamaha President Eguchi announced, "We want to end the H-Y War. It is our fault. Of course there will be competition in the future but it will be based on a mutual recognition of our respective positions."

Honda didn't go unscathed either. The company's sales and service network was severely disrupted, requiring additional investment before it returned to a stable footing. However, so decisive was its victory that Honda effectively had as much time as it wanted to recover. It had emphatically defended its title as the world's largest motorcycle producer and done so in a way that warned Suzuki and Kawasaki not to challenge that leadership. Variety had won the war.

Time-Based Competitive Advantage

The strength of variety as a competitive weapon raises an interesting question. How could Japanese companies accommodate such rapid rates of change? In Honda's case, there could be only three possible answers. The company did one of the following:

1. Began the development of more than 100 new models 10 to 15 years before the attack.
2. Authorized a sudden, massive spending surge to develop and manufacture products on a crash basis.
3. Used structurally different methods to develop, manufacture, and introduce new products.

In fact, what Honda and other variety-driven competitors pioneered was time-based competitiveness. They managed structural changes that enabled their operations to execute their processes much faster. As a consequence, time became their new source of competitive advantage.

While time is a basic business performance variable, management seldom monitors its consumption explicitly—almost never with the same precision accorded sales and costs. Yet time is a more critical competitive yardstick than traditional financial measurements.

Today's new-generation companies compete with flexible manufacturing and rapid-response systems, expanding variety and increasing innovation. A company that builds its strategy on this cycle is a more powerful competitor than one with a traditional strategy based on low wages, scale, or focus. These older, cost-based strategies require managers to do whatever is necessary to drive down costs: move production to or source from a low-wage country; build new facilities or consolidate old plants to gain economies of scale; or focus operations down to the most economic subset of activities. These tactics reduce costs but at the expense of responsiveness.

In contrast, strategies based on the cycle of flexible manufacturing, rapid response, expanding variety, and increasing innovation are time based. Factories are close to the customers they serve. Organization structures enable fast responses rather than low costs and control. Companies concentrate on reducing if not eliminating delays and using their response advantages to attract the most profitable customers.

Many—but certainly not all—of today's time-based competitors are Japanese. Some of them are Sony, Matsushita, Sharp, Toyota, Hitachi, NEC, Toshiba, Honda, and Hino; time-based Western companies include Benetton, The Limited, Federal Express, Domino's Pizza, Wilson Art, and McDonald's. For these leading competitors, time has become the overarching measurement of performance. By reducing the consumption of time in every aspect of the business, these companies also reduce costs, improve quality, and stay close to their customers.

Breaking the Planning Loop

Companies are systems; time connects all the parts. The most powerful competitors understand this axiom and are breaking the debilitating loop that strangles much of traditional manufacturing planning.

Traditional manufacturing requires long lead times to resolve conflicts between various jobs or activities that require the same resources. The long lead times, in turn, require sales forecasts to guide planning. But sales forecasts are inevitably wrong; by definition they are guesses, however informed. Naturally, as lead times lengthen, the accuracy of sales forecasts declines. With more forecasting errors, inventories balloon and the need for safety stocks at all levels increases. Errors in forecasting also mean more unscheduled jobs that have to be expedited, thereby crowding out scheduled jobs. The need for longer lead times grows even greater and the planning loop expands even more, driving up costs, increasing delays, and creating system inefficiencies.

Managers who find themselves trapped in the planning loop often respond by asking for better forecasts and longer lead times. In other words, they treat the symptoms and worsen the problem. The only way to break the planning loop is to reduce the consumption of time throughout the system; that will, in turn, cut the need for lead time, for estimates, for safety stocks, and all the rest. After all, if a company could ever drive its lead time all the way to zero, it would have to forecast only the next day's sales. While that idea of course is unrealistic, successful time-based competitors in Japan and in the West have kept their lead times from growing and some have even reduced them, thereby diminishing the planning loop's damaging effects.

Thirty years ago, Jay W. Forrester of MIT published a pioneering article in *HBR*, "Industrial Dynamics: A Major Breakthrough for Decision Makers" (July–August 1958), which established a model of time's impact on an organization's performance. Using "industrial dynamics"—a concept originally developed for shipboard fire control systems—Forrester tracked the effects of time delays and decision rates within a simple business system consisting of a factory, a factory warehouse, a distributors' inventory, and retailers' inventories. The numbers in the illustration "Time in the planning loop" are the delays in the flow of information or product, measured in weeks. In this example, the orders accumulate at the retailer for three weeks, are in the mail for half a week, are delayed at the distributor for two weeks, go back into the mail for another half a week, and need eight weeks for

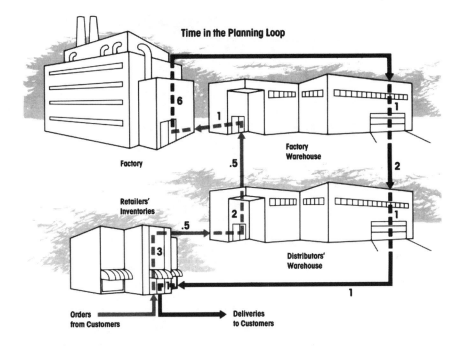

Time in the Planning Loop

processing at the factory and its warehouse. Then the finished product begins its journey back to the retailer. The cycle takes 19 weeks.

The system in this example is very stable—as long as retail demand is stable or as long as forecasts are accurate 19 weeks into the future. But if unexpected changes occur, the system must respond. The following chart, also taken from the Forrester article, shows what happens to this system when a simple change takes place: Demand goes up 10%, then flattens. Acting on new forecasts and seeking to cut delivery delays, the factory first responds by ramping up production 40%. When management realizes—too late—that it has overshot the mark, it cuts production 30%. Too late again it learns that it has overcorrected. This ramping up and cutting back continue until finally the system stabilizes, more than a year after the initial 10% increase.

What distorts the system so badly is time: the lengthy delay between the event that creates the new demand and the time when the factory finally receives the information. The longer that delay, the more distorted is the view of the market. Those distortions reverberate throughout the system, producing disruption, waste, and inefficiency.

These distortions plague business today. To escape them, companies have a choice: They can produce to forecast or they can reduce the time

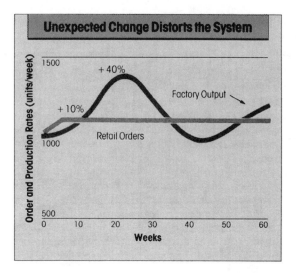

delays in the flow of information and product through the system. The traditional solution is to produce to forecast. The new approach is to reduce time consumption. Because time flows throughout the system, focusing on time-based competitive performance results in improvements across the board. Companies generally become time-based competitors by first correcting their manufacturing techniques, then fixing sales and distribution, and finally adjusting their approach to innovation. Ultimately, it becomes the basis for a company's overall strategy.

Time-Based Manufacturing

In general, time-based manufacturing policies and practices differ from those of traditional manufacturers along three key dimensions: length of production runs, organization of process components, and complexity of scheduling procedures.

When it comes to lot size, for instance, traditional factories attempt to maximize production runs while time-based manufacturers try to shorten their production runs as much as possible. In fact, many Japanese companies aim for run lengths of a single unit. The thinking behind this is as simple as it is fundamental to competitive success: reduced run lengths mean more frequent production of the complete mix of products and faster response to customers' demands.

Factory layout also contributes to time-based competitive advantage. Traditional factories are usually organized by process technology centers. For example, metal goods manufacturers organize their factories into shearing, punching, and braking departments; electronic assemblers have stuffing, wave soldering, assembly, testing, and packing departments. Parts move from one process technology center to the next. Each step consumes valuable time: parts sit, waiting to move; then move; then wait to be used in the next step. In a traditional manufacturing system, products usually receive value for only .05% to 2.5% of the time that they are in the factory. The rest of the time products sit waiting for something to happen.

Time-based factories, however, are organized by product. To minimize handling and moving of parts, the manufacturing functions for a component or a product are as close together as possible. Parts move from one activity to the next with little or no delay. Because the production process eliminates the need to pile and repile parts, they flow quickly and efficiently through the factory.

In traditional factories, scheduling is also a source of delay and waste. Most traditional factories use central scheduling that requires sophisticated materials resource planning and shop-floor control systems. Even though these systems are advanced, they still waste time: Work orders usually flow to the factory floor on a monthly or weekly basis. In the meantime, parts can sit idle.

In time-based factories, local scheduling enables employees to make more production control decisions on the factory floor, without the time-consuming loop back to management for approval. Moreover, the combination of the product-oriented layout of the factory and local scheduling makes the total production process run more smoothly. Once a part starts through the production run, many of the requirements between manufacturing steps are purely automatic and require no intermediate scheduling.

These differences between traditional and time-based factories add up. Flexible factories enjoy big advantages in both productivity and time: labor productivity in time-based factories can be as much as 200% higher than in conventional plants; time-based factories can respond eight to ten times faster than traditional factories. Flexible production means significant improvements in labor and net-asset productivity. These, in turn, yield reductions of up to 20% in overall costs and increases in growth for much less investment.

Toyota offers a dramatic example of the kinds of improvements that leading time-based competitors are making. Dissatisfied with the response time of a supplier, Toyota went to work. It took the supplier 15 days to turn out a component after arrival of the raw materials at its factory. The first step was to cut lot sizes, reducing response time to six days. Next Toyota streamlined the factory layout, reducing the number of inventory holding points. The response time fell to three days. Finally Toyota eliminated all work-in-progress inventories at the supplier's plant. New response time: one day. Toyota, of course, is not alone in improving manufacturing response times. Matsushita cut the time needed to make washing machines from 360 hours to just 2; Honda slashed its motorcycle fabricating time by 80%; in North America, companies making motor controllers and electrical components for unit air conditioners have improved their manufacturing response times by 90%.

Time-Based Sales and Distribution

A manufacturer's next challenge is to avoid dissipation of factory performance improvements in other parts of the organization. In Jay Forrester's example of the planning loop, the factory and its warehouse accounted for roughly one-half of the system's time. In actuality today, the factory accounts for one-third to one-half of the total time—often the most "visible" portion of time. But other parts of the system are just as important, if less apparent. For example, in the Forrester system, sales and distribution consume as much or more time than manufacturing.

What Forrester modeled, the Japanese experienced. By the late 1970s, leading Japanese companies were finding that inefficient sales and distribution operations undercut the benefits of their flexible manufacturing systems. Toyota, which at that time was divided into two separate companies, Toyota Motor Manufacturing and Toyota Motor Sales, again makes this point.

Toyota Motor Manufacturing could manufacture a car in less than two days. But Toyota Motor Sales needed from 15 to 26 days to close the sale, transmit the order to the factory, get the order scheduled, and deliver the car to the customer. By the late 1970s, the cost-conscious, competition-minded engineers at Toyota Manufacturing were angry at their counterparts at Toyota Motor Sales, who were frittering away the advantage gained in the production process. The sales and distribution function was generating 20% to 30% of a car's cost to the customer— more than it cost Toyota to manufacture the car!

Finally, in 1982 Toyota moved decisively to remedy the problem. The company merged Toyota Motor Manufacturing and Toyota Motor Sales. The company announced that it wanted to become "more marketing driven." While Toyota assured the public that the reorganization only returned it to its configuration in the 1950s, within 18 months all the Toyota Motor Sales directors retired. Their jobs were left vacant or filled by executives from Toyota Motor Manufacturing.

The company wasted no time in implementing a plan to cut delays in sales and distribution, reduce costs, and improve customer service. The old system, Toyota found, had handled customer orders in batches. Orders and other crucial information would accumulate at one step of the sales and distribution process before dispatch to the next level, which wasted time and generated extra costs.

To speed the flow of information, Toyota had to reduce the size of the information batches. The solution came from a company-developed computer system that tied its salespeople directly to the factory scheduling operation. This link bypassed several levels of the sales and distribution function and enabled the modified system to operate with very small batches of orders.

Toyota expected this new approach to cut the sales and distribution cycle time in half—from four to six weeks to just two to three weeks across Japan. (For the Tokyo and Osaka regions, which account for roughly two-thirds of Japan's population, the goal was to reduce cycle time to just two days.) But by 1987 Toyota had reduced system responsiveness to eight days, including the time required to make the car. In the Forrester example, this achievement is equivalent to cutting the 19-week cycle to six weeks. The results were predictable: shorter sales forecasts, lower costs, happier customers.

Time-Based Innovation

A company that can bring out new products three times faster than its competitors enjoys a huge advantage. Today, in one industry after another, Japanese manufacturers are doing just that to their Western competition:

- In projection television, Japanese producers can develop a new television in one-third the time required by U.S. manufacturers.

- In custom plastic injection molds, Japanese companies can develop the molds in one-third the time of U.S. competitors and at one-third the cost.

- In autos, Japanese companies can develop new products in half the time—and with half as many people—as the U.S. and German competition.

To accomplish their fast-paced innovations, leading Japanese manufacturers have introduced a series of organizational techniques that precisely parallel their approach to flexible manufacturing:

- In manufacturing, the Japanese stress short production runs and small lot sizes. In innovation, they favor smaller increments of improvement in new products, but introduce them more often—versus the Western approach of more significant improvements made less often.

- In the organization of product development work, the Japanese use factory cells that are cross-functional teams. Most Western new product development activity is carried out by functional centers.

- In the scheduling of work, Japanese factories stress local responsibility, just as product development scheduling is decentralized. The Western approach to both requires plodding centralized scheduling, plotting, and tracking.

The effects of this time-based advantage are devastating; quite simply, American companies are losing leadership of technology and innovation—supposedly this country's source of long-term advantage. Unless U.S. companies reduce their new product development and introduction cycles from 36–48 months to 12–18 months, Japanese manufacturers will easily out-innovate and outperform them. Taking the initiative in innovation will require even faster cycle times.

Residential air conditioners illustrate the Japanese ability to introduce more technological innovation in smaller increments—and how in just a few years these improvements add up to remarkably superior products. The Japanese introduce innovations in air conditioners four times faster than their American competitors; in technological sophistication the Japanese products are seven to ten years ahead of U.S. products.

Look at the changes in Mitsubishi Electric's three-horsepower heat pump between 1975 and 1985. From 1975 to 1979, the company did nothing to the product except change the sheet metal work, partly to improve efficiency but mostly to reduce materials costs. In 1979, the technological sophistication of the product was roughly equal to that of the U.S. competition. From this point on, the Japanese first established, and then widened, the lead.

In 1980, Mitsubishi introduced its first major improvement: a new product that used integrated circuits to control the air-conditioning cycle. One year later, the company replaced the integrated circuits with microprocessors and added two important innovations to increase consumer demand. The first was quick-connect Freon lines. On the old product (and on the U.S. product), Freon lines were made from copper tubing and cut to length, bent, soldered together, purged, and filled with Freon—an operation requiring great skill to produce a reliable air conditioner. The Japanese substituted quick-connect Freon lines—precharged hoses that simply clicked together. The second innovation was simplified wiring. On the old product (and still today on the U.S. product) the unit had six color-coded wires to connect. The advent of microprocessors made possible a two-wire connection with neutral polarity.

These two changes did not improve the energy-efficiency ratio of the product; nor were they intended to. Rather, the point was to fabricate a unit that would be simpler to install and more reliable, thereby broadening distribution and increasing demand. Because of these innovations, white-goods outlets could sell the new product, and local contractors could easily install it.

In 1982, Mitsubishi introduced a new version of the air conditioner featuring technological advances related to performance. A high-efficiency rotary compressor replaced the outdated reciprocating compressor. The condensing unit had louvered fins and inner fin tubes for better heat transfer. Because the balance of the system changed, all the electronics had to change. As a result, the energy-efficiency ratio improved markedly.

In 1983, Mitsubishi added sensors to the unit and more computing power, expanding the electronic control of the cycle and again improving the energy-efficiency ratio.

In 1984, Mitsubishi came out with another version of the product, this time with an inverter that made possible an even higher energy-efficiency ratio. The inverter, which requires additional electronics for the unit, allows unparalleled control over the speed of the electric motor, dramatically boosting the appliance's efficiency.

Using time-based innovation, Mitsubishi transformed its air conditioner. The changes came incrementally and steadily. Overall they gave Mitsubishi—and other Japanese companies on the same track—the position of technological leadership in the global residential air-conditioning industry.

In 1985, a U.S. air conditioner manufacturer was just debating whether to use integrated circuits in its residential heat pump. In view of its four- to five-year product development cycle, it could not have introduced the innovation until 1989 or 1990—putting the American company 10 years behind the Japanese. Faced with this situation, the U.S. air conditioner company followed the example of many U.S. manufacturers that have lost the lead in technology and innovation: It decided to source its air conditioners and components from its Japanese competition.

Time-Based Strategy

The possibility of establishing a response-time advantage opens new avenues for constructing winning competitive strategies. At most companies, strategic choices are limited to three options:

1. *Seeking coexistence with competitors.* This choice is seldom stable, since competitors refuse to cooperate and stay put.

2. *Retreating in the face of competitors.* Many companies choose this course; the business press fills its pages with accounts of companies retreating by consolidating plants, focusing their operations, outsourcing, divesting businesses, pulling out of markets, or moving upscale.

3. *Attacking, either directly or indirectly.* The direct attack involves the classic confrontation—cut price and add capacity, creating head-on competition. Indirect attack requires surprise. Competitors either do not understand the strategies being used against them or they do understand but cannot respond—sometimes because of the speed of the attack, sometimes because of their inability to mount a response.

Of the three options, only an attack creates the opportunity for real growth. Direct attack demands superior resources; it is always expensive and potentially disastrous. Indirect attack promises the most gain for the least cost. Time-based strategy offers a powerful new approach for successful indirect attacks against larger, established competitors.

Consider the remarkable example of Atlas Door, a 10-year-old U.S. company. It has grown at an average annual rate of 15% in an industry with an overall annual growth rate of less than 5%. In recent years, its pretax earnings were 20% of sales, about five times the industry average. Atlas is debt free. In its tenth year the company achieved the number one competitive position in its industry.

The company's product: industrial doors. It is a product with almost infinite variety, involving limitless choices of width and height and material. Because of the importance of variety, inventory is almost useless in meeting customer orders; most doors can be manufactured only after the order has been placed.

Historically, the industry had needed almost four months to respond to an order for a door that was out of stock or customized. Atlas's strategic advantage was time: It could respond in weeks to any order. It had structured its order-entry, engineering, manufacturing, and logistics systems to move information and products quickly and reliably.

First, Atlas built just-in-time factories. These are fairly simple in concept. They require extra tooling and machinery to reduce changeover times and a fabrication process organized by product and scheduled to start and complete all of the parts at the same time. But even the performance of the factory—critical to the company's overall responsiveness—still only accounted for 2½ weeks of the completed product delivery cycle.

Second, Atlas compressed time at the front end of the system, where the order first entered and was processed. Traditionally, when customers, distributors, or salespeople called a door manufacturer with a request for price and delivery, they would have to wait more than one week for a response. If the desired door was not in stock, not in the schedule, or not engineered, the supplier's organization would waste even more time, pushing the search for an answer around the system.

Recognizing the opportunity to cut deeply into the time expenditure in this part of the system, Atlas first streamlined, then automated its entire order-entry, engineering, pricing, and scheduling processes. Today Atlas can price and schedule 95% of its incoming orders while the callers are still on the telephone. It can quickly engineer new special orders because it has preserved on computer the design and production data of all previous special orders—which drastically reduces the amount of reengineering necessary.

Third, Atlas tightly controlled logistics so that it always shipped only fully complete orders to construction sites. Orders require many components. Gathering all of them at the factory and making sure that they are with the correct order can be a time-consuming task. It is even more time-consuming, however, to get the correct parts to the job site after they have missed the initial shipment. Atlas developed a system to track the parts in production and then purchased parts for each order, ensuring arrival of all necessary parts at the shipping dock in time—a just-in-time logistics operation.

When Atlas started operations, distributors were uninterested in its product. The established distributors already carried the door line of a larger competitor; they saw no reason to switch suppliers except, perhaps, for a major price concession. But as a start-up, Atlas was too small to compete on price alone. Instead, it positioned itself as the door supplier of last resort, the company people came to if the established supplier could not deliver or missed a key date.

Of course, with industry lead times of almost four months, some calls inevitably came to Atlas. And when it did get a call, Atlas commanded a higher price because of its faster delivery. Atlas not only got a higher price but its time-based processes also yielded lower costs: It thus enjoyed the best of both worlds.

In 10 short years, the company replaced the leading door suppliers in 80% of the distributors in the country. With its strategic advantage the company could be selective, becoming the house supplier for only the strongest distributors.

In the wake of this indirect attack, the established competitors have not responded effectively. The conventional view is that Atlas is a "garage shop operator" that cannot sustain its growth: Competitors expect the company's performance to degrade to the industry average as it grows larger. But this response—or nonresponse—only reflects a fundamental lack of understanding of time as the source of competitive advantage. The extra delay in responding only adds to the insurmountable lead the indirect time-based attack has created. While the traditional companies track costs and size, the new competitor derives advantage from time, staying on the cutting edge, leaving its rivals behind.

COMPETING ON CAPABILITIES: THE NEW RULES OF CORPORATE STRATEGY*

GEORGE STALK, JR., PHILIP B. EVANS, AND LAWRENCE E. SHULMAN, 1992

In the 1980s, companies discovered time as a new source of competitive advantage. In the 1990s, they will learn that time is just one piece of a more far-reaching transformation in the logic of competition.

---

* Reprinted by permission of *Harvard Business Review.* "Competing on Capabilities: The New Rules of Corporate Strategy" by George Stalk, Philip Evans, and Lawrence E. Shulman (March–April 1992).

Companies that compete effectively on time—speeding new products to market, manufacturing just-in-time, or responding promptly to customer complaints—tend to be good at other things as well: for instance, the consistency of their product quality, the acuity of their insight into evolving customer needs, the ability to exploit emerging markets, enter new businesses, or generate new ideas and incorporate them in innovations. But all these qualities are mere reflections of a more fundamental characteristic: a new conception of corporate strategy that we call *capabilities-based competition.*

For a glimpse of the new world of capabilities-based competition, consider the astonishing reversal of fortunes represented by Kmart and Wal-Mart: In 1979, Kmart was king of the discount retailing industry, an industry it had virtually created. With 1,891 stores and average revenues per store of $7.25 million, Kmart enjoyed enormous size advantages. This allowed economies of scale in purchasing, distribution, and marketing that, according to just about any management textbook, are crucial to competitive success in a mature and low-growth industry. By contrast, Wal-Mart was a small niche retailer in the South with only 229 stores and average revenues about half of those of Kmart stores— hardly a serious competitor.

And yet, only ten years later, Wal-Mart had transformed itself and the discount retailing industry. Growing nearly 25% a year, the company achieved the highest sales per square foot, inventory turns, and operating profit of any discount retailer. Its 1989 pretax return on sales was 8%, nearly double that of Kmart.

Today Wal-Mart is the largest and highest-profit retailer in the world—a performance that has translated into a 32% return on equity and a market valuation more than ten times book value. What's more, Wal-Mart's growth has been concentrated in half the United States, leaving ample room for further expansion. If Wal-Mart continues to gain market share at just one-half its historical rate, by 1995 the company will have eliminated all competitors from discount retailing with the exception of Kmart and Target.

The Secret of Wal-Mart's Success

What accounts for Wal-Mart's remarkable success? Most explanations focus on a few familiar and highly visible factors: the genius of founder Sam Walton, who inspires his employees and has molded a culture of service excellence; the greeters who welcome customers at the door; the motivational power of allowing employees to own part of the business; the strategy of "everyday low prices" that offers the customer a better deal and saves on merchandising and advertising costs. Economists also point to Wal-Mart's big stores, which offer economies of scale and a wider choice of merchandise.

But such explanations only redefine the question. Why is Wal-Mart able to justify building bigger stores? Why does Wal-Mart alone have a cost structure low enough to accommodate everyday low prices and greeters? And what has enabled the company to continue to grow far beyond the direct reach of Sam Walton's magnetic personality? The real secret of Wal-Mart's success lies deeper, in a set of strategic business decisions that transformed the company into a capabilities-based competitor.

The starting point was a relentless focus on satisfying customer needs. Wal-Mart's goals were simple to define but hard to execute: to provide customers access to quality goods, to make these goods available when and where customers want them, to develop a cost structure that enables competitive pricing, and to build and maintain a reputation for absolute trustworthiness. The key to achieving these goals was to make the way the company replenished inventory the centerpiece of its competitive strategy.

This strategic vision reached its fullest expression in a largely invisible logistics technique known as *cross-docking*. In this system, goods are continuously delivered to Wal-Mart's warehouses, where they are selected, repacked, and then dispatched to stores, often without ever sitting in inventory. Instead of spending valuable time in the warehouse, goods just cross from one loading dock to another in 48 hours or less.

Cross-docking enables Wal-Mart to achieve the economies that come with purchasing full truckloads of goods while avoiding the usual inventory and handling costs. Wal-Mart runs a full 85% of its goods through its warehouse system—as opposed to only 50% for Kmart. This reduces Wal-Mart's costs of sales by 2% to 3% compared with the industry average. That cost difference makes possible the everyday low prices.

But that's not all. Low prices in turn mean that Wal-Mart can save even more by eliminating the expense of frequent promotions. Stable prices also make sales more predictable, thus reducing stockouts and excess inventory. Finally, everyday low prices bring in the customers, which translates into higher sales per retail square foot. These advantages in basic economics make the greeters and the profit sharing easy to afford.

With such obvious benefits, why don't all retailers use cross-docking? The reason: It is extremely difficult to manage. To make cross-docking work, Wal-Mart has had to make strategic investments in a variety of interlocking support systems far beyond what could be justified by conventional ROI criteria.

For example, cross-docking requires continuous contact among Wal-Mart's distribution centers, suppliers, and every point of sale in every store to ensure that orders can flow in and be consolidated and executed within a matter of hours. So Wal-Mart operates a private satellite-communication system that daily sends point-of-sale data directly to Wal-Mart's 4,000 vendors.

Another key component of Wal-Mart's logistics infrastructure is the company's fast and responsive transportation system. The company's 19 distribution centers are serviced by nearly 2,000 company-owned trucks. This dedicated truck fleet permits Wal-Mart to ship goods from warehouse to store in less than 48 hours and to replenish its store shelves twice a week on average. By contrast, the industry norm is once every two weeks.

To gain the full benefits of cross-docking, Wal-Mart has also had to make fundamental changes in its approach to managerial control. Traditionally in the retail industry, decisions about merchandising, pricing, and promotions have been highly centralized and made at the corporate level. Cross-docking, however, turns this command-and-control logic on its head. Instead of the retailer pushing products into the system, customers "pull" products when and where they need them. This approach places a premium on frequent, informal cooperation among stores, distribution centers, and suppliers—with far less centralized control.

The job of senior management at Wal-Mart, then, is not to tell individual store managers what to do but to create an environment where they can learn from the market—and from each other. The company's information systems, for example, provide store managers with detailed information about customer behavior, while a fleet of airplanes regularly ferries store managers to Bentonville, Arkansas, headquarters for meetings on market trends and merchandising.

As the company has grown and its stores have multiplied, even Wal-Mart's own private air force hasn't been enough to maintain the necessary contacts among store managers. So Wal-Mart has installed a video link connecting all its stores to corporate headquarters and to each other. Store managers frequently hold videoconferences to exchange information on what's happening in the field, like which products are selling and which ones aren't, which promotions work and which don't.

The final piece of this capabilities mosaic is Wal-Mart's human resources system. The company realizes that its frontline employees play a significant role in satisfying customer needs. So it set out to enhance its organizational capability with programs like stock ownership and profit sharing geared toward making its personnel more responsive to customers. Even the way Wal-Mart stores are organized contributes to this goal. Where Kmart has 5 separate merchandise departments in each store, Wal-Mart has 36. This means that training can be more focused and more effective, and employees can be more attuned to customers.

Kmart did not see its business this way. While Wal-Mart was finetuning its business processes and organizational practices, Kmart was following the classic textbook approach that had accounted for its original success. Kmart managed its business by focusing on a few productcentered strategic business units, each a profit center under strong centralized line management. Each SBU made strategy—selecting merchandise, setting prices, and deciding which products to promote. Senior management spent most of its time and resources making line decisions rather than investing in a support infrastructure.

Similarly, Kmart evaluated its competitive advantage at each stage along a value chain and subcontracted activities that managers concluded others could do better. While Wal-Mart was building its ground transportation fleet, Kmart was moving out of trucking because a subcontracted fleet was cheaper. While Wal-Mart was building close relationships with its suppliers, Kmart was constantly switching suppliers in search of price improvements. While Wal-Mart was controlling all the departments in its stores, Kmart was leasing out many of its departments to other companies on the theory that it could make more per square foot in rent than through its own efforts.

This is not to say that Kmart managers do not care about their business processes. After all, they have quality programs too. Nor is it that Wal-Mart managers ignore the structural dimension of strategy: They focus on the same consumer segments as Kmart and still have to make traditional strategic decisions like where to open new stores. The difference is that Wal-Mart emphasizes behavior—the organizational practices and business processes in which capabilities are rooted—as the primary object of strategy and therefore focuses its managerial attention on the infrastructure that supports capabilities. This subtle distinction has made all the difference between exceptional and average performance.

Four Principles of Capabilities-Based Competition

The story of Kmart and Wal-Mart illustrates the new paradigm of competition in the 1990s. In industry after industry, established competitors are being outmaneuvered and overtaken by more dynamic rivals.

In the years after World War II, Honda was a modest manufacturer of a 50-cc engine designed to be attached to a bicycle. Today it is challenging General Motors and Ford for dominance of the global automobile industry.

Xerox invented xerography and the office copier market. But between 1976 and 1982, Canon introduced more than 90 new models, cutting Xerox's share of the midrange copier market in half. Today Canon is a key competitor not only in midrange copiers but also in high-end color copiers.

The greatest challenge to department store giants like Macy's comes neither from other large department stores nor from small boutiques but from The Limited, a $5.25 billion design, procurement, delivery, and retailing machine that exploits dozens of consumer segments with the agility of many small boutiques.

Citicorp may still be the largest U.S. bank in terms of assets, but Banc One has consistently enjoyed the highest return on assets in the U.S. banking industry and now enjoys a market capitalization greater than Citicorp's.

These examples represent more than just the triumph of individual companies. They signal a fundamental shift in the logic of competition, a shift that is revolutionizing corporate strategy.

When the economy was relatively static, strategy could afford to be static. In a world characterized by durable products, stable customer needs, well-defined national and regional markets, and clearly identified competitors, competition was a "war of position" in which companies occupied competitive space like squares on a chessboard, building and defending market share in clearly defined product or market segments. The key to competitive advantage was where a company chose to compete. How it chose to compete was also important but secondary, a matter of execution.

Few managers need reminding of the changes that have made this traditional approach obsolete. As markets fragment and proliferate, owning any particular market segment becomes simultaneously more difficult and less valuable. As product life cycles accelerate, dominating existing product segments becomes less important than being able to create new products and exploit them quickly. Meanwhile, as globalization breaks down barriers between national and regional markets, competitors are multiplying and reducing the value of national market share.

In this more dynamic business environment, strategy has to become correspondingly more dynamic. Competition is now a "war of movement" in which success depends on anticipation of market trends and quick response to changing customer needs. Successful competitors move quickly in and out of products, markets, and sometimes even entire businesses—a process more akin to an interactive video game than to chess. In such an environment, the essence of strategy is not the structure of a company's products and markets but the dynamics of its behavior. And the goal is to identify and develop the hard-to-imitate organizational capabilities that distinguish a company from its competitors in the eyes of customers.

Companies like Wal-Mart, Honda, Canon, The Limited, or Banc One have learned this lesson. Their experience and that of other successful companies suggests four basic principles of capabilities-based competition:

1. The building blocks of corporate strategy are not products and markets but business processes.

2. Competitive success depends on transforming a company's key processes into strategic capabilities that consistently provide superior value to the customer.

3. Companies create these capabilities by making strategic investments in a support infrastructure that links together and transcends traditional SBUs and functions.

4. Because capabilities necessarily cross functions, the champion of a capabilities-based strategy is the CEO.

A capability is a set of business processes strategically understood. Every company has business processes that deliver value to the customer. But few think of them as the primary object of strategy. Capabilities-based competitors identify their key business processes, manage them centrally, and invest in them heavily, looking for a long-term payback.

Take the example of cross-docking at Wal-Mart. Cross-docking is not the cheapest or the easiest way to run a warehouse. But seen in the broader context of Wal-Mart's inventory-replenishment capability, it is an essential part of the overall process of keeping retail shelves filled while also minimizing inventory and purchasing in truckload quantities.

What transforms a set of indvidual business processes like cross-docking into a strategic capability? The key is to connect them to real customer needs. A capability is strategic only when it begins and ends with the customer.

Of course, just about every company these days claims to be "close to the customer." But there is a qualitative difference in the customer focus of capabilities-driven competitors. These companies conceive of the organization as a giant feedback loop that begins with identifying the needs of the customer and ends with satisfying them.

As managers have grasped the importance of time-based competition, for example, they have increasingly focused on the speed of new product development. But as a unit of analysis, new product development is too narrow. It is only part of what is necessary to satisfy a customer and, therefore, to build an organizational capability. Better to think in terms of new product realization, a capability that includes the way a product is not only developed but also marketed and serviced. The longer and more complex the string of business processes, the harder it is to transform them into a capability—but the greater the value of that capability once built because competitors have more difficulty imitating it.

Weaving business processes together into organizational capabilities in this way also mandates a new logic of vertical integration. At a time when cost pressures are pushing many companies to outsource more and more activities, capabilities-based competitors are integrating vertically to ensure that they, not a supplier or distributor, control the performance of key business processes. Remember Wal-Mart's decision to own its transportation fleet in contrast to Kmart's decision to subcontract.

Even when a company doesn't actually own every link of the capability chain, the capabilities-based competitor works to tie these parts into its own business systems. Consider Wal-Mart's relationships with its suppliers. In order for Wal-Mart's inventory-replenishment capability to work, vendors have to change their own business processes to be more responsive to the Wal-Mart system. In exchange, they get far better payment terms from Wal-Mart than they do from other discount retailers. At Wal-Mart, the average "days payable," the time between the receipt of an invoice from a supplier and its payment, is 29 days. At Kmart, it is 45.

Another attribute of capabilities is that they are collective and cross-functional—a small part of many people's jobs, not a large part of a few. This helps explain why most companies underexploit capabilities-based competition. Because a capability is "everywhere and nowhere," no one executive controls it entirely. Moreover, leveraging capabilities requires a panoply of strategic investments across SBUs and functions far beyond what traditional cost-benefit metrics can justify. Traditional internal accounting and control systems often miss the strategic nature of such investments. For these reasons, building strategic capabilities cannot be treated as an operating matter and left to operating managers, to corporate staff, or still less to SBU heads. It is the primary agenda of the CEO.

Only the CEO can focus the entire company's attention on creating capabilities that serve customers. Only the CEO can identify and authorize the infrastructure investments on which strategic capabilities depend. Only the CEO can insulate individual managers from any short-term penalties to the P&Ls of their operating units that such investments might bring about.

Indeed, a CEO's success in building and managing capabilities will be the chief test of management skill in the 1990s. The prize will be companies that combine scale and flexibility to outperform the competition along five dimensions:

Speed. The ability to respond quickly to customer or market demands and to incorporate new ideas and technologies quickly into products.

Consistency. The ability to produce a product that unfailingly satisfies customers' expectations.

Acuity. The ability to see the competitive environment clearly and thus to anticipate and respond to customers' evolving needs and wants.

Agility. The ability to adapt simultaneously to many different business environments.

Innovativeness. The ability to generate new ideas and to combine existing elements to create new sources of value.

Becoming a Capabilities-Based Competitor

Few companies are fortunate enough to begin as capabilities-based competitors. For most, the challenge is to become one.

The starting point is for senior managers to undergo the fundamental shift in perception that allows them to see their business in terms of strategic capabilities. Then they can begin to identify and link together essential business processes to serve customer needs. Finally, they can reshape the organization—including managerial roles and responsibilities—to encourage the new kind of behavior necessary to make capabilities-based competition work.

The experience of a medical-equipment company we'll call Medequip illustrates this change process. An established competitor, Medequip recently found itself struggling to regain market share it had lost to a new competitor. The rival had introduced a lower-priced, lower-performance version of the company's most popular product. Medequip had developed a similar product in response, but senior managers were hesitant to launch it.

Their reasoning made perfect sense according to the traditional competitive logic. As managers saw it, the company faced a classic no-win situation. The new product was lower priced but also lower profit. If the company promoted it aggressively to regain market share, overall profitability would suffer.

But when Medequip managers began to investigate their competitive situation more carefully, they stopped defining the problem in terms of static products and markets. Increasingly, they saw it in terms of the organization's business processes.

Traditionally, the company's functions had operated autonomously. Manufacturing was separate from sales, which was separate from field service. What's more, the company managed field service the way most companies do—as a classic profit center whose resources were deployed to reduce costs and maximize profitability. For instance, Medequip assigned full-time service personnel only to those customers who bought enough equipment to justify the additional cost.

However, a closer look at the company's experience with these steady customers led to a fresh insight: At accounts where Medequip had placed one or more full-time service representatives on-site, the company renewed its highly profitable service contracts at three times the rate of its other accounts. When these accounts needed new equipment, they chose Medequip twice as often as other accounts did and tended to buy the broadest mix of Medequip products as well.

The reason was simple. Medequip's on-site service representatives had become expert in the operations of their customers. They knew what equipment mix best suited the customer and what additional equipment the customer needed. So they had teamed up informally with Medequip's salespeople to become part of the selling process.

Because the service reps were on-site full-time, they were also able to respond quickly to equipment problems. And of course, whenever a competitor's equipment broke down, the Medequip reps were on hand to point out the product's shortcomings.

This new knowledge about the dynamics of service delivery inspired top managers to rethink how their company should compete. Specifically, they redefined field service from a stand-alone function to one part of an integrated sales and service capability. They crystallized this new approach in three key business decisions.

First, Medequip decided to use its service personnel not to keep costs low but to maximize the life-cycle profitability of a set of targeted accounts. This decision took the form of a dramatic commitment to place at least one service rep on-site with selected customers—no matter how little business each account currently represented.

The decision to guarantee on-site service was expensive, so choosing which customers to target was crucial; there had to be potential for considerable additional business. The company divided its accounts into three categories: those it dominated, those where a single competitor dominated, and those where several competitors were present. Medequip protected the accounts it dominated by maintaining the already high level of service and by offering attractive terms for renewing service contracts. The company ignored those customers dominated by a single competitor—unless the competitor was having serious problems. All the remaining resources were focused on those accounts where no single competitor had the upper hand.

Next Medequip combined its sales, service, and order-entry organizations into cross-functional teams that concentrated almost exclusively on the needs of the targeted accounts. The company trained service reps in sales techniques so they could take full responsibility for generating new sales leads. This freed up the sales staff to focus on the more strategic role of understanding the long-term needs of the customer's business. Finally, to emphasize Medequip's new commitment to total service, the company even taught its service reps how to fix competitors' equipment.

Once this new organizational structure was in place, Medequip finally introduced its new low-priced product. The result: The company has not only stopped its decline in market share but also increased share by almost 50%. The addition of the lower-priced product has reduced profit margins, but the overall mix still includes many higher-priced products. And absolute profits are much higher than before.

This story suggests four steps by which any company can transform itself into a capabilities-based competitor: Shift the strategic framework to achieve aggressive goals. At Medequip, managers transformed what looked like a no-win situation—either lose share or lose profits—into an opportunity for a major competitive victory. They did so by abandoning the company's traditional function, cost, and profit-center orientation and by identifying and managing the capabilities that link customer needs to customer satisfaction. The chief expression of this new capabilities-based strategy was the decision to provide on-site service reps to targeted accounts and to create cross-functional sales and service teams.

Organize around the chosen capability and make sure employees have the necessary skills and resources to achieve it. Having set this ambitious competitive goal, Medequip managers next set about reshaping the company in terms of it. Rather than retaining the existing functional structure and trying to encourage coordination through some kind of matrix, they created a brand-new organization—Customer Sales and Service—and divided it into cells with overall responsibility for specific customers. The company also provided the necessary training so that employees could understand how their new roles would help achieve new business goals. Finally, Medequip created systems to support employees in their new roles. For example, one information system uses CD-ROMs to give field-service personnel quick access to information about Medequip's product line as well as those of competitors.

Make progress visible and bring measurements and reward into alignment. Medequip also made sure that the company's measurement and reward systems reflected the new competitive strategy. Like most companies, the company had never known the profitability of individual customers. Traditionally, field-service employees were measured on overall service profitability. With the shift to the new approach, however, the company had to develop a whole new set of measures—for example, Medequip's "share-by-customer-by-product," the amount of money the company invested in servicing a particular customer, and the customer's current and estimated lifetime profitability. Team members' compensation was calculated according to these new measures.

Do not delegate the leadership of the transformation. Becoming a capabilities-based competitor requires an enormous amount of change. For that reason, it is a process extremely difficult to delegate. Because capabilities are cross-functional, the change process can't be left to middle managers. It requires the hands-on guidance of the CEO and the active involvement of top line managers. At Medequip, the heads of sales, service, and order entry led the subteams that made the actual recommendations, but it was the CEO who oversaw the change process, evaluated their proposals, and made the final decision. His leading role ensured senior management's commitment to the recommended changes.

This top-down change process has the paradoxical result of driving business decision making down to those directly participating in key processes—for example, Medequip's sales and service staff. This leads to a high measure of operational flexibility and an almost reflexlike responsiveness to external change.

A New Logic of Growth: The Capabilities Predator

Once managers reshape the company in terms of its underlying capabilities, they can use these capabilities to define a growth path for the corporation. At the center of capabilities-based competition is a new logic of growth.

In the 1960s, most managers assumed that when growth in a company's basic business slowed, the company should turn to diversification. This was the age of the multibusiness conglomerate. In the 1970s and 1980s, however, it became clear that growth through diversification was difficult. And so, the pendulum of management thinking swung once again. Companies were urged to "stick to their knitting"—that is, to focus on their core business, identify where the profit was, and get rid of everything else. The idea of the corporation became increasingly narrow.

Competing on capabilities provides a way for companies to gain the benefits of both focus and diversification. Put another way, a company that focuses on its strategic capabilities can compete in a remarkable diversity of regions, products, and businesses and do it far more coherently than the typical conglomerate can. Such a company is a "capabilities predator"—able to come out of nowhere and move rapidly from nonparticipant to major player and even to industry leader.

Capabilities-based companies grow by transferring their essential business processes—first to new geographic areas and then to new businesses. Wal-Mart CEO David Glass alludes to this method of growth when he characterizes Wal-Mart as "always pushing from the inside out; we never jump and backfill." Strategic advantages built on capabilities are easier to transfer geographically than more traditional competitive advantages. Honda, for example, has become a manufacturer in Europe and the United States with relatively few problems. The quality of its cars made in the United States is so good that the company is exporting some of them back to Japan.

In many respects, Wal-Mart's move from small towns in the South to large, urban, northern cities spans as great a cultural gap as Honda's move beyond Japan. And yet, Wal-Mart has done it with barely a hiccup. While the stores are much bigger and the product lines different, the capabilities are exactly the same. Wal-Mart simply replicates its system as soon as the required people are trained. The company estimates that it can train enough new employees to grow about 25% a year.

But the big payoff for capabilities-led growth comes not through geographical expansion but through rapid entry into whole new businesses. Capabilities-based companies do this in at least two ways. The first is by cloning their key business processes. Again, Honda is a typical example.

Most people attribute Honda's success to the innovative design of its products or the way the company manufactures them. These factors are certainly important. But the company's growth has been spearheaded by less visible capabilities.

For example, a big part of Honda's original success in motorcycles was due to the company's distinctive capability in dealer management, which departed from the traditional relationship between motorcycle manufacturers and dealers. Typically, local dealers were motorcycle enthusiasts who were more concerned with finding a way to support their hobby than with building a strong business. They were not particularly interested in marketing, parts-inventory management, or other business systems.

Honda, by contrast, managed its dealers to ensure that they would become successful businesspeople. The company provided operating procedures and policies for merchandising, selling, floor planning, and service management. It trained all its dealers and their entire staffs in these new management systems and supported them with a computerized dealer-management information system. The part-time dealers of competitors were no match for the better-prepared and better-financed Honda dealers.

Honda's move into new businesses, including lawn mowers, outboard motors, and automobiles, has depended on re-creating this same dealer-management capability in each new sector. Even in segments like luxury cars, where local dealers are generally more service-oriented than those in the motorcycle business, Honda's skill at managing its dealers is transforming service standards. Honda dealers consistently receive the highest ratings for customer satisfaction among auto companies selling in the United States. One reason is that Honda gives its dealers far more autonomy to decide on the spot whether a needed repair is covered by warranty.

But the ultimate form of growth in the capabilities-based company may not be cloning business processes so much as creating processes so flexible and robust that the same set can serve many different businesses. This is the case with Wal-Mart. The company uses the same inventory-replenishment system that makes its discount stores so successful to propel itself into new and traditionally distinct retail sectors.

Take the example of warehouse clubs, no-frills stores that sell products in bulk at a deep discount. In 1983, Wal-Mart created Sam's Club to compete with industry founder Price Club and Kmart's own PACE Membership Warehouse. Within four years, Sam's Club sales had passed those of both Price and PACE, making it the largest wholesale club in the country. Sam's 1990 sales were $5.3 billion, compared with $4.9 billion for Price and $1.6 billion for PACE. What's more, Wal-Mart has repeated this rapid penetration strategy in other retail sectors, including pharmacies, European-style hypermarkets, and large, no-frills grocery stores known as superstores.

While Wal-Mart has been growing by quickly entering these new businesses, Kmart has tried to grow by acquisition, with mixed success. In the past decade, Kmart has bought and sold a number of companies in unrelated businesses such as restaurants and insurance—an indication the company has had difficulty adding value.

This is not to suggest that growth by acquisition is necessarily doomed to failure. Indeed, the company that is focused on its capabilities is often better able to target sensible acquisitions and then integrate them successfully. For example, Wal-Mart has recently begun to supplement its growth "from the inside out" by acquiring companies— for example, other small warehouse clubs and a retail and grocery distributor—whose operations can be folded into the Wal-Mart system.

It is interesting to speculate where Wal-Mart will strike next. The company's inventory-replenishment capability could prove to be a strong competitive advantage in a wide variety of retail businesses. In the past decade, Wal-Mart came out of nowhere to challenge Kmart. In the next decade, companies such as Toys "R" Us (Wal-Mart already controls as much as 10% of the $13 billion toy market) and Circuit City (consumer electronics) may find themselves in the sights of this capabilities predator.

The Future of Capabilities-Based Competition

For the moment, capabilities-based companies have the advantage of competing against rivals still locked into the old way of seeing the competitive environment. But such a situation won't last forever. As more and more companies make the transition to capabilities-based competition, the simple fact of competing on capabilities will become less important than the specific capabilities a company has chosen to build. Given the necessary long-term investments, the strategic choices managers make will end up determining a company's fate.

If Wal-Mart and Kmart are good examples of the present state of capabilities-based competition, the story of two fast-growing regional banks suggests its future. Wachovia Corporation, with dual headquarters in Winston-Salem, North Carolina, and Atlanta, Georgia, has superior returns and growing market share throughout its core markets in both states. Banc One, based in Columbus, Ohio, has consistently enjoyed the highest return on assets in the U.S. banking industry. Both banks compete on capabilities, but they do it in very different ways.

Wachovia competes on its ability to understand and serve the needs of individual customers, a skill that manifests itself in probably the highest "cross-sell ratio"—the average number of products per customer—of any bank in the country. The linchpin of this capability is the company's roughly 600 "personal bankers," frontline employees who provide Wachovia's mass-market customers with a degree of personalized service approaching what has traditionally been available only to private banking clients. The company's specialized support systems allow each personal banker to serve about 1,200 customers. Among those systems: an integrated customer-information file, simplified work processes that allow the bank to respond to almost all customer requests by the end of business that day, and a five-year personal banker training program.

Where Wachovia focuses on meeting the needs of individual customers, Banc One's distinctive ability is to understand and respond to the needs of entire communities. To do community banking effectively, a bank has to have deep roots in the local community. But traditionally, local banks have not been able to muster the professional expertise, state-of-the-art products, and highly competitive cost structure of large national banks like Citicorp. Banc One competes by offering its customers the best of both these worlds. Or in the words of one company slogan, Banc One "out-locals the national banks and out-nationals the local banks."

Striking this balance depends on two factors. One is local autonomy. The central organizational role in the Banc One business system is played not by frontline employees but by the presidents of the 51 affiliate banks in the Banc One network. Affiliate presidents have exceptional power within their own region. They select products, establish prices and marketing strategy, make credit decisions, and set internal management policies. They can even overrule the activities of Banc One's centralized direct-marketing businesses. But while Banc One's affiliate system is highly decentralized, its success also depends on an elaborate, and highly centralized, process of continuous organizational learning. Affiliate presidents have the authority to mold bank products and services to local conditions, but they are also expected to learn from best practice throughout the Banc One system and to adapt it to their own operations.

Banc One collects an extraordinary amount of detailed and current information on each affiliate bank's internal and external performance. For example, the bank regularly publishes "league tables" on numerous measures of operating performance, with the worst performers listed first. This encourages collaboration to improve the weakest affiliates rather than competition to be the best. The bank also continuously engages in workflow reengineering and process simplification. The 100 most successful projects, known as the "Best of the Best," are documented and circulated among affiliates.

Wachovia and Banc One both compete on capabilities. Both banks focus on key business processes and place critical decision-making authority with the people directly responsible for them. Both manage these processes through a support system that spans the traditional functional structure, and senior managers concentrate on managing this system rather than controlling decisions. Both are decentralized but focused, single-minded but flexible.

But there the similarities end. Wachovia responds to individual customers en masse with personalization akin to that of a private banker. Banc One responds to local markets en masse with the flexibility and canniness of the traditional community bank. As a result, they focus on different business processes: Wachovia on the transfer of customer-specific information across numerous points of customer contact; Banc One on the transfer of best practices across affiliate banks. They also empower different levels in the organization: the personal banker at Wachovia, the affiliate president at Banc One.

Most important, they grow differently. Because so much of Wachovia's capability is embedded in the training of the personal bankers, the bank has made few acquisitions and can integrate them only very slowly. Banc One's capabilities, by contrast, are especially easy to transfer to new acquisitions. All the company needs to do is install its corporate MIS and intensively train the acquired bank's senior officers, a process that can be done in a few months, as opposed to the much longer period it takes Wachovia to train a new cadre of frontline bankers. Banc One has therefore made acquisitions almost a separate line of business.

If Banc One and Wachovia were to compete against each other, it is not clear who would win. Each would have strengths that the other could not match. Wachovia's capability to serve individual customers by cross-selling a wide range of banking products will in the long term probably allow the company to extract more profit per customer than Banc One. On the other hand, Wachovia cannot adapt its products, pricing, and promotion to local market conditions the way Banc One can. And Wachovia's growth rate is limited by the amount of time it takes to train new personal bankers.

Moreover, these differences are deep-seated. They define each of the two companies in ways that are not easy to change. Capabilities are often mutually exclusive. Choosing the right ones is the essence of strategy.

REENGINEERING BUMPS INTO STRATEGY

JONATHAN L. ISAACS, 1994

It's about to become a full-blown problem. The reengineers are bumping into strategy, but still calling it reengineering. They are in danger of causing their firms to miss strategic advantages as well as undermining their own methodology. Before long the reality will be clear to all—reengineering is not strategy nor is it *a* strategy. Instead, reengineering needs strategy.

Reengineering is enormously popular, and its reach inside companies is growing. In some quarters, the word *reengineering* is so well received, you can get almost any project approved under its banner. Reengineering sells.

The result, however, is that reengineering is increasingly overextended and misused. Firms caught up with reengineering are falling victim to two different but related errors:

- Confusing reengineering with strategy by allowing reengineering's focus on how to do things divert attention from what things to do

- Letting reengineering's familiar benchmarking and empowerment procedures mask the need for other, more analytical and inventive ways of thinking

A telecommunications company, beset by rising costs and falling profitability, sought to reengineer its customer acquisition and service processes. Familiar with the methodology from other successes, cross-functional teams set about to map some processes, benchmark others, and devise faster and more efficient procedures. They generated exciting ideas for improvement, but all were based on serving the market in its present condition.

In reality, the challenge included two quite different sets of needs:

- A reengineering part: improving the speed and accuracy of order entry, billing, and service functions. This is what reengineering does best. For this they could learn from others and heed the experience of frontline employees.

- A strategic part: discovering which customer groupings are most profitable and growing, hence which to pursue most vigorously. These were new choices requiring new insights. For this, they needed strategic analysis and original data gathering. No competitor had worked the problem quite this way previously, so a real competitive advantage could be built on this new, proprietary information.

The company needed to uncover the costs, probabilities, and time lags of attracting and retaining different types of customers. Knowing the differing cash streams among customers, they could develop differentiated marketing and pricing programs to get more of the best customers and fewer of the worst.

The original reengineering program would have missed the point—and the new opportunity—by lumping both parts together under the single heading and approach.

How could such missteps arise? Arguably, it's a logical outgrowth of the origins and success of the reengineering movement.

The Reengineering Scale-Up

Reengineering is probably the hottest current idea in North American business. Its aims are clear: increased competitiveness and profitability via simpler, leaner, more productive business systems and processes. Its methods are also clear: cross-functional teams, mapping, benchmarking, learning from frontline employees, customer input, throwing out old paradigms in favor of new ones. Most major firms have reengineered at least some parts of their business—usually with dramatic impact.

At first, managers applied the reengineering concept to the basic routines of the business. The question was mainly how to do them most effectively and productively. Greater speed and reduced head count regularly followed. Building on success, firms then extended the reengineering concept. What started as reengineering of order processing became a reassessment of all customer service.

At this point, besides asking how to do it better, one must also determine what to do and for whom to do it. These are classic strategy choices, and it's vital to get them right.

Unfortunately, much of the reengineering methodology has trouble coping with these questions. While benchmarking works well for bringing inside the best practices of others, it often amounts to strategy by mimicry. It's not very good for devising an original best practice that doesn't already exist. Cross-functional teams are good at pooling existing knowledge, breaking down barriers, and finding new ways to work inside the existing game. But these same teams often shy away from more speculative data gathering, blue-sky brainstorming, and going outside the box to change the rules of the game itself. Few team members want to risk embarrassment and failure by going out on a limb that others may not even be able to perceive. Yet that's often what's required to create a strong and original strategy. And so it is that the reengineers are rediscovering the need for strategy.

A business wag once asked, "Once the trains are running on time, where should they go?" That's the question more and more firms are facing even after their reengineering efforts are done. Finding the answer takes more than just reengineering. It takes strategy.

Compatibility without Blind Spots

The same is true in reverse. Like reengineering, strategy analysis by itself is also not enough. A strategic review can declare a business uncompetitive based on its current way of doing business, yet reengineering can revitalize that business by changing its basic operating premises.

In one instance, a manufacturer's strategy analysis confirmed that parts of two key product lines were lagging in growth and returns. The customers described the products as top-notch, highly differentiated, and already highly priced, but they also complained of long and unreliable lead times, especially on custom and specialty items. Could reengineering change this picture?

A reengineering review showed large opportunities to improve returns by focusing on reducing time-to-market and streamlining the order-to-delivery process across the board. Eventually, the company made these new capabilities the centerpiece of a new process-oriented strategy. The firm went from being the least to the most flexible competitor in the industry with a new price schedule capturing the value of its fast customization.

The reengineering efforts revitalized the product lines, leading to faster sales growth, even greater profitability growth, and new platforms for the future. Reengineering triumphed where strategy alone could not.

Reengineering needs strategy, and vice versa. Alone, each may be the blind spot of the other. Together, the two are quite different but highly compatible. Like the yin and the yang, each needs the other to be balanced and complete.

STRATEGY AND THE NEW ECONOMICS OF INFORMATION*

PHILIP B. EVANS AND THOMAS S. WURSTER, 1997

A fundamental shift in the economics of information is under way—a shift that is less about any specific new technology than about the fact that a new behavior is reaching critical mass. Millions of people at home and at work are communicating electronically using universal, open standards. This explosion in connectivity is the latest—and, for business strategists, the most important—wave in the information revolution.

Over the past decade, managers have focused on adapting their operating processes to new information technologies. Dramatic as those operating changes have been, a more profound transformation of the business landscape lies ahead. Executives—and not just those in high-tech or information companies—will be forced to rethink the strategic fundamentals of their business. Over the next decade, the new economics of information will precipitate changes in the structure of entire industries and in the ways companies compete.

Early signs of this change are not hard to find. Consider the recent near-demise of *Encyclopædia Britannica*, one of the strongest and best-known brand names in the world. Since 1990, sales of *Britannica*'s multivolume sets have plummeted by more than 50%. CD-ROMs came from nowhere and devastated the printed encyclopedia business as we traditionally understand it.

How was that possible? *Britannica* sells for somewhere in the region of $1,500 to $2,200. An encyclopedia on CD-ROM, such as Microsoft Encarta, sells for around $50. And many people get Encarta for free because it comes bundled with personal computers or CD-ROM drives. The cost of producing a set of encyclopedias—printing, binding, and physical distribution—is about $200 to $300. The cost of producing a CD-ROM is about $1.50. This is a spectacular, if small, example of the way information technologies and new competition can disrupt the conventional value proposition of an established business.

Imagine what the people at *Britannica* thought was happening. The editors probably viewed CD-ROMs as nothing more than electronic versions of inferior products. Encarta's content is licensed from the Funk & Wagnalls encyclopedia, which was historically sold in supermarkets. Microsoft merely spruced up that content with public-domain illustrations and movie clips. The way *Britannica*'s editors must have seen it, Encarta was not an encyclopedia at all. It was a toy.

Judging from their initial inaction, *Britannica*'s executives failed to understand what its customers were really buying. Parents had been buying *Britannica* less for its intellectual content than out of a desire to do the right thing for their children. Today, when parents want to do the right thing, they buy their kids a computer.

The computer, then, is *Britannica*'s real competitor. And along with the computer come a dozen CD-ROMs, one of which happens to be—as far as the customer is concerned—a more-or-less perfect substitute for the *Britannica*. When the threat became obvious, *Britannica* did create a CD-ROM version—but to avoid undercutting its sales force, the company bundled it with the printed version and charged $1,000 for the stand-alone disc. Revenues continued to decline. The best salespeople left. And *Britannica*'s owner, a trust controlled by the University of Chicago, finally sold out. Under new management, the company is now trying to rebuild the business around the Internet.

Britannica's downfall is more than a parable about the dangers of complacency. It demonstrates how quickly and drastically the new economics of information can change the rules of competition, allowing new players and substitute products to render obsolete such traditional sources of competitive advantage as a sales force, a supreme brand, and even the world's best content.

When managers hear this story, many respond, "Interesting, but it has nothing to do with my business. *Britannica* is in an information business. Thank goodness, I'm not." They feel less secure, however, when they learn that the largest chunk of *Britannica*'s cost structure was not the editorial content—which constituted only about 5% of costs—but the direct sales force. *Britannica*'s vulnerability was due largely to its dependence on the economics of a different kind of information: the economics of intensive personal selling. A whole host of businesses fit that description, among them automobiles, insurance, real estate, and travel.

Every Business Is an Information Business

In many industries not widely considered information businesses, information actually represents a large percentage of the cost structure. About one-third of the cost of health care in the United States—some $300 billion—is the cost of capturing, storing, and processing information relating to, for example, patient records, physicians' notes, test results, and insurance claims.

More fundamentally, information is the glue that holds together the structure of all businesses. A company's value chain consists of all the activities it performs to design, produce, market, deliver, and support its product. The value chains of companies that supply and buy from each other collectively make up an industry's value chain, its particular configuration of competitors, suppliers, distribution channels, and customers.*

When we think about a value chain, we tend to visualize a linear flow of physical activities. But the value chain also includes all the information that flows within a company and between a company and its suppliers, its distributors, and its existing or potential customers. Supplier relationships, brand identity, process coordination, customer loyalty, employee loyalty, and switching costs all depend on various kinds of information.

When managers talk about the value of customer relationships, for example, what they really mean is the proprietary information that they have about their customers and that their customers have about their company and its products. Brands, after all, are nothing but the information—real or imagined, intellectual or emotional—that consumers have in their heads about a product. And the tools used to build brands—advertising, promotion, and even shelf space—are themselves information or ways of delivering information.

Similarly, information defines supplier relationships. Having a relationship means that two corporations have established certain channels of communication built around personal acquaintance, mutual understanding, shared standards, electronic data interchange (EDI) systems, or the synchronization of production systems.

In any buyer-seller relationship, information can determine the relative bargaining power of the players. Auto dealers, for example, know the best local prices for a given model. Customers—unless they invest a lot of time shopping around—generally do not. Much of the dealer's margin depends on that asymmetry of information.

Not only does information define and constrain the relationship among the various players in a value chain, but in many businesses it forms the basis for competitive advantage—even when the cost of that information is trivial and the product or service is thoroughly physical. To cite some of the best-known examples, American Airlines for a long time used its control of the SABRE reservation system to achieve higher capacity utilization than its competitors. Wal-Mart Stores has exploited its EDI links with suppliers to increase its inventory turns dramatically.

---

* For a complete discussion of the value chain concept, see Michael Porter's *Competitive Advantage* (Free Press, 1985). Differences in value chains—that is, differences in how competitors perform strategic activities or in which activities they choose to perform—are the basis for competitive advantage.

And Nike has masterfully employed advertising, endorsements, and the microsegmentation of its market to transform sneakers into high-priced fashion goods. All three companies compete as much on information as they do on their physical product.

In many ways, then, information and the mechanisms for delivering it stabilize corporate and industry structures and underlie competitive advantage. But the informational components of value are so deeply embedded in the physical value chain that, in some cases, we are just beginning to acknowledge their separate existence.

When information is carried by things—by a salesperson or by a piece of direct mail, for example—it goes where the things go, and no further. It is constrained to follow the linear flow of the physical value chain. But once everyone is connected electronically, information can travel by itself. The traditional link between the flow of product-related information and the flow of the product itself, between the economics of information and the economics of things, can be broken. What is truly revolutionary about the explosion in connectivity is the possibility it offers to unbundle information from its physical carrier.

The Tradeoff between Richness and Reach

Let's back up for a minute to consider why this is such a revolutionary proposition. To the extent that information is embedded in physical modes of delivery, its economics are governed by a basic law: the tradeoff between richness and reach. *Reach* simply means the number of people, at home or at work, exchanging information. *Richness* is defined by three aspects of the information itself. The first is bandwidth, or the amount of information that can be moved from sender to receiver in a given time. Stock quotes are narrowband, a film is broadband. The second is the degree to which the information can be customized. A TV ad is far less customized, but reaches far more people, for example, than a personal sales pitch. The third is interactivity. Dialogue is possible for a small group, but to reach millions of people the message must be a monologue.

In general, the communication of rich information has required proximity and dedicated channels whose costs or physical constraints have limited the size of the audience to which the information could be sent. Conversely, the communication of information to a large audience has required compromises in bandwidth, customization, and interactivity. (See the graph on page 107.) This pervasive tradeoff has

The Traditional Economics of Information

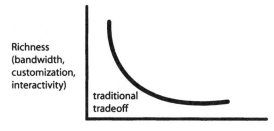

shaped how companies communicate, collaborate, and conduct transactions internally and with customers, suppliers, and distributors.

A company's marketing mix, for example, is determined by apportioning resources according to this tradeoff. A company can embed its message in an advertisement, a piece of customized direct mail, or a personal sales pitch—alternatives increasing in richness but diminishing in reach.

When companies conduct business with each other, the number of parties they deal with is inversely proportional to the richness of the information they need to exchange: Citibank can trade currencies with hundreds of other banks each minute because the data exchange requires little richness; conversely, Wal-Mart has narrowed its reach by moving to fewer and larger long-term supplier contracts precisely because such contracts allow a richer coordination of marketing and logistical systems.

Within a corporation, traditional concepts of span of control and hierarchical reporting are predicated on the belief that communication cannot be rich and broad simultaneously. Jobs are structured to channel rich communication among a few people standing in a hierarchical relationship to one another (upward or downward), and broader communication is effected through the indirect routes of the organizational pyramid. Indeed, there is an entire economic theory (pioneered by Ronald H. Coase and Oliver E. Williamson*) that suggests the boundaries of the corporation are set by the economics of exchanging information: organizations enable the exchange of rich

---

* Coase, R. 1937, "The Nature of the Firm," *Economica*, vol. 4, no. 4, pp. 386–405. Williamson, O. 1975, *Markets and Hierarchies: Analysis and Antitrust Implications*. Free Press, New York.

information among a narrow, internal group; markets enable the exchange of thinner information among a larger, external group. The point at which one mode becomes less cost-effective than the other determines the boundaries of the corporation.

The tradeoff between richness and reach, then, not only governs the old economics of information but is also fundamental to a whole set of premises about how the business world works. And it is precisely this tradeoff that is now being blown up.

The rapid emergence of universal technical standards for communication, which is allowing everybody to communicate with everybody else at essentially zero cost, constitutes a sea change. And it is as much the agreement on standards as the technology itself that is making this change possible. It's easy to get lost in the technical jargon, but the important principle here is that the same technical standards underlie all the so-called net technologies—the Internet, which connects everyone; extranets, which connect companies to each other; and the intranets, which connect individuals within companies.

Those emerging open standards and the explosion in the number of people and organizations connected by networks are freeing information from the channels that have been required to exchange it, making those channels unnecessary or uneconomical. Although the standards may not be ideal for any one application, users are finding that they are good enough for most purposes today. And they are improving exponentially. Over time, corporations and individuals will be able to extend their reach by many orders of magnitude, with often a negligible sacrifice of richness.

Where once a sales force, a system of branches, a printing press, a chain of stores, or a delivery fleet served as formidable barriers to entry because it took years and heavy investment to build them, in this new world, they could suddenly become expensive liabilities. New competitors on the Internet will be able to come from nowhere to steal customers. Similarly, the replacement of expensive proprietary, legacy systems with inexpensive open extranets will make it easier and cheaper for companies to bid for supply contracts, join a virtual factory, or form a competing supply chain.

Inside large corporations, the emergence of universal, open standards for exchanging information over intranets encourages the emergence of cross-functional teams and accelerates the demise of hierarchical functions and their proprietary information systems.

THE END OF CHANNELS AND HIERARCHIES

In today's world, rich content passes through media with limited reach, which we call *channels*. The existence of channels creates *hierarchy*, both of choice (people have to gather rich information in an order dictated by the structure of the channels) and of power (some people have better access to rich information than do others). Hierarchy of choice is illustrated by the decision tree along which consumers are compelled to do their shopping in the physical world: They must choose a street, then a shop, then a department, then a shelf, then a product. They cannot select in any other sequence. They can return to the street and search along a different path, of course, but only by expending time and effort.

Hierarchy of power is illustrated by the traditional organization chart, where senior executives have a wider span of knowledge than do their subordinates.

Hierarchy enables richness, but constrains choice and creates asymmetries in information. The alternative to hierarchy is markets, which are symmetrical and open to the extent that they are perfect. But traditional markets trade only in less-rich information.

When the tradeoff between richness and reach is eliminated, channels are no longer necessary: Everyone communicates richly with everyone else on the basis of shared standards. This might be termed *hyperarchy*.

The World Wide Web is a hyperarchy. So are a deconstructed value chain within a business and a deconstructed supply chain within an industry. So are intranets. So are concepts of fluid, team-based collab-

Hierarchical Decision Tree

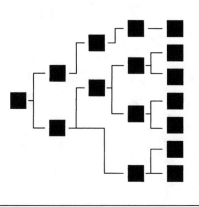

Hierarchical Organization

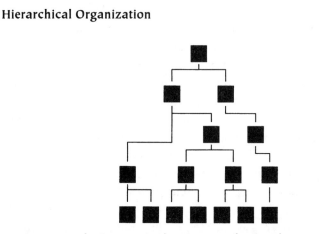

oration at work. So, too, is the pattern of amorphous and permeable corporate boundaries characteristic of the companies in Silicon Valley. (So, too, incidentally, are the architectures of object-oriented programming in software and of packet switching in telecommunications.)

Hyperarchy challenges *all* hierarchies, whether of logic or of power, with the possibility (or the threat) of random access and information symmetry. It challenges all markets with the possibility of exchanging information far richer than the mere trading of products and certificates of ownership. The principles of hyperarchy will provide a better way to understand not just strategies for positioning within business and industry, but issues of corporate organization and even identity.

Hyperarchy

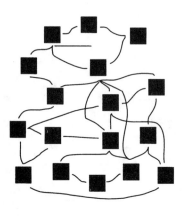

The Deconstruction of the Value Chain

The changing economics of information threatens to undermine established value chains in many sectors of the economy, requiring virtually every company to rethink its strategy—not incrementally, but fundamentally. What will happen, for instance, to category killers such as Toys "R" Us and The Home Depot when a search engine on the Internet gives consumers more choice than any store? What will be the point of having a supplier relationship with General Electric when it posts its purchasing requirements on an Internet bulletin board and entertains bids from anybody inclined to respond? What will happen to health care providers and insurers if a uniform electronic format for patient records eliminates a major barrier that today discourages patients from switching hospitals or doctors?

Consider the future of newspapers that, like most businesses, are built on a vertically integrated value chain. Journalists and advertisers supply copy, editors lay it out, presses create the physical product, and an elaborate distribution system delivers it to the reader each morning.

Newspaper companies exist as intermediaries between the journalist and the reader because there are enormous economies of scale in printing and distribution. But when high-resolution electronic tablets advance to the point that readers consider them a viable alternative to newsprint, those traditional economies of scale will become irrelevant. Editors—or even journalists—will be able to e-mail content directly to readers.

Freed from the necessity of subscribing to entire physical newspapers, readers will be able to mix and match content from a virtually unlimited number of sources. News could be downloaded daily from different electronic news services. Movie reviews, recipes, and travel features could come just as easily from magazine or book publishers. Star columnists, cartoonists, or the U.S. Weather Service could send their work directly to subscribers. Intermediaries—search engines, alert services, formatting software, or editorial teams—could format and package the content to meet readers' individual interests. It does not follow that all readers will choose to unbundle all the current content of the physical newspaper, but the principal logic for that bundle—the economics of printing—will be gone.

This transformation is probably inevitable but distant. As newspaper executives correctly point out, the broadsheet is still an extraordinarily cheap and user-friendly way to distribute information. Little electronic tablets are not going to replace it very soon.

However, the timing of total deconstruction is not really the issue. Pieces of the newspaper can be unbundled today. Classified advertising is a natural on-line product. Think how much easier it would be to pay for, update, search through, and respond to classified ads. Stripping away classifieds, however, would remove 25% of the typical newspaper's revenues but less than 10% of its costs.

Newspaper companies have moved aggressively into the electronic classifieds business. They have exploited their incumbent advantage as makers of the original print marketplace to provide an integrated print and electronic offering that reaches the widest population of buyers and sellers, thus preserving the 60% to 80% margins they need from classifieds to cover their fixed printing costs.

But as more and more people use the electronic medium, companies focused on targeted segments of the electronic classifieds market (operating on, say, 15% margins) will gain share. The greater their share, by definition, the more attractive they will become to buyers and sellers. Eventually, the newspapers will either lose business, or (more likely) retain it by settling for much lower margins.

Either way, the subsidy that supports the fixed costs of the print product will be gone. So newspapers will cut content or raise prices to readers and advertisers, accelerating their defection. That, in turn, will create opportunities for another focused competitor to pick off another part of the value chain. Thus the greatest vulnerability for newspapers is not the total substitution of a new business model, but a steady erosion through a sequence of partial substitutions that will make the current business model unsustainable.

Retail banking is ripe for a similar upheaval. The current business model depends on a vertically integrated value chain through which multiple products are originated, packaged, sold, and cross-sold through proprietary distribution channels. The high costs of distribution drive economies of utilization and scale and thus govern strategy in retail banking as it works today.

Home electronic banking looks at first glance like another, but cheaper, distribution channel. Many banks see it that way, hoping that widespread adoption might enable them to scale down their higher-cost physical channels. Some are even offering proprietary software and electronic transactions for free. But something much deeper has happened than the emergence of a new distribution channel. Customers now can access information and make transactions in a variety of new ways.

Some 10 million people in the United States regularly use personal financial-management software such as Intuit's Quicken or Microsoft Money to manage their checkbooks and integrate their personal financial affairs. Current versions of these programs can use modems to access electronic switches operated by CheckFree or VISA Interactive, which in turn route instructions or queries to the customer's bank. Such a system lets customers pay bills, make transfers, receive electronic statements, and seamlessly integrate account data into their personal financial plan. In addition, almost all financial institutions supply information at their Web sites, which anybody on-line can access using a browser.

No single software program can achieve both richness and reach, yet. Quicken, Money, and proprietary bank software permit rich exchanges but only with the customer's own bank. Web browsers do much less but reach the entire universe of financial institutions. However, the software vendors and switch providers have the resources, and ultimately will have the motivation, to form alliances with financial institutions to eliminate this artificial tradeoff. Bridges between personal financial-management software and the Web, combined with imminent advances in reliability, security, digital signatures, and legally binding electronic contracts, will enable financial Web sites to provide the full range of banking services.

If that happens, the tradeoff between richness and reach will be broken. Customers will be able to contact any financial institution for any kind of service or information. They will be able to maintain a balance sheet on their desktop, drawing on data from multiple institutions. They will be able to compare alternative product offerings and to sweep funds automatically between accounts at different institutions. Bulletin boards or auctioning software will allow customers to announce their product requirements and accept bids. Chat rooms will permit customers to share information with each other or get advice from human experts.

The sheer breadth of choice will create the need for third parties to play the role of navigator or facilitating agent. For example, some companies will have an incentive to create (or simply make available) databases on interest rates, risk ratings, and service histories. Others will create insurance and mortgage calculators or intelligent-agent software that can search for and evaluate product offerings. Still other companies will authenticate the identity of counterparties or serve as guarantors of performance, confidentiality, or creditworthiness. (See the diagram on page 114.)

The Transformation of Retail Banking. In Today's Integrated Business Model, the Retail Bank Stands between the Customer and the Full Range of Financial Services. But Soon, through Internet Technologies, Customers Will Have Direct Access to Product Providers. As Choices Proliferate, Totally New Businesses Will Arise to Help Customers Navigate through the Expanded Range of Banking Options

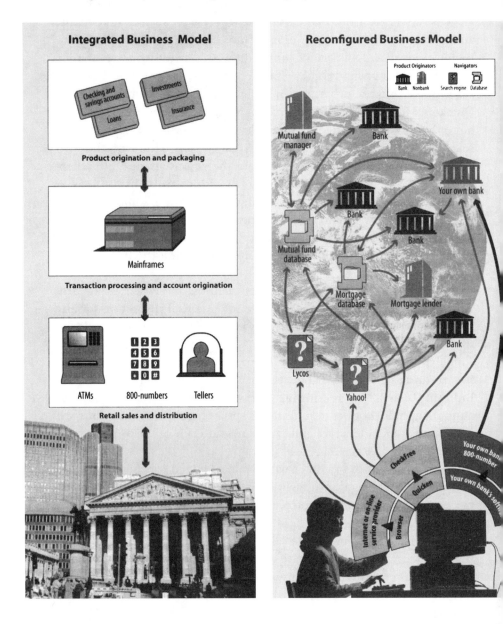

As it becomes easier for customers to switch from one supplier to another, the competitive value of one-stop shopping and established relationships will drop. Cross-selling will become more difficult. Information about the customer's needs or behavior will be harder for the provider to obtain. Competitive advantage will be determined product by product, and therefore providers with broad product lines will lose ground to focused specialists.

In this new world, distribution will be done by the phone company; statements by personal financial-management software, facilitation by different kinds of agent software, and origination by any number of different kinds of product specialists. The integrated value chain of retail banking will have been deconstructed.

Deconstructed, but not destroyed. All the old functions will still be performed, as well as some new ones. Banks will not become obsolete, but their current business definitions will—specifically, the concept that a bank is an integrated business where multiple products are originated, packaged, sold, and cross-sold through proprietary distribution channels.

Many bankers—like encyclopedia executives—deny all this. They argue that most customers do not have personal computers, and many who do are not choosing to use them for banking. They point out that people worry about the security of on-line transactions, and that consumers trust banks more than they trust software companies. All true. However, on-line technology is advancing inexorably. And because they generate a disproportionate share of deposits and fees, the 10% of the population that currently use personal financial-management software probably account for 75% of the profit of the banking system.

Market research suggests that Quicken users are more likely to be loyal to their software than to their banks. In one study, half of them said that if they were changing banks anyway, they would require their new bank to support the software, that is, allow them to transact their business on-line using Quicken. Now, bank accounts churn at the rate of about 10% a year. If a bank that doesn't support Quicken loses half the new Quicken-using customers it might otherwise attract every year, and such customers churn at the average rate, then it follows that the bank will lose 3% to 5% of its retail-customer margin per year. Refusal to support Quicken (or provide an acceptable alternative) could undermine the entire value of a franchise within just a few years.

The deconstruction of the value chain in banking is not unprecedented. Fifteen years ago, corporate banking was a spread business, that is, banks made money by charging a higher interest rate for loans than they paid for deposits. Their business model required them to form deep relationships with their corporate customers so that they could pump their own products through that distribution system. But then, thanks to technology, corporate customers got access to the same financial markets that the banks used. Today, corporate banking consists of small businesses that largely stand alone (even when they function under the umbrella of a big bank) and compete product by product. Credit flows directly from ultimate lender to ultimate borrower, facilitated by bankers who rate the risk, give advice, make markets, and serve as custodians. The bankers make money through the fees they charge for these individual services. Clients no longer bundle their purchases, and relationships are more volatile. Once critical, an advantage in distribution today counts for little.

Newspapers and banking are not special cases. The value chains of scores of other industries will become ripe for unbundling. The logic is most compelling—and therefore likely to strike soonest—in information businesses where the cost of physical distribution is high—newspapers, ticket sales, insurance, financial information, scientific publishing, software, and of course encyclopedias. But in any business where the physical value chain has been compromised for the sake of delivering information, there is an opportunity to unbundle the two, creating a separate information business and allowing (or compelling) the physical one to be streamlined. All it will take to deconstruct a business is a competitor that focuses on the vulnerable sliver of information in its value chain.

WHAT WILL HAPPEN TO YOUR BUSINESS?

All businesses will eventually be affected by the shifting economics of information, but not all at the same rate or in the same way. Answers to the following questions are a first step in determining how a business could be restructured.

1. How and where in the current value chain of this business is information a component of value?
2. Where are tradeoffs currently being made between richness and reach in this business?

3. In what situations will these tradeoffs be eliminated?
4. Which critical activities—especially informational activities— could be peeled off as stand-alone businesses?
5. Could the underlying physical businesses be run more efficiently if the information functions were stripped away?
6. What new activities—especially facilitating-agent roles— might be required?
7. Among the successor businesses, how would risks and rewards be distributed?
8. How would losing control over key activities affect the profitability of the current business model?
9. Which current strategic assets could become liabilities?
10. What new capabilities are needed to dominate the new businesses that will emerge?

Implications for Competitive Advantage

Deconstructing a vertically integrated value chain does more than transform the structure of a business or an industry—it alters the sources of competitive advantage. The new economics of information therefore present threats to established businesses but also represent a new set of opportunities. Every industry will shift according to its own dynamics, and those shifts will occur at different speeds and with varying intensity. No single set of predictions can be applied across the board, but some fundamental strategic implications of the changing economics of information can be drawn.

Existing value chains will fragment into multiple businesses, each of which will have its own sources of competitive advantage. When individual functions having different economies of scale or scope are bundled together, the result is a compromise of each—an averaging of the effects. When the bundles of functions are free to re-form as separate businesses, however, each can exploit its own sources of competitive advantage to the fullest.

Take car retailing in the United States. Dealerships provide information about products in showrooms and through test-drives. They hold inventory and distribute cars. They broker financing. They make a market in secondhand cars. They operate maintenance and repair services. Although most of these activities are physical, the bundle of functions is held together by the classic informational logic of one-stop shopping. A dealer's competitive advantage is therefore based on a mixture of location, scale, cost, sales force management, quality of service, and affiliations with car manufacturers and banks.

Bundling these functions creates compromises. Each step in the value chain has different economies of scale. If the functions were unbundled, specialty companies that offer test-drives could take cars to prospective buyers' homes. Distributors of new cars could have fewer, larger sites in order to minimize inventory and transportation costs. Providers of after-sales service would be free to operate more and smaller local facilities to furnish better service. Auto manufacturers could provide product information via the Internet. And car purchasers could obtain financing by putting their business out for bid via an electronic broker. Eliminate the informational glue that combines all these functions in a single, compromised business model, and the multiple businesses that emerge will evolve in radically different directions.

Some new businesses will benefit from network economies of scale, which can give rise to monopolies. In a networked market, the greater the number of people connected, the greater the value of being connected, thus creating network economies of scale. There is no point, for example, in being the only person in the world who owns a telephone. As the number of people who own telephones rises, the value of hooking up for any one individual progressively increases.

This self-reinforcing dynamic builds powerful monopolies. Businesses that broker information, make markets, or set standards are all taking advantage of this dynamic. The implication: The first company to achieve a critical mass often will take all, or nearly all—although the continuing battle between first-mover Netscape and Microsoft in the market for network browsers illustrates that the lead of the first mover is not always insurmountable.

Reaching critical mass can be an enormous challenge. General Electric may have solved the problem of critical mass by using its own enormous purchasing power. GE has opened its internal electronic-procurement system to other buyers of industrial goods, turning its own sourcing system into a market-making business.

As value chains fragment and reconfigure, new opportunities will arise for purely physical businesses. In many businesses today, the efficiency of the physical value chain is compromised for the purposes of delivering information. Shops, for example, try to be efficient warehouses and effective merchandisers simultaneously and are often really neither.

The new economics of information will create opportunities to rationalize the physical value chain, often leading to businesses whose physically based sources of competitive advantage will be more sustainable.

Consider the current battle in bookselling. Amazon.com, an electronic retailer on the Web, has no physical stores and very little inventory. It offers an electronic list of 2.5 million books, ten times larger than that of the largest chain store, and customers can search through that list by just about any criterion. Amazon orders most of its books from two industry wholesalers in response to customers' requests. It then repacks and mails them from a central facility.

Amazon.com cannot offer instant delivery; nor can customers physically browse the shelves the way they can in a traditional bookstore. Its advantages are based on superior information and lower physical costs. Customers can, for example, access book reviews. They have greater choice and better searching capabilities. And Amazon.com saves money on inventory and retail space.

But Amazon's success is not a given. The discount chains are aggressively launching their own Web businesses. There is nothing defensible about Amazon's wide selection since it really comes from the publishers' and wholesalers' databases. By double-handling the books, Amazon still incurs unnecessary costs.

In fact, the wholesalers in the book industry could probably create the lowest-cost distribution system by filling customers' orders directly. If competition pushes the industry in that direction, electronic retailers would become mere search engines connected to somebody else's database—and that would not add much value or confer on them much of a competitive advantage. The wholesalers could be the big winners.

When a company focuses on different activities, the value proposition underlying its brand identity will change. Since a brand reflects its company's value chain, deconstruction will require new brand strategies. For instance, the importance of branches and automated teller machines today leads many banks to emphasize *ubiquity* in their brand image (Citibank, for example). However, the reconfiguration of financial services might lead a company to focus on being a product provider. For such a strategy, *performance* becomes the key message, as it is for Fidelity. Another brand strategy might focus on helping customers navigate the universe of third-party products. The key message would be *trust*, as it is for Charles Schwab.

New branding opportunities will emerge for third parties that neither produce a product nor deliver a primary service. Navigator or agent brands have been around for a long time. The *Zagat Survey* of restaurants and *Consumer Reports* are two obvious examples. It's the *Zagat Survey*'s own brand—its credibility in restaurant reviewing—that steers its readers toward a particular establishment.

Recently, the Platform for Internet Content Selection (PICS) was established. This is a way of embedding third-party ratings into searchable information about any Web site. It enables anybody to rate anything, and it makes those ratings ubiquitous, searchable, sortable, and costless.

The dramatic proliferation of networked markets increases the need for navigators and other facilitating agents, for example those that guarantee a product's performance or assume risk. Thus there will be many new opportunities to develop brands.

Bargaining power will shift as a result of a radical reduction in the ability to monopolize the control of information. Market power often comes from controlling a choke point in an information channel and extracting tolls from those dependent on the flow of information through it. For example, sellers to retail customers today use their control over the information available to buyers to minimize comparison shopping and maximize cross-selling. But when richness and reach extend to the point where such channels are unnecessary, that game will stop. Any choke point could then be circumvented. Buyers will know their alternatives as well as the seller does. Some new intermediaries—organizers of virtual markets—may even evolve into aggregators of buying power, playing suppliers off against one another for the benefit of the purchasers they represent.

WHERE THE NEW BUSINESSES WILL EMERGE

In a world of limited connectivity, choices at each point in the value chain are, by definition, finite. In contrast, broadband connectivity means infinite choice. But infinite choice also means infinite bewilderment. This navigation problem can be solved in all sorts of ways, and each solution is a potential business.

The navigator could be a database. The navigator could be a search engine. The navigator could be intelligent-agent software. The navigator could be somebody giving advice. The navigator could be a brand providing recommendations or endorsements.

The logic of navigation can be observed in a number of businesses in which choice has proliferated. People often react to clutter by going back to the tried and true. Customer research indicates that people faced with complex choices either gravitate toward dominant brands or confine their search to narrow formats, each offering a presorted set of alternatives. In the grocery store, for example, where the number of products has quadrupled over the last 15 years, hundreds of segmented specialty brands have gained market share in almost every category. But so have the one or two leading brands. The proliferation of choice has led to the fragmentation of the small brands and the simultaneous concentration of the large ones. The losers are the brands in the middle.

Similarly, television viewers seem to flock to the hit shows without caring which network those shows are on. But they select specialty programming, such as nature documentaries or music videos, by tuning in to a cable channel offering that format. In essence, the viewer selects the channel, and the channel selects the content. In the first case, the product's brand pulls volume through the channel; in the second, the channel's brand pushes content toward receptive viewers.

Those two approaches by the consumer yield different patterns of competitive advantage and profitability. Networks need hit shows more than the hit shows need any network: The producers have the bargaining power and therefore receive the higher return. Conversely, producers of low-budget nature documentaries need a distributor more than the distributor needs any program, and the profit pattern is, therefore, the reverse. In one year, the popular comedian Bill Cosby earned more than the entire CBS network; the Discovery Channel probably earns more than all of its content providers put together. Despite the fact that CBS's 1996 revenues were about six times those of the Discovery Channel, Discovery's 52% profit margin dwarfed CBS's 4%.

The economics playing out in the television industry are a model for what will likely emerge in the world of universal connectivity. Think of it as two different value propositions: one is a focus on popular content; the other, a focus on navigation.

Navigation might have been the right strategy for *Encyclopædia Britannica* in responding to the threat from CD-ROMs. Its greatest competitive asset, after all, was a brand that certified high-quality, objective information. Given the clutter of cyberspace, what could be more compelling than a *Britannica*-branded guide to valuable information on the Internet?

If *Britannica*'s executives had written off their sales force, if they had built alliances with libraries and scientific journals, if they had built a Web site that had hot links directly to original sources, if they had created a universal navigator to valuable and definitive information validated by the *Encyclopædia Britannica* brand, they would have been heroes. They might have established a monopoly, following the example of Bill Gates. In fact, he might have been forced to acquire them.

Customers' switching costs will drop, and companies will have to develop new ways of generating customer loyalty. Cmmon standards for exchanging and processing information and the growing numbers of individuals accessing networks will drastically reduce switching costs.

Proprietary electronic data interchange systems, for example, lock companies into their supply relationships. But extranets linking companies with their suppliers using the Internet's standard protocols make switching almost costless. The U.S. auto industry is creating such an extranet, called the Automotive Network eXchange (ANX). Linking together auto manufacturers and several thousand automotive suppliers, the system is expected to save its participants a billion dollars a year, dramatically reduce errors, and speed the flow of information to second- and third-tier suppliers. By reducing switching costs and creating greater symmetry of information, ANX will also intensify competition at every level of the supply chain.

Incumbents could easily become victims of their obsolete physical infrastructures and their own psychology. Assets that traditionally offered competitive advantages and served as barriers to entry will become liabilities. The most vulnerable companies are those currently providing information that could be delivered more effectively and inexpensively electronically—for example, the physical parts of sales and distribution systems, such as branches, shops, and sales forces. As with newspapers, even the loss of a small portion of customers to new distribution channels or the migration of a high-margin product to the electronic domain can throw a business with high fixed costs into a downward spiral.

It may be easy to grasp this point intellectually, but it is much harder for managers to act on its implications. In many businesses, the assets in question are integral to a company's core competence. It is not easy psychologically to withdraw from assets so central to a company's identity. It is not easy strategically to downsize assets that have high fixed costs when so many customers still prefer the current business model. It is not easy financially to cannibalize current profits. And it is certainly not easy to squeeze the profits of distributors to whom one is tied by long-standing customer relationships or by franchise laws.

Newcomers suffer from none of these inhibitions. They are unconstrained by management traditions, organizational structures, customer relationships, or fixed assets. Recall the cautionary tale of *Encyclopædia Britannica*. Executives must deconstruct their own businesses. If they don't, someone else will.

PART THREE

The Practice of Business Strategy

The Customer: Segmentation and Value Creation

THE PRACTICE OF business strategy must begin with the customer, for without customers with needs to be met, the business has no raison d'être. Strategy issues arise when customer groups with distinct needs emerge from what was previously thought of as a single, homogeneous group.

Business segments can be defined along several dimensions: by customer group (needs), by the economics of serving these groups (cost/ price), and/or by the players who choose to serve them (competitive dynamics). Segments are like ecological niches, which some see as defined by the environment and others by the species that occupy them. The interplay of the dimensions makes segmentation an art.

BCG began exploring business segmentation with its clients in the early 1970s. The first insights were analytical. Different needs among customer groups entailed different costs to serve. We helped our clients deaverage their costs, identify the needs and economics of each segment, and align their value propositions with customer needs. We modeled the costs of the players serving each segment to identify potential competitive threats and opportunities. These analytical approaches, described in the first four *Perspectives* in this section, remain valid and useful.

The revolution in the economics of information added new dimensions to segmentation in the late 1980s. In consumer goods and services, information technology enables detailed tracking and analysis of transactions. In combination with flexible manufacturing, companies can now use information on buying behavior to customize both their communications and their product and service offerings to reach and serve segments as small as a single consumer. In industrial markets, information technology enables closer coordination and, ultimately, tighter relationships between venders and suppliers. The next four *Perspectives* in this section represent early contributions to the thinking on these trends.

Recently, growth has reemerged to the top of most companies' agendas. But many companies have found that, in the wake of the reengineering flurry, they have lost the aptitude for identifying growth opportunities. The final three *Perspectives* in this section offer imaginative ways to create growth through segmentation. These *Perspectives* validate BCG's belief that there is no such thing as a mature business.

SEGMENTATION AND STRATEGY

SEYMOUR TILLES, 1974

Segmentation problems often go unrecognized. Each of the managers quoted below focused on something else as the critical factor.

- "In this business the key to success is the broad product line. However, we are losing business to small producers who are cherry-picking at key accounts."

- "We are the Cadillac of our industry and recognized as the leader in quality. However, our competitors seem to be growing more rapidly than we are. Lately our profitability has been declining."

- "We seem to do a lot better in some regions than others. It's probably the result of differences in sales capability, although recently we shifted some sales assignments and our performance didn't change much."

Segmentation is a critical aspect of corporate strategy. It is essential in visualizing the competitive arena and analyzing the preferred strategic emphasis. The goal is to find a way to convert differences from competitors into a cost differential that can be maintained.

For commodity products the basic segment boundary is the cost differential for serving different classes of customers. Cost differences between customers often can be easily determined—differences in logistics or packaging are obvious. Other cost differences may be even more important but more difficult to measure. The cost of customization, the disadvantage of maintaining a broad product line, or the cost of technical service are examples.

For differentiated products, the basis of segmentation is the combination of the features built into the product and their cost/price ratio. For example, Cadillacs, Torinos, and Volkswagens are all very different in their price-feature relationships and for that reason do not compete directly with each other. The segmentation of markets for differentiated products rests on the relationship between the cost features to the producer and the value of features to the customer.

In considering differentiation, it is important to include all of the conditions of the transaction, as well as the product itself. Service, reliability of vendor, and delivery times are likely to be as important as inherent product characteristics. There are often highly differentiated suppliers in markets for commodity products.

A differentiated product remains a differentiated product only until the emergence of the first follower. After that it begins to behave as a commodity.

Over time, all products tend to become commodities. With the evolution of the market, pioneering companies face the choice of becoming limited-volume, high-priced, high-cost specialty producers or high-volume, low-cost producers of standard products. There is no obvious answer to which is best. The choice is dependent upon the predilections and financial resources of the individual company.

It is possible to serve both segments with great benefits in lowering average cost. However, to do this it must be possible to sell at different prices to each segment. Cost to the customer must match value in each segment. Different value requires different prices to cover different costs.

Powerful competitive strategies often can be constructed to force a competitor to choose one segment or the other. The alternative, in the absence of a price differential, is to sell below cost in one segment and be noncompetitive in the other, because a price must be charged based on average cost.

Measuring profitability by customer group is important. The inability to monitor profitability by customer group is extremely hazardous since it permits major changes in competitive position within a given group of customers to go undetected. Averages hide more than they disclose.

The base for a strategy is identification of products and customer groups that will achieve and sustain an economic advantage with respect to competitors. This requires:

- An assessment of the relationship between cost and value to the customer by both product group and customer group

- An assessment of cost on a comparative basis with selected competitors by product group and customer group

- An assessment of the eventual effects on cost and volume of changing the definition of the segment and consequently its potential market size

Competitive segmentation is a competitor-specific process. There is always a leading competitor in any area. The classic segmentation forces that specific competitor to choose between parts of the segment. If he chooses either alternative, he must abandon the rest or serve it at a loss. This choice is virtually unavoidable where a common price must be offered to customers who have quite different service or support costs. The same choice is forced where small-volume customers will pay high margins for special features but high-volume customers will pay nothing extra for such characteristics.

The infinite variety of factor combinations make segmentation an extremely difficult decision process to optimize. This is also why the competitive strategy rewards are potentially so great.

STRATEGIC SECTORS

BRUCE D. HENDERSON, 1975

A strategic sector is one in which you can obtain a competitive advantage and exploit it. Strategic sectors are defined entirely in terms of competitive differences. Strategic-sector analysis performs the same function as cost-effectiveness analysis. Cost-effectiveness analysis optimizes value versus cost. Strategic-sector analysis optimizes margin relative to competition.

Strategic-sector analysis, like cost-effectiveness analysis, ignores the administrative unit until the objective and its feasibility have been evaluated. The resources and the program component are assigned as necessary to administrative units in order to accomplish the mission.

Strategic sectors cut across profit centers, strategic business units, groups, divisions, departments, markets, and all other administrative units. The boundary of a strategic sector is defined by the maximum rate of change of relative competitive margin as you cross that boundary.

Strategic sectors exist because the same product can be made in many variations and supplied with many related services. Each feature and each service has a cost. But the value added by such increments varies from customer to customer. It affects product design, manufacturing capability, and distribution practices. Every change in these affects both cost and value simultaneously.

Design requires focus on the strategic sector to be served. Yet every compromise of that focus either adds cost or reduces value.

Manufacture requires focus on the strategic sector to be served. Compromises and variety produce the same consequences on cost and value. No job shop can match the cost of a full-scale focused factory.

A given strategic sector can rarely use more than one distribution channel. Since different channels have different costs and provide different services, they appeal to different customers. Therefore, customers of one channel tend to be in a different strategic sector from those served by other channels. Competitors who try to serve both strategic sectors at the same price are handicapped by a too-high price in one sector and a too-high cost in the other sector.

Profit centers and strategic business units are self-defeating profit-wise unless the whole company is the profit center. GM can be the most profitable competitor because the whole company is the business unit, while internal administrative units are tailored to focus on value added in strategic sectors in which they can be the largest factor.

Profit centers originated when companies became too big and complex to manage by individual function. Decentralization, however, led to suboptimization and loss of internal financial mobility that is critical to strategic concentration.

Strategic business units were devised to reverse the effects of over-fragmentation into profit centers. So-called SBUs attempted to aggregate all the strategy decisions in an administrative unit. The critical factor, cash flow, cannot be delegated to any SBU. If it is, then the parent is merely a lockbox holding company without strategic options as a company except divestment or acquisition.

Strategic sectors are the key to strategy because the strategic sector's frame of reference is competition.

The very largest competitor in an industry can be unavoidably unprofitable if the individual strategic sectors are dominated by smaller competitors. Market share in the strategic sector, is what determines profitability not size of company.

SPECIALIZATION

RICHARD K. LOCHRIDGE, 1981

All competitors are specialists. No two competitors can serve exactly the same customers, at exactly the same time, in exactly the same way, at exactly the same cost. The differences between competitors are the measure of their specialization.

The greater the differences, the greater the specialization. Customers place a value on the differences through their purchasing behavior—how much they buy and at what price. In some markets specialization is highly valued. In others it is not.

When differentiation is costly, the specialist competitor will make adequate returns only if its customers are willing to pay a premium. If the costs of providing product or services are highly dependent on volume (because of either experience effects or scale economies, for example), the cost of differentiation may be doubly great. Not only the cost of differentiation but the cost of reduced volume must be added to the price customers must pay to provide adequate returns. In price-sensitive, commodity-type businesses this can be disastrous.

In other businesses, the reward for specialization is much greater. Both variety in customer preferences and lower cost of differentiation favor specialization. Not all customers want the same thing. Particularly in well-supplied markets, customers generally prefer products or services that are tailored to their needs. The variety can be expressed in terms of product or service features, service levels, quality levels, or something else. If the cost of serving the different needs of different customer groups is a large part of the value added, specialization is almost inevitable.

In a crude way, costs can be divided into two broad categories. The first is those costs required for basic participation in a business. These include, for example, the minimum level of ingredients or supplies, manufacturing or service, direct and variable costs, and sufficient overhead to manage the business.

The second category is discretionary costs. These costs are a function of the segments being served. They may be as specific as more expensive ingredients to add quality; advertising to reach specific customer groups; or service levels, sales support, and delivery systems valued highly by a portion of the market. The discretionary, or segment-specific, costs also include less obvious expenses, such as the cost of flexibility in manufacturing processes or the cost of complexity in overheads and other levels of value added to serve a variety of customer needs.

When the discretionary costs are a large part of the value added, opportunities for segment focus arise. One competitor can focus on a portion of the market and adjust its costs to meet the needs of that group and that group alone. Not only are the discretionary costs of flexibility and complexity reduced, but scale economies in segment-specific costs may be achieved. Thus the focused competitor achieves real advantage versus other competitors in serving the chosen segment's needs.

By corollary, when discretionary costs are a large part of the value added, basic costs will be a relatively small part. Thus the small penalty of higher basic costs due to lower volume, fewer scale economies, and less experience is outweighed by advantages in discretionary costs for the segment being served. If few cost differences exist between competitors in basic costs, then specialization-induced cost reduction in discretionary costs is even more valuable.

The competitor who can serve a segment at the lowest cost relative to other competitors will have a competitive advantage. If scale economies are important in segment-specific costs, the leader in each segment will be more profitable than the followers. Often, segment-specific costs are among the most scale-intensive. Advertising cost per unit, for example, is cut in half with each doubling of unit volume. When these costs are a large part of the value added, large differences in return by competitor by segment will result.

Superior specialization strategies should result in sufficient cost advantage so that a portion of that advantage can be passed on to consumers in either added quality/service or reduced price. This effectively raises the barriers to competitive attack. The specialist thrives, capturing a larger portion of the market, and expands the boundaries of the segment to encompass a larger area of competitive advantage.

For each dimension in which competitive advantage can be achieved, there will be a specialist supplier. It is the differences between competitors, not customers, that define segment boundaries. Customers merely place a value on the area of relative advantage. A competitor can be either a low-cost commodity specialist (with a minimum of discretionary costs) or a higher-priced specialist with higher levels of discretionary costs. Higher price realization in the latter segments will be valuable only if the added price more than covers the added cost. This is often true only for the leader in the segment.

Specialization is the result of both variety in customer needs and competitors' willingness to serve those needs. Specialization is a strategy to achieve competitive advantage in a portion of the market. Doing business outside the area of advantage will reduce the specialist's average returns. Worse, it may obscure the value of focus. Because accounting systems rarely capture discretionary costs by segment, they average costs and returns across segments. Thus even a successful specialist may not perceive its advantage or the segment boundaries. This misperception results in dispersion of effort and, eventually, eroded advantage as others with superior perceptions gain ground on the segment leader.

Specialization is a means of survival in a rich, but competitive, market. Competitive advantage cannot be achieved in all cases, with all customers, relative to all competitors. Where it is achieved, however, the rewards can be exceptional.

SPECIALIZATION: COST REDUCTION OR PRICE REALIZATION

ANTHONY J. HABGOOD, 1981

Specialization businesses are becoming increasingly significant. Fewer and fewer businesses can be run purely on the basis of overall volume. By specializing in particular areas, small companies can often coexist successfully with a much larger industry leader. Two quite different kinds of specialization are possible, each with its own strategies and risk profiles. Some specialist companies compete by reducing cost and cutting price, others by adding significant amounts of cost and achieving higher price realization.

Successful cost-reduction specialization is not achieved by reducing the level of important cost components but by totally eliminating one part of the industry leader's cost structure. Private-label producers do not owe their prosperity to lower costs of production but rather to the elimination of branding and distribution costs. Laker has not found a cheaper way to fly from London to New York; rather it has avoided all the costs associated with the IATA airlines' ticketing and full-route and customer coverage. Amdahl competes with IBM not by producing mainframe computers cheaply but by eliminating the operating system costs.

By eliminating a significant portion of the leader's cost structure, the specialist can often cut price between 20 and 40 percent. Theoretically, a vigorous response by the leader could drive out the specialist. In practice, organizational and structural constraints on the leader make many of these specialists quite secure. Market dynamics normally favor the specialists, although too rapid a shift toward the specialist's segment might force the market leader to react early, when the small company is most vulnerable.

Successful price-realization specialists, in contrast, compete by achieving a high price that is supported by additional costs that the leader may not incur at all. One often sees a wide range of price levels in these businesses. In cosmetics or automobiles, for example, there may be a tenfold cost difference between mass-market products and those designed, produced, packaged, distributed, and promoted for small, high-quality niches. The upmarket products are often produced by specialist companies like Daimler-Benz or BMW, which can compete successfully around the far larger producers of standard products.

Such specialists can achieve economic security against competition from the overall market leader by establishing an advantage in the significant scale-intensive cost elements specific to their high-quality niche. The risks lie in the market. A shift in consumer taste or user economics can change the size of a niche dramatically while hardly affecting the overall market. The customers almost always have the choice of shifting down-market.

Successful specialization may be based on either cost reduction or price realization. The two types of specialists face different risks and require different strategies. Cost-reduction specialists must concentrate on their areas of strength: focusing, keeping costs down, and resisting the temptation to enter other parts of the market less suited to their approach. Price-realization specialists must understand and optimize the relationship between the costs they incur to serve their segment and the price they can realize. They must monitor the market closely, for it is in market-segment dynamics that their risks and opportunities lie.

SEGMENT-OF-ONE®
MARKETING

RICHARD WINGER AND DAVID EDELMAN, 1989

Remember back when predictions of the computer age conjured up an Orwellian landscape of impersonal robots dispensing mechanized service and standardized products? In fact, the opposite has happened.

Across a wide range of industries, computers have personalized, not standardized, the way companies serve their customers. For example, in a leading hotel chain personnel greet customers by name and remember special requirements. They are prompted by telephone consoles that flash up customers' names when a line rings, aided by a database that stores customers' personal requirements.

Ten years ago mass marketers discovered they could narrow their focus and create products for specific customer segments. Now a segment can be trimmed down to an individual.

Like most breakthroughs, Segment-of-One marketing brings together in a working relationship two formerly independent concepts: information retrieval and service delivery. On one side is a proprietary database of customers' preferences and purchase behavior; on the other is a disciplined, tightly engineered approach to service delivery that uses the information base to tailor a service package for individual customers.

Carriage-Trade Service

The advantage to the customer is straightforward and powerful. Increasingly, consumers are putting more value on being treated as individuals. They demand customized products and services delivered at the moment of need. They also value the reassurance and stability that comes from an enduring relationship with somebody who understands and can respond to their specific needs.

Of course these values aren't new—but until recently, only the very wealthy could afford them. Information technology has brought the services associated with the carriage trade within reach of the middle class.

At First Wachovia, an innovative and very successful North Carolina bank, the staff serves all of its customers the way it used to serve its best customer. The bank greets all customers by name, providing personalized information about their finances and how they relate to their long-term objectives. Based on this knowledge, Wachovia suggests new products. Commodity retail banking has been turned into a customized, personalized service. The result? More sales at lower marketing costs and powerful switching barriers relative to competition.

Three major investments are behind this seemingly effortless new service level: a comprehensive customer database, accessible wherever the customer makes contact with the bank; an extensive training program that teaches a personalized service approach; and an ongoing personal communications program with each customer.

Technology Surpasses Imagination

The foundation for Segment-of-One marketing is the ability to track and understand individual customer behavior. Thanks to the expansion of data-capture opportunities and lower storage costs, such databases are already cost-effective on a large scale. Indeed, technology is now far ahead of the imagination of many marketers.

But not all marketers. Citicorp is developing a massive database that will track the supermarket shopping behavior of 30 to 50 million households. This will enable packaged goods marketers to fine-tune their promotional efforts to an extent unimaginable today.

The major packaged goods companies will be able to know by name and address, by brand-loyal households and switchers, their own and their competitors' light and heavy users.

The second requirement of Segment-of-One marketing is the ability to use the information system to customize the product and personalize the service to the individual customer. In some cases, personalized service can be designed directly into the information system.

When Noxell introduced its Clarion line of mass-market cosmetics in drugstores, it looked for a way to differentiate the new line in a crowded market. The answer was the Clarion computer, where customers type in the characteristics of their skin and receive a regimen selected from the Clarion line. "Department store–type personal advice without sales pressure in the much more convenient drug channel" became the central customer value. The result? The only successful introduction of a broad line of mass-market cosmetics in recent years.

People and Systems

In most cases, the key to the personalized service bundle is the successful interaction of people and systems. But this interaction has to be carefully engineered. It requires user-friendly information systems and a tightly engineered service approach.

In the boutiques of Yves Rocher, the successful French cosmetics house, the customer shows an ID card and the salesperson flashes up her purchase history on a POS terminal. The salesperson is trained to use this information as the basis for a detailed conversation about the customer's individual experience with the company's products and what she should buy next. Compare that with the canned sales pitch used in many department stores. The result is higher sales and more customer loyalty. Shu Uemura, the large Japanese cosmetics firm, bases its U.S. market entry strategy on a similar concept.

Often, Segment-of-One breakthroughs will come from the ability to perform to exacting service standards at the customer's convenience.

D'Agostino, the large New York grocery retailer, builds shop-by-phone service by storing customers' shopping lists and updating them every time the customer calls in. With every call, ordering becomes more convenient because a standing order needs only to be modified. Over time, a denser and denser web of information ties the customer tighter and tighter to the store. Ultimately, the benefits of personalized convenience will, if not offset, at least mitigate the price signals of competitors and improve margin opportunities across the core customer base.

The ability to gather detailed information about a customer's purchasing behavior coupled with relationship-oriented delivery of services provides a tool and a context for the third element of Segment-of-One marketing: personalized communication.

Personalized Communication

Experience shows that even direct mail, not generally an attractive medium in today's cluttered environment, can work powerfully in the context of the intimate customer relationship of a successful Segment-of-One strategy.

Other media options for personalized communication are beginning to proliferate. Selective binding technology that makes it possible to customize magazines to individual subscribers is on the drawing boards. Videotext, point-of-purchase communication, and targeted co-op mailers are beginning to be available. Addressable cable TV is a technical, if not yet a commercial, reality.

These new options alone will force marketers to come to grips with personalized communications. But they will work most powerfully for

Organizational Imperatives

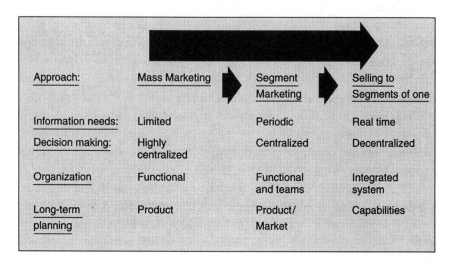

Approach:	Mass Marketing	Segment Marketing	Selling to Segments of one
Information needs:	Limited	Periodic	Real time
Decision making:	Highly centralized	Centralized	Decentralized
Organization	Functional	Functional and teams	Integrated system
Long-term planning	Product	Product/ Market	Capabilities

those who employ them in the context of an integrated Segment-of-One strategy.

A successful Segment-of-One strategy involves more than experiments with databases and direct mail—although these can be first steps. It requires a broad rethinking of the values a company provides to its customers and the way it approaches them. As the following chart indicates, it can also require significant investments in the infrastructure of service and information.

Because establishing this infrastructure represents a major broadening of a company's capabilities, it should blend with and build on existing strengths. But in every case, the constants will be service, information, and the marriage of the two.

From a competitive point of view, the implications will be dramatic. Economies of scale in production or product volume have eroded in many industries. Segment-of-One marketers will reestablish powerful scale economies in information, information management, service, and distribution. As a result, competitive advantage will tilt to those companies that simultaneously own the market and are able to satisfy individual customers' needs.

DISCOVERING YOUR CUSTOMER

MICHAEL J. SILVERSTEIN AND PHILIP SIEGEL, 1991

By now, everyone knows that giving the customer what he or she wants is critical to success. But if everyone is doing this, where is the competitive advantage? The answer is in going one step further and deeper. This means knowing your most important customers' business systems so well that you see opportunities before they do and are able to provide some useful ideas. When you serve your customers by helping them discover untapped potential in their businesses, you both reap the rewards.

Discovery is real work. It's not just asking your customers or their customers what they want. It entails learning the strategic and economic factors driving your customer's business and turning them into ideas, products, and services that benefit you and your customer. It's not just traditional marketing dressed up in help-your-customer clothes. It requires analytic skills, an open mind, curiosity, follow-through, and confidence in your company's adaptive and creative capabilities. Because it takes a lot of effort, you can afford to do it only for significant customers. The idea is to team with your customer to learn something of major value to him or her, then help make it happen.

How Does Discovery Work?

Discovery can be done in both consumer and industrial goods. One packaged-food producer worked with a supermarket chain to do in-store research on how browsing shoppers first notice, then select, particular items from the growing assortment of refrigerated food products. What they learned over two months led the store to radically change the way refrigerated items were displayed in the chilled case, including doing away with the glass door that deterred shoppers from examining the product packages. The changes triggered strong increases in sales of these high-margin items across the chain. All this was at the initiative of the producer, not the store.

This first round of discovery triggered more discoveries. The packaged-food company went on to tailor promotional programs to the unique demographics of each major store in the chain. The two parties now have an annual calendar of cooperative business-building activities where the benefits are monitored and shared.

A large commercial printer in the Middle West used discovery to create new value for major customers and for itself. Often, high-volume printing jobs, like catalogues and telephone books, are considered commodity businesses: The low-priced vendor wins. By understanding the business economics of a few key customers, however, this company uncovered a variety of revenue innovations and cost reductions for them. The company worked with one customer for three months in a five-step process:

- It analyzed the customer's core business practices—how it decides what products and services to offer consumers, how it merchandises these offerings, how it buys printing services, and so on.

- It discovered where the customer wasn't taking advantage of the extraordinary flexibility and speed of its printing process. More services to consumers at higher margins to the customer were possible.

- It tested and funded much of the R&D in the new-product development phase to become the only vendor that could deliver the full program.

- It monitored the sales response and customer satisfaction results of the new program and was the force behind execution.

- It used this success to reinforce the customer relationship and expand its base business as well. The new business revealed by the discovery was worth millions to both parties—more than 20 times the cost of the discovery effort.

In both these examples, the discovery team and the customer cooperated at several organizational levels—from field sales to top management. The work involved sharing sensitive internal information, including cost and profit data and customer-by-customer sales histories. You conduct deep discovery only for customers with whom there is mutual trust and respect.

Discovery is applicable in many settings. Good candidates will be large customers with varied needs. They must be strong enough in their markets to capture and keep the added business you are helping them get. Otherwise the benefits flow quickly to others.

The Rules of Discovery

To conduct a successful discovery process, you should:

- Make sure top management supports the partnership, but allow your salesperson to own the results. He or she is crucial to keeping the effort moving through the inevitable bumps in the road.

- Carefully select and train the teams of people that perform the discovery. Use only good people who are experienced in all the critical disciplines: reading customers for what they need but don't say, analyzing the economics of a business, knowing how to mobilize an organization to do something new.

- Follow through on the new ideas you and the customer decide to pursue with all the capabilities and resources of your company. You want to play this game only if you are thoroughly committed.

- Compensate those people in your organization who generate ideas from the discovery process and are able to make them work. Working with customers in new, unstructured ways will bring out the best in your people.

Simply listening to customers is not enough to sustain partnerships. You need to understand the structure and economics of their businesses and offer them a stream of creative ideas that tap their full capabilities. Discovery is a great opportunity to get more of your good people into direct contact with your customers' businesses. Discovery will unlock your organization and stimulate more rounds.

You can choose to be "just" a vendor. You can submit proposals to specifications. You can play golf and entertain. You can focus on friendships. You can win some, you can lose some.

Or you can learn about your customers' vulnerabilities, dreams, business-process blocks, decision-making weaknesses, and major growth targets. You can grow with luck or you can grow through knowledge and innovation.

THE NEW VERTICAL INTEGRATION

JOHN R. FRANTZ AND THOMAS M. HOUT, 1993

When Henry Ford set out to make the lowest-cost car in America, he integrated vertically. Turning iron ore into automobiles, Ford eliminated almost all inventories, reduced costs and prices, and was able to raise wages—until less-integrated competitors proved better at providing what customers wanted. Vertical integration as a business concept fell under a cloud from which it has not emerged.

Until now. Leading-edge companies are beginning to reinvent the vertically integrated enterprise. They are getting the same advantages of low cost and fast turns, but they are also giving customers more of what they want and sooner.

The new vertical integration does not involve ownership or exclusive relationships. Instead, it is about eliminating barriers and costs between independent companies.

The new integration starts by thinking of your business as part of a supply chain made up of several companies. But instead of the conventional view of separate companies transacting with each other, visualize one continuous business system. Most companies just manage their suppliers and serve their customers. But today's leaders consider their suppliers' suppliers and their customers' customers part of their business. And they understand that the only way to eliminate inventory is to coordinate actions across this system through the imaginative use of information.

Most overhead is incurred in dealing day to day with customers and suppliers—forecasting, placing and accepting orders, scheduling, stocking, shipping, warehousing, billing and collecting—and then changing it all daily to cope with surprises. The objective of the new integration is to collapse this cost structure.

To implement the new integration, companies generally progress through three stages. First, two companies decide to lower some of the barriers that separate them and begin to operate as one business. Second, they build a customized relationship, expanding on the new opportunities they have discovered. Third, they extend their new approach to the entire chain of companies surrounding their business and take some risks by dramatically changing the rules that govern how they all work with each other. The later the stages, the bigger the organizational challenge to make it happen, but the greater the total impact on the business.

Working as one usually starts with basics, such as paring the duplicate buffer inventories that have built up over time. The customer then starts to share product and point-of-sale information with the supplier. Together, these actions can cut inventories by at least 20 percent. Another variation finds a manufacturer running a full product mix through a flexible plant every day and shipping every night to a wholesaler or an end customer. This can triple the customer's inventory turn.

Logistics leaders in most industries are already getting these basics done, but even this is often not easy. Getting to this level takes trust and some new metrics. For example, when one manufacturer began to ship to its wholesalers every night regardless of the size of their orders, the transportation manager was not convinced that the policy made good business sense. He saw only that his departmental costs went up as trucks left half empty each night. He was not aware that overnight shipments were reducing inventory costs for both the manufacturer and the wholesaler and bringing down order-processing and scheduling costs as well.

Top management soon realized that opposition to daily shipments by the transportation manager and others stemmed from the company's failure to develop metrics that fit the strategy. The two missing metrics were total inventory turn for the manufacturer and wholesaler combined and total order-processing costs for the manufacturer, from order entry and scheduling through shipment. Once these metrics were in place and explained, everyone began to understand the big picture and could support the changes.

Companies like Helene Curtis have gone to the next level by customizing the delivery process, saving the customer costs that have always been thought of as fixed. With its ability to meet each customer's unique packing and delivery requirements without special handling, Helene Curtis has steadily gained share in the personal care business. Its warehouse data system manages the loading process right down to the order of cartons on the truck. All this costs no more at the sending end and saves money at the receiving end.

Customizing logistics between companies is organizationally demanding. It usually takes a permanent cross-functional team organized around a customer or customer group. Otherwise, there is too much reliance on standard solutions. The best customizing comes from hunches, idea fragments, and brave experiments. For these to go anywhere, everyone on the team has to have the same incentive, namely, "This is our baby and we had better make it work."

The ultimate form of partnership is when a supply chain of three or four companies recognizes the value of managing itself as a single logistics system. This is the third stage. One such group is Du Pont (fibers), Spring Mills (a fabric maker), Warren Featherbone (a children's apparel maker), and Mercantile Stores. They first got together to defend themselves against imported clothing and began by sharing point-of-sale information to reduce inventory and shorten lead times. Later they started to cooperate in planning product-line introductions.

The keys to the apparel business are keeping the retail shelf turning fast and avoiding markdowns. Domestic producers' only advantage against imports is logistics: the capability to quickly make more of what is selling and stop making what is not. The result of the cooperation among these companies has been spectacular. Markdowns are a third of the industry average, gross profit margins rose through the past recession, and share of market has increased.

Having learned to work with each other, these companies are now pushing the frontiers of cooperation. One possibility is that they will move together to execute one coordinated vertical order—whatever was sold off the shelf today would be replenished at each level in the chain at once. Each company would produce just the right amount and ship it to its customer immediately. Such coordination is now possible with fast information and flexible production. Current inventory turns in the system could double.

Going further, a well-integrated chain could eventually decide, for example, that no one gets paid until the final product is sold at retail. This is the ultimate discipline and test—but the rewards in overhead reduction would be great. Combining automatic replenishment with one-time payment for everyone would reduce costs across the board—billing, ordering, promotions, working capital, and so on—to a fraction of current levels.

Getting started is the hardest part, because so much of what is routine in companies must be overcome. Functional and company boundaries break the business into separate parts, each of which is managed by a person who is evaluated largely on the performance of that piece only. This discourages risk taking across the parts. Also, conventional accounting data hide rather than reveal radical logistics opportunities. ("Fixed cost" is one of the most misleading phrases in our language.)

The best place to start the integration process is at the top. However, it will take more than getting a group of people in a room together. The number of obstacles and setbacks you encounter rises sharply when multiple companies are involved. Trust is fragile in the early stages. You need continuous project management at senior levels across all the companies. And you need to create new sets of numbers and new language, like *total-system inventory* and *vertical cycle time.*

Vertically integrated supply chains can achieve extraordinary customer responsiveness with minimum inventories. We will see it accomplished in the 1990s by companies that buy and sell from each other as they push the frontiers of cooperation.

TOTAL BRAND MANAGEMENT

DAVID C. EDELMAN AND MICHAEL J. SILVERSTEIN, 1993

A business revolution has come to brands. From every side, traditional brands appear to be under attack. Costs are escalating. Consumer loyalty is eroding. Retailers are competing through private label. Store brands are commandeering valuable niches. Some observers are even speculating about "the end of brands."

No, brands won't disappear. But what a brand is and how best to manage it are changing. Increasingly, a brand is far more than just a name on a product. Winning brands are carefully designed business systems. These systems stretch from the choice of raw materials to final service with the customer. And it is the total system that the customer purchases, not just the product.

When brands become business systems, brand management becomes far too important to leave to the marketing department. It cuts across functions and business processes. It requires decisions and actions at every point along the value chain. It is central to a company's overall business strategy. That's why we call it *total brand management.*

Escalating Investments, Increased Focus

Total brand management can take a variety of forms:

- In some cases, the brand extends beyond the actual product to include the infrastructure supporting it. For example, high-end brands such as Lexus or Infiniti, and even midmarket brands such as General Electric appliances, have invested heavily in information systems that support customer service and serve as marketing attributes enhancing the core product.

- In other cases, well-crafted umbrella brands like Gillette or Levi's stretch across many related products, enabling their owners to leverage materials innovations, marketing investments, and trade promotions more effectively.

- In still other cases, the entire retail system itself is the brand. At The Body Shop, for example, the way products are sourced (all-natural ingredients), developed (no animal testing), and sold (in distinctive Body Shop boutiques) is as important to the company's marketing image as the actual products.

Regardless of the particular form, total brand management has two fundamental imperatives. The first is a major escalation in the amount and kind of investments necessary to support a successful brand. It's no longer enough simply to increase the advertising budget. Companies have to invest in a broad range of costly capabilities—proprietary research methodologies for understanding subtle shifts in consumer attitudes, intertwined manufacturing and logistics networks providing superior retail service at lower cost, retail information processing capability to optimize inventory costs, and product development functions to speed innovative products.

But the total brand manager must also remember that such investments are only table stakes that allow entry into the game. It takes more than deep pockets to win. In particular, companies must concentrate on three key high-leverage activities.

Maximize synergies across a coherent brand portfolio. Financing a massive build-up in new capabilities requires spreading investments over many brands, cascading across price points and channels. Practitioners of total brand management, therefore, focus not on individual brands but on a coherent brand portfolio.

French cosmetics maker L'Oréal, for example, knew that increased R&D was essential to competing in the new brand environment. So over a five-year period, L'Oréal doubled its R&D budget. This major investment helped spark a key innovation: the company's new "anti-aging complex," a breakthrough in skin care that slows the onset and spread of wrinkles. But L'Oréal was able to afford this massive increase in R&D spending only because it could spread the costs over several brands in its portfolio at different price points and positions. The company introduced its anti-aging complex under the Lancôme brand, then moved it into the Vichy range and finally into broad distribution with Plénitude. It has been a tremendously successful innovation, yet couldn't have been done with one brand alone.

The key word in "coherent brand portfolio" is coherent. It's no good to cobble together a collection of unrelated brands. This only leads to higher overhead costs, fragmented business processes, and duplication of resources.

Not all brands contribute equally to enhancing the value of your brand portfolio. Brand managers must evaluate each existing brand along two dimensions: fit with core capability and potential for value generation. Such an assessment reshuffles the brands into four categories of investment priority, ranging from good fit/high value to low fit/low value.

Strengthen the brand portfolio through innovation. As the L'Oréal example suggests, innovation is now more important than ever. Other forms of growth, such as acquisitions and expanding margins, have been largely played out. Spending on retailers or consumers is becoming too expensive for all but the biggest budgets. What's more, consumers are becoming more sophisticated and harder to reach. Mere bells and whistles won't sell anymore.

But the kind of innovation that matters is not what managers might expect. It's not the creation of new brands, an increasingly expensive proposition. Rather, it is the reinvention of existing brands through three basic techniques: repositioning, extension, and transformation.

For example, SmithKline Beecham repositioned Lucozade, once considered a medicinal remedy, by directing it at anybody who cares about a healthy life, particularly athletes. Today, Lucozade is Britain's number one noncola drink. Unilever extended Flora, originally a "healthy fat" margarine low in polyunsaturates, across product categories to become an umbrella brand for a whole range of health-food oils and dairy products. And by moving quickly to exploit a technological breakthrough, Procter & Gamble transformed its traditional Pert Shampoo brand by launching a two-in-one shampoo/conditioner known as PertPlus.

Secure the brand through close relationships with customers and the trade. Increasingly, customers value the reassurance and stability that comes from an enduring relationship with someone who understands and can respond to their specific needs. But this requires a broad rethinking of the value a company provides for its customers, as well as of the specific products and services it provides.

Not long ago, for example, Japanese video game maker Nintendo found itself in a dying market with too many players and limited shelf space. The challenge: to discover a new way to hold its brand name with customers. So the company launched two new business initiatives: Nintendo Power, a $15-a-year magazine that receives 40,000 letters a month, and a 900-number line on game strategy that receives 10,000 calls a week. Both proved to be powerful customer-relationship vehicles that cut across hardware, software, education, product development, and customer service. But even more important, the magazine and 900 number have opened a direct line of communication from the customer back to new product development, which has enabled the company to forecast sales of a new product within 10 percent. Today, with annual sales of $5 billion, Nintendo is Japan's most profitable company.

For many brands, the most important customer is the trade. To fend off private-label growth, brand managers must find ways to create value for the trade without simply giving away more margin. A leading office products producer, for example, has been able to work with a superstore chain to create new packaging, replenishment, and stocking systems that provide more margin to the superstore than private-label products would. With its interlocking business systems, the manufacturer is now able to secure its brand franchise and to increase margins in a win-win relationship with a heavily deal-driven retailer.

The Role of the Total Brand Manager: Making Choices along the Entire Value Chain

As brand managers manage portfolios of brands, customer segments, and retailers across an entire business system, their role has become more cross-functional and strategic. Indeed, total brand management often involves redesigning the business through new partnerships, better cross-functional linkages, and innovation. To that end, brand managers must make choices at every point along the value chain, not just in marketing and sales.

This more strategic conception of brands means that the stakes involved in launching, maintaining, and evolving a brand are higher. But so are the potential payoffs. Companies that innovate new brand-building strategies will reap long-term rewards. Those that do not will slowly disappear.

MICHAEL J. SILVERSTEIN, 1995

Behind every successful innovation is an unexpected insight. When it finds expression as a new business breakthrough, markets take off and competitors don't know what hit them. And yet, even at the best companies most attempts at innovation fail. Lacking a systematic process for developing new ideas, organizations rely too much on the random inspiration of individuals.

It doesn't have to be this way. Insight can be made to flourish. Genius isn't required; ordinary mortals can generate breakthrough ideas—systematically. What it takes is a rigorous methodology for conceiving new opportunities and a customer-driven discovery process for testing and refining them.

1. *Expand your business definition and map it exhaustively.* Focus may enable flawless execution, but it can impede insight. The way you see your market today can blind you to tomorrow's possibilities. Start by expanding your business definition—from "cellular phones" to "mobile communications," from "enamel paints" to "industrial coating systems," from "mutual funds" to "retirement services." The new definition may seem arbitrary. It may even sound a bit pretentious. It doesn't matter, as long as it jump-starts creative thinking. Focus can come later.

Exhaustively map the opportunity space described by these expanded boundaries. Visual representation helps. One company regularly charts opportunities on a cube whose axes list potential users of a product category, potential uses to which products might be put, and the range of benefits they might deliver. Each cell represents a possible opportunity. By identifying unoccupied cells and conceiving products that could fill them, the company uses the cube to give structure and direction to its innovation process.

Contrast this to traditional market-research techniques where, typically, a single idea is tested against the total user population. Mapping the terrain of diverse customer needs segment by segment allows you to explore a panoply of possibilities.

2. *Get inside the customer experience to tap core dissatisfactions.* Done properly, the mapping process will reveal more opportunities than most companies can pursue. How do you decide which ones to develop?

Don't rely on asking customers what they want. They almost never really know. It's the rare individual who can predict his or her own behavior or understand the inchoate emotions that motivate action. And few consumers can forecast the premium they'll be willing to pay for a unique new value proposition.

What they can do is articulate their dissatisfactions. Let these dissatisfactions guide you to the most promising cells of the opportunity cube. What matters most aren't so much the specific deficiencies of existing products as the broad customer disaffections—for example, frustrations born of time scarcity, inconvenience, or unfulfilled yearnings for affiliation.

Probe for how customers see current offerings in the context of these deeper dissatisfactions. They represent the grain of sand around which the pearl of a new innovation can grow.

You get to these dissatisfactions through intensive, face-to-face interactions with customers. Settle for nothing less than unfiltered, real-time contact. Watch how customers use your products where they live, work, or play. The goal isn't just getting close to the customer; it's getting inside the customer experience.

Doing so requires getting outside the cocoon of the executive suite. If you're a senior auto industry executive, for instance, pass up the perquisite of having your next new car ordered by your secretary, and experience firsthand what the typical buyer endures at the hands of your dealer sales-and-service organization. You will gain an invaluable stimulus to new insight.

Shop the way your customers shop. In fact, study the total buying and use process. In an industrial business, look at how a product is engineered, sourced, bought, received and stocked, installed and repaired, and recycled once it reaches the end of its useful life. In a consumer business, examine how consumers shop for the product, use it, and clean up or put it away afterward. Learn how customers really use your product, how they routinely ignore or modify instructions, how they discover unimagined uses for your product, and how they define quality and superior performance.

Understanding the customer's total experience offers clues for new ways to bundle products, shorten time requirements, or deliver a solution more directly. It's how you get behind taken-for-granted tradeoffs of quality, cost, and time to identify fundamentally new value propositions.

3. *Don't delegate responsibility for insight.* All this demands enormous personal energy. New ideas are hard to come by and easy to kill. The

obstacle course they must run to win approval too often reduces them to a sterile lowest common denominator. That's why companies that excel at innovation ensure that senior managers don't delegate responsibility for insight.

Those closest to the customer may have the most firsthand data to contribute, but too often it doesn't get through. Those at the top bring a perspective that comes with experience and a degree of distance from the trenches. It's often easier for them to help the organization hear what customers are really saying and draw the frame-breaking conclusion. And of course, senior executives are freer to take risks and to see their convictions through to reality.

Breakthrough innovators design top-management engagement into every stage of the idea-generation process. Senior executives continuously challenge the organization to expand business concepts; they spend time face-to-face with customers; and they actively participate in exploring the opportunity space.

When they take responsibility for insight, executives discover that there is no such thing as a mature business—you can grow any business from the insight out.

CAPITALIZING ON ANOMALIES

LAWRENCE E. SHULMAN, 1997

Sometimes the best opportunities lie hidden in something that, at first glance, makes no sense. Idiosyncratic customer preferences or employee behavior can lead to aberrations in business results. How do you deal with these anomalies?

One common response is to ignore them. Most organizations try to contain or suppress anomalies for fear they will draw attention to departures from standard operating practice. When senior managers learn of anomalies, they generally dismiss them as random, one-time events.

That's too bad. Anomalies can reveal what your customers really want—and what your organization is capable of delivering in response. Paying attention to them may point you to major opportunities to grow your business, by doing on a broad scale what some part of your company is already doing on a small scale.

Wise executives capitalize on anomalies. They dig into them and look for ways to exploit them, asking: What's really going on? How can we learn from this? Is there an insight buried here that can move the business to a whole new level?

Inadvertent Next-Day Delivery

At one broad-line manufacturer, the business-altering anomaly was in the behavior of its distributors in a single geographic market. In most manufacturing businesses, distributors tend to carry the products of only one or two suppliers, and suppliers tend to do business with only a few key distributors in any given market. But in Chicago, a large market with many distributors, the company found that it was selling its specialty products to nearly every distributor in town. This didn't make sense. Why were all these Chicago distributors willing to buy from the same manufacturer?

The initial answers—"Chicago is just different" and "We've got a great sales rep there"—weren't much help. But patient digging revealed the real explanation: The company's factory was located only 200 miles from Chicago, and Chicago was on the way to almost all of the company's other markets. The frequent shipping runs through the area had inadvertently created a system of next-day delivery in and around Chicago. Distributors could stock a broader range at dramatically higher inventory turns, simultaneously enhancing their economics and allowing them to be more responsive to their customers.

Once they saw it, company executives began thinking about their business differently. They realized they could replicate the pattern in other markets. They assigned pairs of drivers to each truck and increased the overnight service range to 600 miles. They added order-entry and logistics systems that allowed them to make overnight delivery of high-tonnage orders. They expanded product variety to exploit new opportunities for even wider market access. Over time, they tripled or quadrupled market share in a half dozen Midwest cities and improved the product mix. Profits increased eightfold. Recently, the company acquired a new factory in another part of the country and is rolling out the same strategy in this new region.

Traffic-Jam Sales and Service

At a maker of high-tech health care diagnostic machines, the key anomaly was in the unusual performance of a local sales-and-service unit. A curious manager noticed that in Manhattan, the company had an extremely high capture rate for lucrative service contracts to maintain and repair the complex technology. What's more, customers there were buying all their new equipment from the company, even in product lines where the company's market share was normally quite low.

Closer inspection revealed that the Manhattan sales-and-service unit was the only one in the company assigning full-time, on-site service engineers to customer locations. Constant contact bred close relationships with both the buyers and the users of the equipment, and an in-depth understanding of their needs. Master technicians had become the company's most productive salespeople. Was the decision to locate the service engineers on the customers' premises a brilliant strategic decision? Hardly. The local service manager was simply trying to avoid having highly paid service technicians waste time in Manhattan traffic jams going from site to site. But understanding the anomaly did lead to a winning strategy. By assigning on-site technicians to customers in other regions, the company added 8 points of market share and boosted margins by 25 percent. It also gained a first-mover advantage over its rivals.

From Serendipity to System

The innovations at these two companies were serendipitous. What does it take to capitalize on anomalies systematically?

For starters, you need to have metrics and information systems that are sufficiently refined to identify anomalies in the first place. Knowing the average margins and market share isn't enough; look at the entire range of outcomes—across customers, geographies, products, and the like. This allows you to surface out-of-the-ordinary results for closer inspection.

The next step is to separate wheat from chaff: those anomalies that signal a potential business opportunity from those that are merely one-time events. The key is to examine the pattern of unusual performance over time. The customer who consistently buys high volumes or the market that outperforms the average year after year are, by definition, not random. Is there an underlying cause that can be identified and then replicated elsewhere?

Finally, you need to understand the precise mechanisms that animate the anomalies you identify. Why is the unusual pattern of performance happening? What specific features of the product or the local environment or the customer experience are bringing it about? Don't accept the usual first-order explanations. It's not enough to know that a particular customer has been loyal for years; find out precisely why.

It's up to senior management to create the forum for asking why and to persist until the question is answered with genuine insight. Business-unit personnel may be closest to the details of the anomaly in question, but they are usually too caught up in the day-to-day demands of the business to recognize the strategic significance of unusual patterns and practices. It often takes someone one step removed—regularly scanning the business for unexpected results—to notice and act on anomalies. It also takes an appreciation of differences, a lively sense of curiosity, and a willingness to play with the taken-for-granted rules of the business.

Timing is important. The worst time to look for anomalies is during a budget review, when everyone is worried about control numbers. A much better time is in a strategic review, when everyone should be prepared to think creatively about the future. Companies that consistently exploit anomalies plan for their future by reflecting on their past. A retrospective look at their strategy and business results allows them to take advantage of the serendipitous in a highly systematic way. As one executive put it, "We innovate from our own accidents."

Taking advantage of anomalies is an opportunity to inject into your company some of the experimentation and vitality characteristic of start-ups. Every day, entrepreneurs are working to reinvent your business and carve out a piece of it for themselves. By capitalizing on anomalies, you can harness the same kind of creative energy and put growth back on your company's agenda.

BREAKING COMPROMISES

GEORGE STALK, JR., DAVID K. PECAUT, AND BENJAMIN BURNETT, 1997

Many companies today are searching for growth. How and where should they look? One powerful way to grow is through innovations that break the fundamental compromises of a business. When a company successfully breaks a compromise, it releases enormous trapped value. Breakaway growth can be the result.

Compromises are concessions demanded of consumers by most of the companies in an industry. They occur when the industry imposes its own operating constraints on customers. Usually, customers accept these compromises as just the way the business works—inevitable trade-offs that have to be endured.

But a compromise is different from a tradeoff. In choosing a hotel room, for instance, a customer can trade off luxury for economy by choosing between a Ritz-Carlton and a Best Western. Until recently, however, most hotels forced all customers to compromise by not permitting check-in before 4:00 P.M. No law of nature or economics decrees that hotel rooms can't be ready before late afternoon.

Uncompromising Opportunity

The idea of compromises can be a useful organizing principle to focus an entire company on growth. It provides a systematic way to search for growth opportunities that are logical extensions of a company's existing business system.

Take the example of Circuit City's recent foray into the used-car business through the creation of a network of used-car superstores under the brand name CarMax. Annual used-car sales in North America top $200 billion, making it the third-largest consumer spending category behind food and clothing. What's more, few experiences are more fraught with compromises. Shopping for a used car is extremely time-consuming. And the buyer is at a fundamental disadvantage, ignorant about the actual condition of the product and subject to high-pressure sales tactics.

Circuit City concluded that many of the distinguishing capabilities of its consumer-electronics business could be used to break the compromises imposed on used-car buyers. Circuit City is known for the wide variety of its merchandise. CarMax takes the same approach. The typical used-car dealer has only 30 vehicles in stock, CarMax sites have up to 1,500. That makes it easy for customers to compare makes and styles. CarMax further enhances customer choice and lowers search costs by harnessing Circuit City's considerable expertise in information systems. At CarMax, customers have access to easy-to-use computer kiosks that allow them to review the inventory of available cars at all the CarMax stores in the region.

CarMax hasn't hesitated to deviate from the Circuit City model when the strategic logic requires it. For instance, Circuit City pays percentage-of-sales commissions to its consumer electronics sales force, but CarMax does not. Because a key compromise in used cars is pressure selling, the unit has created a compensation system that encourages no-haggle pricing and no-hassle guarantees. The result: an integrated business system that offers a fundamentally different experience to used-car buyers, and a business model that has allowed CarMax to capture roughly 15 points of share in the markets where it is active.

A Pathway to Growth

Compromises are inherent in any business. Even when a company breaks one compromise, it usually ends up creating another. By focusing on compromises, a company can continuously uncover fresh opportunities and thus sustain growth over time.

The financial services company Charles Schwab, for example, was founded on the breaking of a compromise. The company began as a discount brokerage in 1975, when the deregulation of U.S. security markets made it unnecessary for individual investors to pay high fees to full-service brokers.

But Schwab didn't stop there. Next, it broke the compromise set up by the discount brokerage houses themselves. Although these new firms offered low prices, most also provided unreliable service. By investing in computer technology that allowed almost immediate confirmation of orders over the telephone, Schwab was able to combine low prices with levels of responsiveness unusual for its industry. Subsequently, Schwab added convenience, flexibility, and ease of transferring funds to its value proposition through the provision of 24-hour-a-day, seven-day-a-week service, the Schwab One cash-management account, and automated phone and electronic trading.

Recently, Schwab has used its compromise-breaking capabilities to enter the mutual fund business. Most people invest in several fund families to achieve diversification. But diversification often comes at the price of frustration. It means dealing with a confusing variety of statements, rules, and sales representatives. In 1992, Schwab introduced OneSource, a single point of purchase for more than 350 no-load mutual funds. In the more than 20 years since its founding, Schwab has evolved from a simple discount broker to a comprehensive self-help financial supermarket, generating an annual growth rate of 20 to 25 percent.

Creativity, Flexibility, and Nerve

For a company to grow by breaking compromises, it must have the creativity to translate customer dissatisfactions into new value propositions, the flexibility to engage in constant reorientation of its business system, and the nerve to challenge business-as-usual in its industry. There are three basic steps.

1. *Get inside the customer experience.* Start by asking your managers and employees to immerse themselves in the customer's experience. It is critical to develop a visceral feel for the compromises consumers encounter when they do business with you.

A compromise often becomes visible when customers have to modify their behavior to use a company's product or service. So pay special attention to the compensatory behaviors customers engage in to get around the constraints that your product or service imposes on them. In the brokerage business, for instance, it was common knowledge that customers often called back a second or even a third time to confirm that their trade had gone through at the price requested. By paying careful attention to this behavior, Schwab realized that the ability to provide immediate confirmation when an order was taken would eliminate the extra calls, saving customers a lot of trouble and giving Schwab a significant advantage over its competitors.

2. *Travel up the hierarchy of compromises.* Once the organization is focused on the customer experience, learn to recognize three different types of compromises, each with increasing potential to create value.

Some of the most obvious can be found in your company's existing products or services. It was Chrysler's awareness of the compromises between station wagons (based on a car platform) and vans (based on a truck platform) that led to the minivan, a van based on a car platform. In the ten years after Chrysler introduced the minivan in 1984, minivan sales grew eight times as fast as industry sales overall.

Other, more powerful compromises can be found at the level of an entire product category. Witness how Nike has transformed the athletic footwear category by combining continuous innovation in shoe design with the proliferation of narrowly defined customer segments. Nike doesn't just make basketball shoes. It makes Air Jordans, Force, and Flight, each designed for a different playing style, with different design requirements and a different image.

The most powerful compromises are often the hardest to identify: broad social dissatisfactions that may have little to do with your product or industry but a lot to do with how your customers live their lives. For example, long-term social and economic trends are causing more and more people to manage their own investments. Yet lack of time and growing economic complexity can make this an immensely frustrating task. Schwab's ability to address that frustration is a big factor in its success.

3. *Reconstruct your value chain.* Defining new value propositions for the customer is necessary but not sufficient. You must also use the compromises you break to redefine the competitive dynamics of your industry to ensure that the economic value liberated by compromise breaking flows to you rather than to your competitors.

Think of compromises as an opportunity to reshape the value chain of your industry to your advantage. When Schwab entered the mutual fund business, its first thought was to create its own family of funds. Careful analysis of the industry value chain, however, revealed an even bigger opportunity: to become an intermediary between its own customer base and a large number of subscale mutual fund companies. Through OneSource, the firm serves the needs of the fund companies by providing them with economies of scale they could not achieve on their own. At the same time, Schwab interposes itself between the funds and the customer. Schwab's ownership of the direct customer relationship now provides a platform for growth in other financial services, such as insurance.

To break compromises, executives must first break with the conventional wisdom of their industry—about customers, about industry practices, and about the economics of the business. When they do, faster growth and improved profitability are the result.

Time-Based Competition

DURING THE 1980s, several BCG vice presidents, following initial work by George Stalk and Tom Hout, expanded on the early insights into flexible manufacturing to develop the strategic concept and tactical underpinnings of time-based competition. Client work, supplemented by extensive independent research, resulted in the Stalk/Hout book, *Competing Against Time*, published by The Free Press in 1990.

In the first chapter of their book, Stalk and Hout describe time-based competition and outline their view of its place in the progression of business thinking:

> In the competitive environment of the latter twentieth century, innovations in competitive strategy have life cycles of ten to fifteen years. Each innovation is followed by major shifts in competitive positions and in corporate fortunes. As these shifts occur, concerned managements struggle to understand the nature of their competitors' newfound advantage. However, like a military secret, the new source of advantage soon becomes understood by all and is thus no longer an exploitable innovation. A new innovation must be found.
>
> Today's innovation is time-based competition. Demanding executives at aggressive companies are altering their measures of performance from competitive costs and quality to competitive costs, quality, and responsiveness. Give customers what they want when they want it. This refocusing of attention is enabling early innovators to become time-based competitors. Time-based competitors are offering greater varieties of products and services, at lower costs and in less time, than are their more pedestrian competitors. In doing so, they are literally running circles around their slower competition.

BCG published a series of *Perspectives* on time-based competition in 1987 and 1988. The best are included here, along with others that extend the concept, plus one final piece that evaluates the results time-based competitors have achieved.

THE TIME PARADIGM

GEORGE STALK, JR., 1988

Time is the secret weapon of business. Advantages in response time provide leverage for all the other competitive differences that make up a company's overall competitive advantage.

Many executives believe that competitive advantage is best achieved by providing the most value for the lowest cost. This is the traditional paradigm for corporate success. Providing the most value for the lowest cost in the least amount of time is the new paradigm for corporate success. An increasing number of companies are achieving success by establishing competitive-response advantages. These time-based competitors belong to a new generation of companies that manage and compete in different ways. New-paradigm companies:

- Choose time consumption as a critical management and strategic measure
- Use responsiveness to stay close to their customers, increasing their customers' dependence on them
- Rapidly redirect their value-delivery systems to the most attractive customers, forcing their competitors toward the less attractive ones
- Set the pace of business innovation in their industries
- Grow faster with higher profits than their competitors

The new generation of competitors is obtaining remarkable results by focusing its organizations on flexibility and responsiveness. The companies in the following table use their response advantages to grow at least three times as fast as their industries and to earn profits more than twice the average of their competitors.

Company	Business	Response advantage	Growth difference	Profit
Wal-Mart	Discount stores	80%	36 vs. 12%	19 vs. 9% ROCE
Atlas Door	Industrial doors	66%	15 vs. 5%	10 vs. 2% ROS
Ralph Wilson Plastics Co.	Decorative laminates	75%	9 vs. 3%	40 vs. 10% RONA
Thomasville	Furniture	70%	12 vs. 3%	21 vs. 11% ROA

Becoming a Time-Based Competitor

You have become a time-based competitor when you have accomplished three tasks:

- Your value-delivery system is two to three times as flexible and responsive as those of your competitors.
- You have determined how your customers value these capabilities and have priced accordingly.
- You have a strategy for surprising your competitors with your time-based advantage.

Make Your Value-Delivery System Flexible and Responsive

Most of the time a product or service is in your value-delivery system is spent waiting. Delays stem from these causes:

- *Procedural constraints,* including minimum production or information-processing batch sizes, scheduling practices, and authorization schedules
- *Quality problems,* including physical and intellectual rework necessitated by inadequate design and attention to details
- *Structural difficulties,* including convoluted flows of product and information, functional handoffs, and interrelated facilities located at different sites

The single greatest cause of inflexibility and slow responsiveness, though, is organizing for economies of scale and control rather than for fast throughput.

To improve its responsiveness a company needs to organize for economies of time and for visibility. To do so, many companies disassemble their functional organizations and reassemble them into permanent, multifunctional teams. The members of these teams focus on entire processes, products, projects, customers, and/or competitors. The teams include everyone who can slow or speed the process and are often in one location. Their performance measures are set to achieve goals rather than efficiency.

One consumer appliance manufacturer formed development teams and challenged them to reduce the company's development cycle from as much as three years to less than 12 months. The teams identified many opportunities. For example, they found that months could be cut from the cycle by transferring several performance tests from the company's central testing laboratories to the design team organization. As the result of such changes, the company is well on its way to achieving its goal.

Price for Value Provided to Your Customers

The customers of time-based competitors obtain special value, although sometimes they do not recognize the value of faster response right away. Flexible, faster response benefits your customers in a number of ways:

- They need less inventory.
- They can make purchase decisions closer to the time of need.
- Their customers are less likely to cancel or change their orders.
- Their cash-flow cycle is speeded up.
- They receive more special services and customized products.

These and others benefits affect customers' economics, thus creating value. Time-based competitors retain some of this increased value in the form of increased prices and market share. For example, a manufacturer of a commodity product improved its responsiveness and is gaining share while earning a 20 percent price premium. Its distributors can pay higher prices and still make more money, because their inventory turns four times as fast as the industry average.

Improved responsiveness creates greater customer dependency and thus increases market share. A supplier of a custom industrial product could not increase its share of customer purchases using traditional means but did so after reducing its response time by 75 percent on every order, including semicustom fabrication. As customers became confident that they could rely on this company as a sole supplier, its share of their purchases increased from 30 to 45 percent.

Surprise Your Competitors

The greatest risk you run in becoming a time-based competitor is that one of your competitors might become one simultaneously. If you increase your responsiveness at equal rates, any advantage either of you achieves will be arbitraged away in the marketplace and only your customers will benefit.

True value and additional profits result only if you can establish a substantial response advantage over your competitors that will be difficult if not impossible for them to close. You can do this by:

- Initiating and executing a determined program to reduce delays in your organization

- Not passing the benefits on to customers until those benefits are substantial (i.e., not tipping your hand early)

- Focusing your marketing and sales resources on the customers that will benefit the most from improved responsiveness and thus be willing to pay a price premium

- Buying time by diverting your competitors' interest in the changes you have made

- Preserving your lead by continuing your internal efforts to improve responsiveness

The Importance of Vision

The journey to becoming a time-based competitor is demanding. It must begin with a vision of what could be. The vision needs to be sufficiently clear and attractive to motivate you and your organization to rethink the structure and activities of your whole value-delivery system so as to maximize its performance.

Initiating and executing a program that improves the responsiveness of an organization rapidly is not easy. Such a program must compete with other programs for attention. Further, the job is difficult to delegate to your subordinates, because improving responsiveness requires breaking down rigidities and delays across, as well as within, functions. Thus, you must stay involved. Finally, sustaining the rate of improvement and the accompanying benefits necessitates a philosophical change. Top management must shift its focus from cost to time and its objectives from control and functional optimization to providing resources to compress time throughout the organization.

You, as the keeper of the vision, must believe that time is your number one competitor.

MAKE DECISIONS LIKE A FIGHTER PILOT*

MARK F. BLAXILL AND THOMAS M. HOUT, 1987

Corporate strategy goes through phases. Companies have been restructuring their business portfolios and operations through the mid-1980s to raise stock prices and cut costs, and many are asking what to do next. How will the next round of competitive advantage be created? Leading-edge companies across a variety of industries are beginning to give the answer: build an organization with fast response time in serving customers and preempting competitors, and you will grow profitably.

Restructuring meant competitive survival rather than competitive advantage for many large older companies. Raiders forced these companies to jettison underperforming business while their Japanese competitors made them downsize and outsource high-cost manufacturing activities. Organizationally, layers of management were collapsed and individual business units made smaller, all to get the company closer to its customers and its managers closer to employees. Useful as this restructuring was, it was only a correction, a catch-up to competitive realities.

Real advantage requires of management something uniquely active and not easily achieved. Consistently greater speed in making management decisions, in developing new products and in delivering orders to customers ahead of the competitor creates that advantage. Fast-response companies are also likely to have lower costs and be more innovative than their competitors.

The best analogy for this kind of highly competitive management comes from the Air Force, which studied why certain pilots consistently won dogfights in wartime. Their findings were that winners complete the so-called O.O.D.A. loop—the cycle of observation, orientation, decision and then action—faster than losers.

The outcome between comparable planes was decided by which pilot could size up the situation and read opportunities in each encounter and then decide and act before the enemy. By preempting an adversary's move, the winner throws the loser into confusion and into a reactive cycle. After gaining this insight the Air Force designed aircraft and trained pilots to process sensory data into decisions faster.

The business world moves faster today. Business competition has become more like an encounter between fighter planes than a chess game, which had been our prevailing analogy. Product life cycles are much shorter. New products that utilize hybrid technologies are more frequent. Mass markets are dissolving into smaller customer segments, making competition messy. New materials and technology are multiplying company choices in how to design, make and distribute a product.

Fast-response companies manage their O.O.D.A. loops, starting with timely observation and orientation. For example, they collect today's sales data at the retail level because wholesale data are too late and distorted. They visit advanced university labs as research is taking shape and do not just read the papers. They study their customers thoroughly from several different points of view. Reactive companies suffer late recognition and disparate views, then incur the extra cost of studies and dispute resolution to fix them.

Fast-response companies accelerate decisions by better preparing the participants. They move senior executives around temporarily, forming new teams to vary the interaction patterns and fracture old assumptions. They move decisions down the corporate ladder and make the small decisions continually, without putting them off. No organizational habit is more insidious than constant formal, upward review and the need to wait for the big decision.

Speed in the action stage of the O.O.D.A. loop requires a particular operations architecture and a lot of high-quality work. The company's operations architecture—how the elements in its value-added chain are designed and interconnected—must be rooted in systems thinking. If each working part of the company is closely linked with others and work is done right the first time, the company will do everything faster than its competitors. When manufacturing people join the product development team, the new product and the process to make it can match, eliminating later redesign and retooling. When new orders enter the plant's production schedule directly, customers get their shipments faster.

Typically, less than 10 percent of the total time devoted to any work in an organization is truly value-added. The rest is wasted because of unnecessary steps or unbalanced operations. A few multifunctional working teams perform better than many departments that separately handle and slow down information. New product development is usually authorized by top management in big, discrete projects, but is done better in a continuous flow.

Fast-response companies not only have marketing advantages, but also tend to have lower costs because when production materials and information move through a company's operation quickly, they collect less overhead and do not accumulate as inventory. Also, the company can innovate more effectively because more new products can be conceived and engineered in a given period, giving customers more choices.

Management's focus on O.O.D.A. loop improvement will heavily influence our concept of business strategy. Competitive strategy has to be dynamic and recognize the systemlike nature of a company. But the planning lexicon has become too reliant on static and positional notions. Our concept of competitive advantage must shift to more of an operations and real-time orientation.

To accomplish this, the analytic questions become: How can my company build faster capability? Where does my current operations architecture and mindset slow the company? What is the performance of my competitor's O.O.D.A. loop?

Governments carefully design aircraft/pilot systems for superior O.O.D.A. loop performance, and companies are starting to follow. The basic building blocks are the flow of information, the organization of work and the perceptual range of people. Building such an organization is not hard science, it is rigorous craft.

The focus of the O.O.D.A. loop will ultimately influence the nation's competitiveness and trade balance. American companies with fast response time and high-quality products will close the gap against imports. But highly competitive foreign companies seeking greater shares of the American market will also be establishing self-sufficient operations in the United States. They will be removing the delays that long distances impose on their own performance in order to quicken their response time in today's fast-changing environment.

TIME AND QUALITY

GARY REINER AND MATTHEW ERICKSEN, 1990

Pity the overwhelmed executive! At any moment, there are 19 priorities—the bottom line, this quarter; human resource development; cost reduction; and several others. Recently, two process management priorities have been added to the list—*quality* and *speed-to-market.*

Quality, in particular, has become a popular umbrella. Many who are focusing on quality have found it useful to compete for the Malcolm Baldrige National Quality Award. Just competing for the award helps raise an organization's consciousness of quality. Indeed, some large companies, including IBM and Motorola, even insist that their vendors apply for the award in order to make them aware of the quality of their processes.

Speed-to-market has also become a popular goal. The earlier a competitor can innovate or fill an order, the more customer loyalty it can command. But the problem for the executive is how to reconcile quality and speed. Quality focuses on doing it right. Speed-to-market means moving faster than competitors. But doesn't haste make waste?

In fact, quality and time compression are consistent. Pursuing one reinforces the other. A focus on time helps a company find its quality problems. Most process quality problems show up in lost time—parts that can't be used, information that didn't arrive, work that must be done again, a customer-service visit that didn't fix the problem. Companies that are fast to market get that way by achieving quality in their processes, from engineering new products to shipping products off the line.

Time is never explicitly mentioned in the Baldrige Award application. Nevertheless, virtually all of the winners cite reduction in cycle times as a key to the award. At the National Quality Forum, Robert Galvin, then chairman of Motorola, reported a drop in the time required to process customer orders from 44 days to 100 minutes and a dramatic decline in defects at the same time. David Kearns of Xerox, another Baldrige winner, cited a cut in new-product development time of 60 percent. Visitors to Milliken, yet another winner, are told of the textile company's success in reducing order-to-delivery time of custom-made carpets from five months to two weeks.

In fact, the fastest developers tend also to be known for high-quality products. Honda is the fastest developer of new cars and is known for product quality and reliability. The same holds true for Compaq in personal computers, Boeing in aircraft, and Microsoft in software.

It should not be too surprising that quality and speed-to-market go together. Look at what companies with good, established quality cultures do. They are the same things that companies focusing on time compression do. The common threads are:

- *Seeing the company as a set of processes.* Executives can always see a company as a set of organizations and control statements. But those pursuing quality and speed also see their companies as a set of processes that need to work right and work together. A corporation that's serious about quality asks the same questions as a company working on cycle-time compression: What are our processes? Where do they interface? How can we make each more reliable? What steps don't we need if we do the essential steps right?

- *Measurement.* Businesses must be able to measure a process before improving it. This applies to order entry as well as shipping, engineering as well as field performance. Motorola measures cycle time of processes just like it measures yields and variances. In developing new products, for instance, the clock starts ticking the moment the product is conceived.

- *Common goals and cross-functional coordination.* Companies are usually organized for administrative convenience—salespeople under one head and pay system, engineers under another head and pay system, and so on. But a customer wouldn't organize his supplier this way. Instead he would have everyone concerned with his business—from the salesperson to the engineer—working together as a unit with one common goal—his order.

  Companies start to improve quality and cycle time once they get their people to view customers in this way. Customer satisfaction is usually the common goal that kicks off both quality and time improvements in companies. The simple question they ask is: What causes a slow-down or error in a customer's order? They usually find that the delays and mistakes are one and the same.

- *Empowering employees.* It is now a cliché that top-management commitment is the first requirement for quality and time improvement. But how is this commitment measured? Number of speeches made or award ceremonies attended? Employees have one very good indicator of senior-management commitment: Do they empower employees to find the problems, develop the solutions, and manage the new processes?

The Baldrige National Quality Award criteria cover everything from technical, field-level definitions of quality like defect rates and statistical quality control to management-level characteristics like planning and leadership. Applicants are graded on seven categories:

- Leadership
- Use of information and analysis
- Planning
- Use of human resources
- Design and control of processes
- Quantitative results
- Customer satisfaction

This is the same list one would put together for a national award on speed and customer responsiveness.

So, quality and time depend on each other. You cannot be more responsive to customers without high-quality processes. And the best way to locate quality problems in processes is to measure and analyze cycle times. Quality is what we all want to have in our companies. Time is the best route to quality.

In order to win the Baldrige National Quality Award, you should do what's necessary to become a time-based competitor. It's the fastest way there.

A NEW PRODUCT EVERY WEEK? LESSONS FROM MAGAZINE PUBLISHING

GARY REINER AND SHIKHAR GHOSH, 1988

In businesses from autos to consumer electronics, American companies need to find ways to develop new products faster. Product life cycles have shortened dramatically over the past decade, thanks in part to improved design technologies, such as CAD/CAM, which speed up the development process, and more flexible components, which permit easy variations on a theme. And aggressive competitors have stepped up the pace by adopting time-oriented management approaches that produce a quantum leap in the rate of product realization.

Fast competitors are going to market with product lines that offer more variety, incorporate newer technology and features, and reflect the latest design trends. They command the sharpest consumer attention and premium prices, thereby improving their market shares and profitability. Some of these competitors are progressive U.S. companies; many are Asian. These companies are building new competitive advantages that transcend low-cost labor.

BCG's work with businesses that develop new products quickly, such as consumer electronics, autos, construction equipment, business equipment, and magazine publishing, suggests that, in a wide variety of industries, the most successful competitors have adopted many of the same principles that enable weekly magazine publishers to hit the newsstands like clockwork the same time every week.

First and foremost, new-product development is a way of life for a weekly magazine. The organization's structure, skills, and systems are all honed to deliver new products over and over, better and better, and closer and closer to real-time events (i.e., the news).

In fast organizations, new products are developed in a steady stream. No one program is make-or-break, and a feature or performance enhancement that is not available for one generation can be rapidly implemented in the next.

> **Lesson 1:** Like a magazine, manage new-product development as a continuing process, not an isolated event.

Second, a weekly magazine never misses its deadline. In fact, time is the key management variable, and the organization is shaped around aggressive time targets.

Fast organizations differentiate themselves from slow ones by putting a high premium on time. Paradoxically, some of the fastest companies, such as Honda and Toyota in automobiles, Compaq in personal computers, and Panasonic in consumer electronics, also have the lowest costs and highest quality levels. Living with a tight and unchangeable schedule drives the organization to do the essentials well.

Lesson 2: To speed new-product development, make time the key variable. Acceptable levels of cost and quality must be maintained, but the clock is king.

Each weekly magazine issue dishes up timely, newsbreaking stories. This could not happen without powerful and highly tuned organizational machinery that makes it possible to move quality from concept to finished product. A shared computer system shows the current status of the magazine instantly. Runners bring layouts to the editors within 15 minutes. Editors give immediate feedback to writers—often by computer. A large, sophisticated library holds information on topics relevant to the publication.

Fast companies invest in capabilities to support rapid product development—for example, design libraries to use the experience gained in previous products, market research and technology development for future product families, and cost-estimation databases to minimize the time required to get a cost estimate. By investing ahead of a specific need, they remove these support functions from the critical path of product development, making it shorter and less risky. A primary role of senior management in fast companies is to build these capabilities so that each development cycle is faster and better than the previous one.

Lesson 3: Companies need to invest actively in the activities that support rapid product development so that they never slow down the process. Directing this investment is a key function of senior management.

Reporters, photographers, and artists work together in close-knit, cross-functional teams to deliver the magazine as quickly as possible, with senior editors empowered to make final decisions. For example, picture choices are made jointly by the picture editors and artists.

Honda, the fastest developer of new autos, incorporates the SED (Sales, Engineering, and Development) system, which calls for a small team consisting of members of each of these three departments whose joint task is to evaluate consumers' needs, design the auto, and plan the factory needs.

Lesson 4: A new-product development project should be managed by a team whose members bring skills from all relevant functions (e.g., product management, design, manufacture).

At a weekly magazine, the team works together and communicates intimately. The entire magazine staff is often on one floor. There are frequent team meetings and decisions are made orally, on the spot.

Successful teams typically have three characteristics. They are located close to each other—in the same room if possible. They are judged only by the overall success of the project—not by individual contributions. And they have the authority to make the key decisions that affect the product.

Lesson 5: Empower the team members to work as a team. They must have common goals and rewards, authority to make decisions, and an elbow-to-elbow environment.

At a weekly magazine, the doers are the decision makers, and they act quickly. Everyone who touches the product adds value directly.

Fast organizations typically minimize the role of staff in the development process. Decisions on the product are made by the people developing it. Senior management focuses on developing the organizational capabilities that will shorten the cycle for future products.

Lesson 6: Members of product teams must have the experience, expertise, training, and authority needed to make important decisions. The role of senior managers is primarily to create an environment that leverages the skills of the teams.

U.S. businesses are frequently exhorted to emulate their Asian competitors in order to reduce costs, increase speed, and improve quality. Mostly this is good advice—certainly with regard to speed. But good models can also be found right here at home. Companies hoping to bring products to market faster can learn a lot about process from some of their neighbors—the ones that have always managed time well, such as weekly magazine publishers.

RULES OF RESPONSE

GEORGE STALK, JR., 1987

Corporate operations—their value-delivery systems—are subject to a challenging set of rules. These are the rules of response. Managements that appreciate the significance of these rules and use them to their benefit can achieve startling gains. The rules of response are:

- The .05 to 5 Rule
- The 3/3 Rule
- The 1/4-2-20 Rule
- The 3 × 2 Rule

The .05 to 5 Rule

Across a spectrum of businesses, the amount of time required to execute a service or to order, manufacture, and deliver a product is far less than the actual time the service or product spends in the value-delivery system. For example, a manufacturer of heavy vehicles takes 45 days to prepare an order for assembly, but only 16 hours to assemble each vehicle. The vehicle is actually being worked on less than 1 percent of the time it spends in the system.

The .05 to 5 Rule highlights the poor time productivity of most organizations. Most products and many services are actually receiving value for only 0.05 to 5 percent of the time they are in the value-delivery systems of their companies.

The 3/3 Rule

During the 95 to 99.95 percent of the time a product or service is not receiving value while in the value-delivery system, the product or service is waiting.

The waiting time has three components. These are the amounts of time lost while waiting for:

- Completion of the batch a particular product or service is part of
- Completion of the batch ahead of the batch a particular product or service is part of

- Management to get around to making and executing the decision to send the batch on to the next step of the value-adding process

Generally, the 95 to 99.95 percent of time lost divides almost equally among these three categories.

The amount of time lost is affected very little by working harder. But working smarter has tremendous impact. Companies that reduce the size of the batches they process—whether the batches are physical goods or packets of information—and streamline the work flows significantly reduce the time lost in their value-delivery systems. For example, when a manufacturer of hospital equipment reduced standard production lot sizes by half, the time required to manufacture the product declined by 65 percent. After the production flow was streamlined to reduce material handling and the number of intermediate events requiring scheduling was reduced, the total time was reduced by another 65 percent.

While these improvements are dramatic, this company barely escaped the .05 to 5 Rule. Its time productivity increased over 200 percent—from 3 percent to 7 percent.

The 1/4-2-20 Rule

Companies that attack the consumption of time in their value-delivery system experience remarkable performance improvements. For every quartering of the time interval required to provide a service or product, the productivity of labor and of working capital can often double. These productivity gains result in as much as a 20 percent reduction in costs.

A U.S. manufacturer of a consumer durable has reduced its time interval from five weeks to slightly more than one week. Labor and asset productivity have more than doubled. Costs are down considerably, and profits are approaching extraordinary levels.

The 3 × 2 Rule

Companies that cut the time consumption of their value-delivery systems turn the basis of competitive advantage to their favor. Growth rates of three times the industry average with two times the industry profit margins are exciting—and achievable—targets.

A manufacturer of a prefinished building material reduced the time required to meet any and all customer orders to less than ten days. Most orders can be on the customer's site one to three days from when they are placed.

The other competitors require 30 to 45 days to fill any and all orders.

The fast-response competitor has grown over 10 percent a year for the last ten years, to become the market leader. The average industry growth rate has been less than 3 percent over the same period. The pretax return on net assets of the fast-response competitor is 80 percent—more than double the industry average.

Summary

The rules of response apply to both service and product businesses. Managements that have invested the time it takes to understand how the rules of response apply to their businesses and that aggressively use the rules to their advantage are:

- Growing much faster and more profitably than their competitors
- Becoming closer and more essential to their customers
- Taking leadership positions in their industries

And perhaps the greatest benefit of all is the excitement of new growth in core businesses.

TIME-BASED RESULTS

THOMAS M. HOUT AND GEORGE STALK, JR., 1993

We first spoke of time-based competition five years ago. The concept was simple: Companies that meet the needs of their customers faster than competitors grow faster and are more profitable than others in their industries. We argued that time could be the next decade's most powerful competitive weapon and management tool for U.S. companies.

We were right. Companies of all sorts and sizes became time-based competitors. By inspecting their processes and organizations through the lens of time these companies have found new ways to operate, satisfy their customers, compete, grow, and invigorate themselves. Consider the results of three very different companies.

Time and Innovation

Chrysler entered the 1990s with only two profitable product lines—minivans and jeeps—and several outdated lines of cars and trucks. It needed a new winner soon, and made the do-or-die decision to reinvent its new-car development process and cut the old time of four to six years to 39 months.

In the company's traditional process, a new-car concept moved sequentially from styling to engineering to parts procurement to manufacturing, with each step carefully planned and scheduled. Under a time-based approach, each new-car platform now has a team of several hundred people working together on everything from the start. Everyone, including vendors, has access to the same information. All functions on the team are housed on one floor of the development building, breaking up the old departmental offices and enabling more face-to-face communication. Each new-car team has a vice president in charge—many with no previous experience managing development on this scale—to make sure old habits and turf issues do not get in the way.

Chrysler made its first move with the LH large-car platform team—nicknamed by the skeptical press The Last Hope. A year ago, the LH models—Intrepid, Vision, New Yorker, and Concorde—were introduced. The team took 25 percent of the time out, cut the dollar investment to 30 percent below that in any previous program, and brought out a car to rave reviews and more orders than any new Chrysler model since the minivan. Recently, Chrysler followed up with the classy-looking subcompact Neon, developed in 31 months.

Time and Service

Because time-based competition started in manufacturing companies, large service organizations initially questioned whether its principles applied to them. Experience in industries ranging from insurance to package delivery to health care proves that these principles do. Take, for example, the case of Karolinska Hospital in Stockholm.

Sweden has provided superior health care for its entire population since World War II. But by the early 1990s, rising costs and a weakened economy were forcing the government to reassess and reduce health care expenditures. In the face of expected cost cuts, Karolinska, one of the country's leading teaching hospitals, wondered if quality care could survive.

Karolinska turned to time-based competition. At first, the doctors were skeptical. How could they save time without imperiling patient care? In fact, they found that poor coordination and scheduling problems were not only reducing efficiency and inflating costs, but also causing patients unnecessary delay, inconvenience, and anxiety.

By redesigning operating procedures and staffing patterns, Karolinska was able to cut the time required for preoperative testing from months to days. It was able to close 2 of 15 operating rooms and still increase the number of operations per day by 30 percent. Doctors could schedule operations in weeks rather than months. The result: better service for patients, with no loss of quality and less overhead.

Time and Integration

Time-based competition may be at its most powerful when suppliers and customers use it to redefine how they do business. That is what happened when textile manufacturer Milliken & Company joined with The Warren Featherbone Company, a children's apparel maker, and Mercantile Stores, a large retail chain, to compete through what they called Quick Response.

In the mid-1980s, it took 66 weeks for the apparel industry to go from yarn at the manufacturer to clothing on the rack. But since no one in the chain knew what would be selling in a month, much less a year, the cost of that lengthy supply cycle was devastating. The industry as a whole lost billions of dollars each year through markdowns on what customers didn't want and by not having enough of what they did want.

The three companies were gaming each other every time they did business. Each level—fabric, garment, retail—carried redundant buffer inventory to protect against shortages caused by others. When demand turned down, each scrambled to avoid holding inventory by slashing orders to its supplier. Long lead times and slow communications between layers made things worse. The result was heavy markdowns at retail that sent cost pressure back through the system.

With Quick Response, the companies got together and reengineered their forecasting, production, reordering, and logistics systems, and in doing so created a new short-cycle replenishment system. Mercantile shares its point-of-sale information with Warren Featherbone and Milliken. Orders down the chain are more frequent and smaller. Inventories carried at each level are lower, eliminating the need to shift them. Any surprises or problems anywhere are communicated along the chain quickly. The result: Retail inventory turns went from three times to five times a year, and markdowns dropped to a third of the industry average.

Reaching this level of integration was hard, because it required each company to make itself more vulnerable to the rest of the chain. Here, time was a unique catalyst. It was the one metric all the partners could easily understand and use that did not pit one against the other. By setting radical time-compression goals, everyone was forced to change old assumptions.

Time and Business Process Reengineering

Time-based competition begins with strategy and ends with process reengineering. Chrysler, Karolinska, and Milliken were all looking for higher revenues, not just lower costs. They focused their thinking first on getting to the customer faster, then reengineered the processes that could help them do this. They engaged the organization in a positive building effort, not a contraction.

For every dollar that can be removed by reengineering cost and time out, several more can be saved by rethinking how to use speed to serve customers better and competitively reposition the company. Now Chrysler has fresh, not old, product. Karolinska avoided cuts in service by increasing throughput. Milliken and its apparel partners raised price realization by eliminating markdowns.

Time-based competition is a reality, not just a concept. It is rapidly becoming the baseline, not the exception.

Performance Measurement

NO BUSINESS STRATEGY, no matter how brilliant, can be brought to fruition unless the tactical support for its execution is in place. One of the primary tactical decisions a manager must make is how performance will be measured: individual, team, SBU, division, group, and company.

Bruce Henderson held a strong conviction that measurements linked only to the short-term profitability of a business would damage its long-term performance. He saw the profit center as the worst organizational offender—it forced a manager to sacrifice his career to the business, or (unfortunately more commonly) to sacrifice the business to his career. Judging performance on the basis of short-term profit alone caused managers to ignore investments to achieve long-term strategic goals.

The *Perspectives* in this section make the case that the metrics employed must be aligned with the strategy that the managers being measured are committed to execute. This requires, first, that information (costs, revenue, cash flow, market share, etc.) be collected in a way that allows progress toward strategic goals to be evaluated objectively. Second, the timing of performance evaluation must match the time horizon of the strategy. If a strategy is meant to play out over five years, managers must be measured against sensible milestones over the entire period. Finally, performance measures need to be evaluated regularly to ensure they are still creating incentives that buttress the strategy. All too frequently, performance measurements remain in place long after strategy or market demands have shifted.

What gets measured gets done—for better or worse. Two recent developments have focused renewed attention on performance measures. The concern for process excellence has motivated the current generation of managers to explore a whole new range of metrics that calibrate their businesses' responsiveness and operational effectiveness. And their preoccupation with enhancing shareholder value has prompted a search for measures that can motivate employees throughout the organization to seek the appropriate kind of results. "Process excellence" has been unfailingly constructive; "shareholder value management" less so, as the popularity of economic value added highlights once again the dangers of trading off growth for short-term profitability. Both are explored in the last two *Perspectives* in this section.

PROFIT CENTER ETHICS

BRUCE D. HENDERSON, 1971

Profit center managers are frequently caught in a cruel dilemma. They are often asked to carry out policies that they strongly feel to be unwise. Yet they know that they will be held responsible for failure, whatever the cause.

The ethics of dissent are a very real issue in profit center management. Is the good of the corporation the overriding concern? Or is it personal survival? How far should dissent be pushed if higher authority neither wants nor accepts advice? What is honorable when either protest or acquiescence lead to unacceptable consequences?

The situation is real even with the best of goodwill on all sides. Differences in perspective lead to far different projections of consequences. Clear-cut orders can be followed and must be followed. But orders to a profit center are rarely clear-cut just because it is a profit center. However, the manager of a profit center receives much advice that must be heeded.

By definition, a profit center is measured on results. In theory, future profit is the measure. In theory, the manager is free to follow his own judgment except within explicit, specific constraints. In theory, current performance is factored by the long-term benefits and the effect of corporate constraints. In fact, none of these conditions are ever wholly true.

Characteristically, profit center managers are measured over a quite moderate time span. The penalty for unsatisfactory absolute performance over the short term is severe. But the proper balance between the known performance and potential future benefits is never clear.

The executive stress is difficult to overstate when there is conflict between policy restrictions, near-term performance, the long-term good of the company, and personal survival.

Logically, a profit center should have a combination of all kinds of goals simultaneously. The management should be judged on the net results of this complex of goals. Yet if this is done, profit is merely a derivative of the interactions of the various goals and constraints over time. It is not a prime index of current performance. It would not be the conventional profit center if it were managed this way.

The manager's situation becomes more difficult when corporate staff becomes deeply involved. Should the manager do what is politically expedient and satisfy the preferences of staff advisers or optimize future performance for which he is held accountable? This can be an excruciating choice.

Corporate staff individually and collectively have their own ideas of how the business should be run. They are in a position to press those ideas hard. They can also significantly bias the evaluation of performance and the imposition of constraints. Failure to obtain their full support means being judged rigidly, even harshly, on near-term results. Yet the disagreement almost always concerns the longer-term consequences. *The most important decisions a manager makes tend to depress short-term reported performance in order to significantly improve long-term results.* The issue becomes, "Should I do what is expedient, or should I fulfill my responsibilities to the best of my ability?" Martyrs are rarely honored in business.

In most corporations the evaluation of the profit center manager is based on current reported profit. Managers know it. Incentive compensation schemes often tend to reinforce this specific measurement over all others.

The problems of ethics are inherently chronic. The manager's problem can be serious enough even in the absence of any constraints. The temptation is great to take the performance measurement at stated face value. It is all too easy to liquidate the future and thereby maximize apparent current performance. In all too many cases this leads to promotion, leaving the aftermath to the hapless successor.

When the overall interests of the company impose constraints or goals that conflict with short-term profit performance, the conflict of interest is compounded. Both count. A balance must be struck. Compliance with the conflicting constraints and contribution to corporate goals are apt to be evaluated in a subjective and often uncertain fashion. Political expediency becomes a necessity.

The problem becomes even more acute when corporate management has a short-term time horizon and profit center optimization requires long-term investments of expense as well as capital. No manager can expect to survive who has a longer time horizon than his superiors. But neither can the business survive if the time horizon is inadequate to encompass the actions required today in order to protect the business in the future.

The worst situation exists when corporate management has a different concept of the requirements for future success from the concepts of the profit center management. The differences in perspective and philosophy can apply both to the profit center itself and to the corporation as a whole.

When any of these conditions exist, then managerial ethics become a real issue.

There are often real tradeoffs between the personal career and the good of the company. There can be real dilemmas where only short-term survival seems possible because of the tradeoffs between long-term and short-term performance. The conflict between expediency and responsibility can become painful.

Regardless of ethics, everyone who aspires to responsibility in a complex organization must strike some balance. Those who are most realistic in their compromises inherit the responsibility and set the pattern for the future. That pattern may be far from the best interests of the company.

Resolution of this conflict can occur only if three conditions are met:

- There must be an explicit corporate strategy. To be useful, the strategy must relate administrative behavior to the allocation of resources over time. Action must be relatable to a value system that all members of management understand and accept.

- There must be an understanding and consensus on the strategy. The consensus must include essentially everyone who is in a position to make decisions and tradeoffs that would affect implementation.

- Profit center profit performance appraisal must encompass a time horizon equal to the strategy time horizon.

Few multidivision corporations have a strategy that is adequate enough to spare their profit center managers the stress implicit in the ethics of dissent.

THE STORY OF JOE (A FABLE)

BRUCE D. HENDERSON, 1977

Joe made himself quite a reputation as a "turnaround" manager. It began when he was put in charge of a very sick division of his very large and diversified company. Within a couple of years he changed it from a big loser to a modest profit maker.

He turned around sick divisions not once, but several times, one after the other. His staff thought he was the best. The corporate management eulogized him. Morale in his operations was high. But Joe's reputation began to tarnish.

After Joe left these divisions and turned them over to someone else, they seemed to go sour. They seemed to drop back slowly and inexorably into their former unprofitability. The managers who succeeded Joe, one by one, convinced top management that major new investment was necessary if their sick operations were ever to be built into something really worthwhile. The suspicion grew that Joe had not really "turned around" those operations.

By then Joe was a high-ranking officer of this great company. Joe was put in charge of one of the company's very large divisions, which over many years failed to realize its promise. Under Joe nothing changed. He tried hard. But nothing changed. He tightened budgets. He cut overhead. He looked for every penny he could save. All this had been done before. Joe failed. This operation continued to slowly sink into mediocrity.

So Joe was fired. It wasn't done lightly. Joe had been a hardworking and loyal employee. No one could find fault with what he had done. He had seemed to be a first-class manager. Yet the facts were clear for all to see. Every operation that Joe managed looked good for awhile but became a disaster eventually. Joe was really bad news.

Some of the younger managers in the company were greatly disturbed. How could Joe look so good and turn out like that? Joe had seemed to be a good man, a good manager, a good businessman, a leader. Why . . . ? So the young men sought out a retired old-timer wise in the ways of people and corporations. They asked him why. And this is what he told them.

"Business is complex. Nobody is really sure what determines success. The only thing that seems sure is results. The bottom right-hand corner of the P&L statement seems real. But it is not real either. It is based on a whole series of assumptions about the future that have been stylized as accounting.

"Joe's company believed its own accounting. It set Joe's goals in short-term budgets. It asked Joe to make those accounts show a profit and do it quickly. Joe did it.

"Joe cut out every expense that didn't have an immediate payback. He cut back on advertising, product development, maintenance, personnel development, training, and all support activities not absolutely essential.

"Joe liquidated every asset he could that had a depreciation charge in excess of current contribution. This not only improved the return on the remaining assets but reduced his excess capacity and left mostly assets with low book values. This was done very early when Joe took charge, since early writeoffs can always be attributed to your predecessor.

"Joe then held prices firm and perhaps a little on the high side. This tended to slowly lose market share, but then, customers do not ordinarily shift suppliers very fast. Meantime, a few percentage points in margin looked very good in a marginal operation.

"Joe did exactly what he should have done. He did exactly what the company's control system asked him to do. He did exactly what the company's incentive plans rewarded.

"Far beyond that in importance, Joe did exactly what the company should have wanted him to do. Joe initiated an orderly liquidation of those businesses that should have been liquidated because they were too poorly situated to really compete."

So why did Joe get fired?

"Joe did what he was told to do, but the results were neither what the company expected nor wanted. The company wanted a weak and poorly positioned operation to be turned around immediately into a profitable one. Joe did that."

But the company wanted and expected this and much more. The company expected the immediate turnaround to be the first step in a long and steady increase in profitability ending in industry leadership. This, of course, was utterly unrealistic.

In fact, there was no way for any of these businesses to be converted into long-term profitable leaders without very substantial long-term investment, which would necessarily be very heavy in the beginning.

The risk would have been high. The end result would have been completely dependent on the established leaders already in place as competitors.

The company had no strategy and confused short-term operating goals with long-term investment decisions and investment evaluation. Neither Joe nor the company knew what they were really doing or what they should have done.

A Requiem for Joe

His company wanted the impossible and expected Joe to get it.

Joe gave his company what they asked for but not what they expected.

Poor Joe, he did the right thing for the wrong reason and was fired for the wrong thing for the wrong reason.

CONTROLLING FOR GROWTH IN A MULTIDIVISION BUSINESS

Patrick Conley, 1968

Profit centers and return on investment have been equally popular concepts for evaluating the performance of a division in a multidivision business. As concepts taken at face value, however, both are inappropriate when a division is engaged in a growth business. ROI and profit centers both imply an absolute current measure of performance: "Profit is good, loss is bad." In a rapidly growing business, this is simply not true unless important—and universally overlooked—riders are attached; as a measure of optimum performance current profit or return are usually downright wrong.

To optimize performance in a growth business, a manager must use, and be measured on, a long-time perspective. Traditional control systems discourage this. Conventional control systems emphasize profits reported now. This is in direct conflict with appropriation evaluation systems that measure discounted cash flow. Cash flows may be far out of phase with reported profits. This becomes critical when dealing with more intangible relationships such as organization development, R&D, or the value of market share.

For example, long-term profitability appears to be a direct function of sustainable relative market share. Growth in market share proceeds fundamentally from better values for the customer than competitors are willing or able to offer. Therefore, improving market share requires a commitment of resources and expense that depresses current reported profits for the sake of the future. It is a fact, though, that the greater the market share over time, the lower the relative costs can be compared to competition: The more you produce, the faster your costs can go down; the greater your total production experience, the greater your cost advantage can be over less-experienced competitors. The more market share you can get, the more market share you can afford to buy—because your costs are going down faster than your competitors'. Your increasing market share represents foreclosed cost-reduction opportunities for competitors.

In this context current profit could be bad and could reflect *poor* performance on the part of a division manager. Maximizing current profit here would require prices and margins higher than the optimum for capturing market share. It would mean funds withheld from investment in market growth and future cost reductions. On the other hand, loss could reflect, instead, investment in a sustainable cost advantage and thus substantial future profits. These future profits can have a discounted present value far higher than the current profits being sacrificed. Investments can be in expenses as well as in capitalizable assets. Investments can also be made in relationships that are created by forgone revenues.

For every product there is an optimum achievable and sustainable market share. Top management should make explicit the appropriate market share for each product. This should be calculated on the long-term value to the company of attaining and keeping the target share. This can be done if there is a characteristic relationship between accumulated experience, cost, price, margin, and market position. If the value of the appropriate share for a product can be determined, then management can determine how much it can afford to spend in forgone current profits in order to invest in market-share growth. Management can also establish some schedule for achieving the target share.

Divisional control can then be effected by computing the cost-decline schedule that corresponds to market projections. Performance can be monitored by cross-checking cost levels achieved and market share achieved to date. By treating changes in short-term profits as changes in investment, it is possible to construct a strategy of competitive behavior that will have the probability of the highest return on investment in terms of present values.

In the long run, all that counts is "cash in versus cash out discounted to present value." Evaluating the changes in the present value of the cash-flow profile is not as easy as accepting conventional "good accounting practice." Yet it is clear that it is worth the effort. It seems obvious that profit centers and return on investment based on conventional accounting practice can lead to gross misinterpretations of current performance.

A multidivision business runs a peculiar and characteristic risk. It is quite likely to rely on primarily financial performance measures in controlling its business. These controls by definition discount any performance or policies that are not reflected in the books of account. If the controls are effective, then other considerations are downgraded.

The result of this can often be that multidivision companies are effective in operating mature businesses but singularly inept in capitalizing on the opportunity of the growth product. In such a situation, the manager of a growth division is vying for corporate funds against appropriation requests for short-term projects and investments in mature businesses with established annual returns. He obviously cannot compete for funds on these terms without there being a completely different frame of reference than the financial controls used in operations.

The only time a multidivision company seems able to fully accommodate both mature and growth businesses is when the growth opportunity becomes so big and so visible that the policy and strategy is set by top management and the financial controls are adjusted to fit—*instead of vice versa.*

For the large multidivision company, explicit strategies and long-term plans would seem to be a prerequisite for growth. This means that nonfinancial goals and performance checkpoints must be established in parallel to the financial controls. These in turn must be the result of optimizing *long-term* financial performance, not current performance necessarily. "Cash in versus cash out discounted to present value" may show quite different plans and policies than maximization of current reported profit and current apparent return on assets invested.

It is becoming increasingly clear that multidivision, multiproduct companies can be extremely efficient competitors if they are able to direct and redirect the flow of capital internally into the *best long-term* returns. The conglomerate is potentially far more efficient at this than the public capital market.

For this potential to be realized, however, a far more sophisticated set of control concepts is required than those that are implicit in the conventional profit center.

MAKING PERFORMANCE MEASUREMENTS PERFORM

ROBERT MALCHIONE, 1991

Performance measurements at most companies are out of step with the business environment. What matters today is meeting rising customer expectations by emphasizing time and quality. Let's look at the characteristics of traditional performance measurements to see why they no longer work.

Traditional performance measurements focus more on internal goals of cost and efficiency than on external realities of customer satisfaction and competitive capabilities.

Company A's customers almost always received their orders when the shipping department promised. Yet the company was losing customers to higher-priced competitors. The problem was that the internal measurement of "ship-to-promise" failed to detect the external reality that customers wanted the product even sooner and would pay a premium to get it. A "ship-to-customer want" measurement would have captured this.

An automotive component company achieved its key customer's highest-quality classification, yet its competitor was gaining market share. It turned out that the competitor was supplying other customers with twice the quality at lower cost. While focusing on one customer's quality criteria, this company neglected to look at what its competitor could do for other customers.

Traditional performance measurements emphasize control at the expense of customer response.

Company C's distribution outlets were measured on their fill rate, that is, how many orders they could fill off the shelf. When the product wasn't in stock, however, some customers went elsewhere. Because the distribution department's measurement tracked only customers who placed orders, the number of orders lost went undetected. In fact, it was to the distribution center manager's disadvantage to persuade the customer to order and wait for delivery because that would count as a stock-out for the distribution center.

Traditional performance measurements focus on the end product and overlook the importance of the process.

Market share and profitability are results. They measure how effectively and efficiently a company has met its customers' needs after the fact. Additionally, a company could focus on the process employed to meet these needs. Such measurements as the percentage of transactions handled in one phone call, time from customer order to delivery, or percentage delivered when customer wanted it would highlight how well an organization's business system was performing against customers' needs.

Traditional performance measurements focus on particular departments or aspects of a business, often at the expense of overall business goals.

When Company D's distribution center ordered parts from the factory, the factory would make more than ordered because it could never be sure of the yield. Because the distribution center was measured on product turns, however, it would take only the number ordered, even if the factory yielded more. If demand was greater than expected and the distribution center ran out of inventory, orders were lost even though the organization had already committed time and money to producing the product.

A specialty material producer, believing its business to be capital-intensive, measured and focused on asset utilization. This resulted in large product backlogs to ensure that machines were kept busy. A smaller competitor observed that many customers needed product quickly and chose to measure time. It put in "excess" capacity to achieve its time objectives. The result: a complete reversal of market shares and profitability for the two.

These four characteristics of typical performance measurements can result in an organization's spending significant effort without making much progress toward its goals.

Measurements That Work

Every business is different, so each should have its own set of performance measurements. But there are some common rules to follow in designing effective measurements.

Start on the outside of your business, not inside the company. Ask yourself: "What do customers really want and when?" "What do our best competitors give customers that we do not?" For example, customers almost always welcome recommendations on how they might make better use of their suppliers. They also want personal relationships to help build commitment from suppliers. But these items aren't high on the agendas of most departments. If you value them, measure them.

Responsiveness to customers overshadows all other marketing goals. Make sure control measures don't get in the way. You have to dismantle control measures that work against customer responsiveness. For example, backlog is a time-honored measurement of a company's strength. Companies are comfortable when backlog is high. Department heads use it to justify hiring more people. But high backlog means slow response to customers. If you're serious about responsiveness, don't reward backlog. Reward throughput.

Think of process and product as equals. Focusing on the end product can cause you to lose sight of the process unless measurements make both equally visible to your people. Most employees think in terms of fixing the product as it goes by. This is because it's easier to spot a flawed product than a flawed process. Make your process explicit. Map and measure it. Reward people who fix the process.

You compete as a company. Don't let overall business goals get lost among the many operating measures. In measuring more processes and more variables, it's easy to lose sight of the overall goal. Beware of losing track of the larger measures that tell you how the customer views you against competitors. Watch customer retention, customer gains, and customer losses. Share this information with your people. If you measure them only on their own piece of the company, they may not look beyond to the larger picture. Train your people to think of the company as one integrated delivery system for the customer's benefit.

Establishing New Measurements

Externally focused, process-oriented, and systemwide performance measurements are essential for encouraging the actions that create competitive advantage today, but they won't happen without strong management support.

The process starts with communication. Convincing an organization to rethink measurements that have been part of its business mindset for years is not an easy undertaking. Rules give people security and a sense of purpose. Changing them arouses anxiety. Some employees will worry about having to work too hard; others will wonder if the company isn't neglecting the bottom line.

Therefore, management has to give the rationale behind the new measurements. Too often, people are told the "what" without the "why." The more employees know about why customer satisfaction, time, and quality really matter, the more they can support the new goals. Once the rationale is clear, give your people a chance to design the new measurements. Let them wrestle with the various options to figure out which make sense and which will just get in the way.

Management also needs to show commitment to the new rules by monitoring them to make sure they are keeping pace with the rapidly changing competitive environment and by sticking to them even if results are slow to materialize.

The purpose of performance measurements is to focus the energy of the organization on its strategic goals, to track progress toward the goals, and to provide feedback. If performance measurements haven't been realigned with the new priorities of the business, they will keep the organization from achieving advantage. When in conflict, the old performance measurements will win out over new goals because measurements, not goals, determine promotions and compensation. Changing the goals without changing the measurements is no change at all.

ECONOMIC VALUE ADDED

ERIC E. OLSEN, 1996

What gets measured gets done—for better or worse. Too many companies chase growth in earnings per share, only to find themselves employing too much capital at too low a rate of return and thereby eroding shareholder value. Economic value added* offers a beguiling solution: an easy-to-understand measure that recognizes improvements in earnings only to the extent that they exceed the cost of the capital employed to secure them.

Eminently sensible but for one critical flaw: EVA discourages growth. The conceptual problems have been there all along; the empirical evidence is beginning to mount. At a time when renewing growth represents the major competitive challenge facing most companies, dependence on EVA can become a major obstacle to building shareholder value. Fortunately, there are better alternatives.

Evaluating EVA

The value financial markets assign to a company reflects its prospects for profitability and growth. A change in value is driven by a change in expectations for one or both. CEOs naturally seek to influence shareholder value. The trick is to pick the right metric—one that tracks the market

---

* Economic Value Added—which we will abbreviate as EVA—is generally calculated as net operating profit (before interest, but after tax) minus a charge for capital employed.

valuation process closely, yet is fairly simple and intuitive—and then drive the management of that metric down through the organization.

EVA is easy to understand and to calculate, but at a cost: It tracks actual market valuations rather poorly (see figure) and introduces three fundamental distortions into managers' decisions:

1. *EVA is biased against new assets.* EVA shares the same bias against new assets as do all conventional accounting-based measures. When an investment is made, its full cost hits the capital charge, and EVA shows artificially low. As the investment depreciates, the capital charge declines proportionally. At maturity, EVA shows artificially high. Inflation exacerbates the tendency, since EVA recognizes its impact on earnings but ignores its impact on the replacement cost of assets.

This has the perverse effect of penalizing managers who bet on growth by investing. Except for the rare case where an investment has an immediate payback, growth-oriented managers take a short-term EVA hit.

2. *EVA encourages managers to milk the business.* Even worse than punishing progrowth behavior, EVA rewards antigrowth behavior. Investing aggressively at rates of return exceeding the cost of capital may be the preferred way to move the EVA needle. But managers quickly learn that the easier way, at least in the short term, is to reduce assets faster than earnings—to milk the business.

Pursued long enough, say three to five years, this strategy creates an EVA trap. Lack of investment can leave managers with such a depreciated asset base that any new investment will have a huge negative impact on EVA. The disincentive—whether to grow or to renew with more productive assets—compounds over time.

Little surprise, then, that the record of longtime EVA converts is one of delivering enhanced returns but not long-term growth in the capital base. Indeed, several have experienced growth rates in their asset bases close to zero and well below those of their peers.

3. *EVA is biased in favor of large, low-return businesses.* EVA is a marginal measure: It represents the incremental earnings above a base level set by the cost of capital employed. This makes EVA heavily biased by size. Large businesses that earn returns only slightly above the cost of capital can have bigger EVAs than smaller businesses earning much higher returns. What's more, the rate of change in EVA is accentuated for businesses whose historical performance hovers around the cost of capital. Small improvements in the performance of a marginal business generate large percentage gains in EVA.

EVA Has a Low Correlation to Shareholder Value. Total Shareholder Return (TSR) Versus % Change in Economic Value Added 1994–1995.

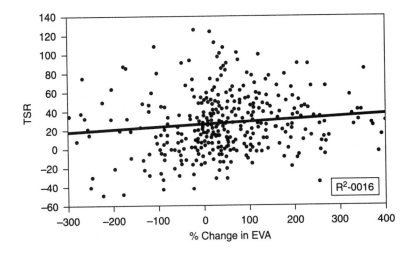

This makes EVA a poor metric for comparing businesses, whether to benchmark performance against peers or to allocate resources across a company's portfolio. Because EVA sends misleading signals about the relative attractiveness of businesses, companies that rely on it run the risk of growing the wrong ones.

Moving beyond EVA

Companies that want to grow must move beyond EVA. There are two viable alternatives. The simpler approach is to adjust the measure to a cash basis by adding depreciation and amortization back to net operating profit and accumulated depreciation back to book capital. You might term this measure *cash value added* (CVA). Because it eliminates the worst of EVA's antigrowth or reinvestment bias, CVA takes an important step beyond EVA. It remains inadequate, however, as a means to compare businesses.

For that reason, more and more companies are going even further. They are evaluating business-unit performance in the same way that investors look at a company's stock or executives size up a potential acquisition. Call this approach *total business return* (TBR). By comparing the beginning value of a business with its ending value, plus free cash flow, TBR effectively replicates total shareholder return inside the company at the level of the individual business unit. (For a more detailed treatment of TBR, see "Meeting the Value Challenge," The Boston Consulting Group, Inc., 1995, and "Shareholder Value Metrics," The Boston Consulting Group, Inc., 1996.)

As one might expect, TBR displays a much more satisfying correlation with observed total shareholder return: 40 percent over one-year periods and 57 percent over three years, roughly double the correlations for EVA. The results are sufficiently convincing that some companies are using TBR directly to peg planning and executive compensation targets. Others are using TBR at the corporate level to set objectives, which they then translate into more familiar accounting-based measures for the operating units. The result is to reward executives for expanding businesses that create value for shareholders.

Aligning your managers' interests with those of the company and its shareholders is critical, especially at a time when the chief imperative— to grow—runs counter to the behavior encouraged by accounting-based measures. Recognize the limits of these measures and move beyond them.

Resource Allocation

BRUCE HENDERSON WROTE a group of *Perspectives* in the 1970s that are now considered to be a classic body of work on corporate resource allocation and investment. Bruce attempted to distill the art of financial decision making into a few simple rules. At the core of these rules is the importance of cash flow in measuring performance.

Bruce observed that many product lines and businesses are cash traps. Companies evaluate performance on near-term reported profit, but this measure understates the cash required to sustain the business. In most cases, only a small number of products and businesses generate cash in excess of the working capital and reinvestment required to fund operations. The net cash that they throw off is too precious to squander—it is the primary source of funding for businesses that represent the company's future. Generally, only a few of a corporation's cash-consuming businesses have the potential to achieve a competitive position that will result in net cash generation when their growth slows. All the others are—or will be—cash traps.

The dynamics of cash flow make diversification a viable corporate strategy. Businesses have life cycles, just as products do. Mature businesses generate much more cash than they can reinvest productively. This excess cash is best used to support new or growth businesses, which have a voracious appetite for cash during their sprint for market leadership. A corporation with a diversified portfolio can balance cash generation and cash use among its businesses most efficiently.

Bruce Henderson's bold writings on corporate portfolio strategy have been both lauded and assailed. How do they hold up today? First, the core of portfolio theory remains valid, though admittedly it has been widely misapplied over the years. Resources must be allocated with steadfast discipline only to those businesses whose competitive positions, current or potential, promise real returns. Second, the diversification thesis is gaining renewed respectability. After years of fixation on conglomerate discounts and breakup values, new research is showing that well-managed diversified companies enjoy real advantages over—and frequently outperform in shareholder value creation—their more focused peers. The portfolio lives.

CASH TRAPS

BRUCE D. HENDERSON, 1972

The majority of the products in most companies are cash traps. They will absorb more money forever than they will generate. This is true even though they may show a profit according to the books of account. Continued investment sends good money after bad. Escape from the trap requires extreme measures. Either stop investing and manage solely to maximize cash withdrawal, or invest so heavily that a leading position is reached in the market.

Reported profit always exceeds payout to owners in any business over time. Much of the reported profit must necessarily be reinvested just to maintain competitive position and finance inflation. If the required reinvestment, including increased working capital, exceeds reported profit plus increase in permanent debt capacity, then it is a cash trap. Cash is rarely ever recovered from a cash trap unless relative competitive performance is improved by obtaining a superior market share.

Historically, the typical manufacturing company with typical growth rates and asset turnover had to have a pretax profit of about 7 percent on sales, or the entire company became a cash trap. Fast-growth sectors of the economy required even higher margins. So did capital-intensive businesses. At any lesser margin, the required increase in assets exceeded the reported profit. This cannot continue unless the permanent debt also increases in the same proportion or new equity is constantly added.

With higher rates of inflation, the minimum required return is increased in proportion. Inflation of assets must be financed and will never be recovered in dividends or liquidation.

Real cash traps are worthless because the owners will never receive a payout. Instead, the owners will put in cash. Reported profit is not payout. Even if you escape from such a cash trap eventually, you have still lost. The longer it takes to escape, the greater the loss in present value of your investment.

It is a fact that most of the net cash generation of virtually all companies comes from a very few products that have a clearly dominant share of their relevant product-market segment. This is inevitable.

Pareto, an Italian economist, discovered this effect many years ago while trying to determine why most of the wealth was concentrated in a few families. It is a familiar pattern: Approximately 20 percent of the items produce approximately 80 percent of the margin. However, when a constant reinvestment requirement is subtracted from all margins, then that 20 percent may well represent 120 percent or more of the actual net cash generation.

Pareto's law alone would lead to most of the net cash generation coming from only a small number of products. The experience curve effect compounds the relationship and couples cash generation to market share. The experience curve effect causes your relative cost to decrease about 20 to 25 percent each time your market share doubles. Both margin and volume increase with increase in market share. The converse is true also, of course. That is why there are many cash traps, and most of them are low-market-share products.

Reported profit is really irrelevant to the shareholder who actually holds the shares. All he will ever receive is a cash payout of either dividends or liquidation value. This is all a corporation receives internally from a product: either net cash throw-off or net liquidation proceeds. Regardless of reported profit, a business or product is worthless unless it compounds and returns the cash invested in it.

In a dynamic economy, almost every business, even slow-growth ones, require reinvestment of a substantial proportion of reported profit. Inflation alone requires financial growth to compensate for inflation in asset values as they turn over. Additional growth in assets employed is required in order to maintain market share as the industry grows with the economy. Consequently, only a portion of the reported profit can ever be available for distribution unless the business is liquidated. If it is liquidated, many assets will prove to be unconvertible into cash at book value.

When profit margins are low, the required reinvestment will often exceed the reported profit indefinitely, even in mature, stable businesses. Do nothing, and such businesses trap cash forever. The longer the delay until liquidation, the greater the loss. If eventual liquidation will produce only a portion of book value, then the reported profit until then is being overstated in proportion. If the company's required threshold on investment return is higher than this deflated profit, then the difference represents the company's annual opportunity cost.

Fast-growth products are even more dangerous cash traps than slow-growth products. Growth compounds the cash input required. But growth alone does not improve relative cost or profit compared to competition. Yet the eventual payout depends on a superior cost compared to competition whose margin is just sufficient to finance growth needed to maintain their own market share. Superior margin is rarely achieved without superior market share. Consequently, growth just compounds the cash drain unless it also leads to superior market share.

The only advantage of a growth product is that share can be shifted more rapidly from one competitor to another by preempting the share of the growth itself. The disadvantage of a growth product is that it usually requires a large negative cash flow just to hold position in the market. Yet failure to achieve a leading position before the growth slows can be fatal to any hope of a cash payout later.

The critical market share seems to be a level about twice that of the largest competitor. At about that point, debt capacity increases with market share even faster than the assets required. The cost level that can be achieved makes it possible to service debt equal to total net assets employed even though competition is selling at cost or below. When this condition is reached, the entire reported profit and more can be withdrawn as cash and reinvested elsewhere or paid out. It is a highly desirable position. This leads to a competitive rule of thumb.

Take at least twice as much of the growth as your leading competitor in any relevant product-market segment. If you cannot, then plan the process of extricating your investment as expeditiously as possible.

Only the largest two or three competitors in any product-market segment can reasonably expect to avoid being a cash trap. However, there are usually several times that many active competitors. *Therefore, the majority of the products in the average company must be cash traps. This means that a majority of the products in the average company are not only worthless but a perpetual drain on corporate resources.*

Prices could be lower to customers and profit could be higher at the same time if all competitors would recognize their cash traps and stop wasting money on them. Anytime there are more than two or three active competitors in a given product-market segment, then someone is making a mistake. The leader may be failing to compete by holding an umbrella over higher-cost competition at his own expense. Or it may be that competitors are caught in cash traps. Either way, there are major opportunities being lost.

THE STAR OF THE PORTFOLIO

BRUCE D. HENDERSON, 1976

The high-growth market leader is a star. Its P&L statement scintillates. But cash is all that counts. Profit is a promise. The star of the portfolio must keep twice the market share of its next competitor or its apparent performance is an illusion.

Cash-flow generation is a function of the differential in cost from competitors. The cost differential should be and usually is a function of market share. The differential can be approximated or predicted by the experience curve on value added. High relative share means high relative cash generation. But high growth also means high required reinvestment. If the financial growth rate exceeds the return on net assets employed, then even the star will not be self-financing.

Growth requires more of everything, but particularly assets. Assets added equal cash investment added. If a star is to be self-financed, then its after-tax return on assets employed must equal physical growth plus inflation. That is a high return where growth is high too in an inflationary environment. It is so high that many competitors will be tempted to settle for less profit if they can finance the required growth by any means. Even the debt capacity of other businesses may be used as long as it increases reported profit.

Reported profit is not net cash throw-off. It may never be. But reported profit is the frame of reference for decision making for many potential competitors. That is why the high-growth, high-share star of the portfolio is rarely allowed the opportunity to both hold market share and be self-financing. Stars are not cash generators.

Challengers of the star must have deep pockets full of cash. Differences of two to one in market share typically result in differentials in cost equal to 5 to 8 percent of value added. This times asset turnover times financial growth in revenue is equal to the added cash input per unit of sales required by a follower to keep the pace of a star in a growth business. Yet many do. Growth and reported earnings attract many competitors who can never hope to recoup their gross cash input, much less the present value.

With the passage of time all stars set. Growth above average is not forever. Cash input requirements subside with growth. But cash-generation capability does not change if the cost differential from competitors remains unchanged. However, if competition is real, the number of competitors becomes fewer and fewer as the higher-cost and underfinanced competitors fall behind. The survivors gain that share. The leader can lose relative market share even if absolute market share is maintained.

The ultimate value of any product or service must be the value of the stream of cash it generates net of its own reinvestment. For the star, that stream of cash will be in the future, sometimes the distant future. For real value, that stream of cash must be discounted back to the present at a rate equal to the return on alternative opportunities. It is the future payoff of the star that counts, not the present reported profit.

For a future worth the wait and the cost, the market share differential must be preserved. The star of the portfolio that loses its market-share differential is a costly investment that will not pay off regardless of its interim reported profit.

ANATOMY OF THE CASH COW

Bruce D. Henderson, 1976

The first objective of corporate strategy is protection of the cash generators. In almost every company a few products and market sectors are the principal source of net cash generated. These are the cash cows.

The cash cows fund their own growth. They pay the corporate dividend. They pay the corporate overhead. They pay the corporate interest charges. They supply the funds for R&D. They supply the investment resource for other products. They justify the debt capacity for the whole company. Protect them.

By definition a cash cow has a return on assets that exceeds the growth rate. Only if that is true will it generate more cash than it uses.

This requires high return and slow growth if the cash generation is to be high. Almost invariably, the cash cow has a high market share relative to the next two or three competitors. The experience curve relationships would predict that.

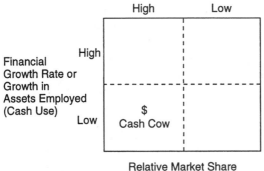

The debt capacity of the cash cow standing alone is always high. The net cash generation provides high interest coverage and debt repayment assurance. Increased market share for the cash cow frequently increases the debt capacity much more than it increases the total assets employed. This makes possible a leveraging of shareholder investment that can be converted either into higher return on net assets or into lower prices in order to buy more market share. Or the leverage can be converted into increased cash generated for use of other businesses.

There is a limit to the market share of the cash cow. The total cost of buying market share gets greater and greater as the share increases, since the margin on total volume is affected. The total value of market share available becomes less and less as the remaining share becomes small. When market share exceeds twice that of the next-largest competitor and four times that of the second-largest competitor, there is rarely any incentive to gain more.

Conversely, market share of a cash cow can be sold off for a very high price in near-term cash flow. A price umbrella converts all the higher price into cash flow and profit multiplied by total volume. However, the competition can increase their growth under a price shelter. The result is a continuing loss of both volume and relative cost potential for the cash cow. Eventually, the growing capability of competitors removes the value of the remaining market share until the cash cow goes dry.

The value of the cash cow's market share is almost always higher than the value of any competitor's market share, point for point. This is because the higher market share can and should produce a lower cost than competitors' on equivalent investment.

If it is properly leveraged to equate risk with higher-cost competitors, the cash cow can be a very high generator of cash and profit on the net investment. Yet the decision to invest or disinvest in a cash cow's market share depends on the alternative opportunities for investment in other parts of the corporate portfolio.

The real value of a cash cow is the discounted present value of the projected cash generated. A high discount rate will almost invariably favor liquidation because of the emphasis on near-term cash flow. The reported profit and net cash flow tend to be parallel and near equal in a low-growth business. Consequently, many cash cows are unwillingly liquidated by short-time-horizon profit budgets even though there is no alternative investment that would yield the same net return on net assets.

The real test of value of a cash cow is the net return on net investment when the cash cow has been leveraged with debt to the point at which its break-even cost as a percent of revenue is the same as the break-even cost of the largest-share alternative competitor. To be valid, this comparison must be made after the competitor has also been leveraged to his optimum debt usage.

This test will frequently show that both competitors have high potential returns on net investment. But if extended to each successively smaller competitor, it will eventually reach the one whose net return is no greater than the GNP growth including inflation. It is then possible to determine the true return for each competitor. Rarely will more than three or four competitors be involved if the market is both stable and competitive.

The marginal competitor whose net cash flow just finances the investment required to maintain his market position is worthless except in liquidation. Yet such a competitor is the ultimate reference. All competitors with superior costs and margins can convert that margin differential into a net cash throw-off. That is how you determine the output of a cash cow.

The value of a cash cow is determined by the rate of return on alternative corporate portfolio investments that must be used as the basic discount rate on the cash cow's output.

Do you wish to buy or sell market share for your cash cow? If you buy share, where will the money come from? If you sell, where will the money that you receive be reinvested?

THE CORPORATE PORTFOLIO

BRUCE D. HENDERSON, 1977

Diversified company portfolios are the normal and natural business form for efficiently channeling investment into the most productive use. All diversified companies, as distinct from holding companies of any kind, have one major characteristic in common. They are able to control the internal allocation of financial resources. In a holding company, each business must be self-financing and independent. In a corporation, cash flow and investment can be rechanneled from one business to another. This is a critical capability.

A diversified business portfolio enables a company to carry the process of business evolution to a higher level of complexity. Instead of developing a family of products, it is able to develop a family of businesses.

All products go through a life cycle. In the beginning they need far more cash input than they can generate. If they succeed, they generate far more cash than they can productively reinvest. Successive, overlapping generations of products smooth out this cash flow to some degree, but even the product family has the same life cycle. Cash input is needed when they are succeeding. Cash generation cannot be reinvested when they have matured successfully. This is what drives many companies to diversify into a family of businesses as well as products.

But businesses as a whole go through the same cycle. They tend to be unprofitable when very new, profitable but undercapitalized when their growth is the fastest, and then generators of cash when they become successful, mature, and slow growing. The problems change with maturity. The young, fast-growing business needs capital to take advantage of its potential growth and exploit its opportunity. The mature business has real problems in finding suitable investments for its cash flow.

The diversified company with a portfolio of businesses is exceedingly well positioned to discharge the function of directing capital investment into the most productive areas. It can be far more efficient and effective than the public capital market is likely ever to be.

Top management of even a far-flung diversified company is better equipped to appraise the potential and characteristics of a growing business than an outside investor. Such a company has staff research capability and access to data that even the most detailed prospectus cannot provide to the general public.

This ability to divert and reinvest the cash flows of a mature business is very important. There is no reason to reinvest the profits of a business in further expansion of the same business merely because it has been successful in the past. General Motors is not the only successful company that would find it difficult to expand faster than its industry.

The U.S. tax structure severely curtails investment funds available for reinvestment, first when they appear as reported profits, and again when they pass through the hands of shareholders as dividends. The value of this advantage is not small. Income taxes would take away about half the reinvestable funds if the cash flow is reported as profit. If paid out in dividends before reinvestment, then only a fraction of this is left for reinvestment.

Any company that can treat its investments in growing businesses as an expense to be offset against other profit has a great advantage in terms of its cost of capital. Also, any company that can obtain its equity from internally generated funds has a far lower effective cost of capital than if it obtained those funds outside from stockholders who can retain only a fraction of the proceeds they eventually receive in dividends.

The diversified company with a portfolio of businesses is in an unexcelled position to obtain capital at the lowest possible cost and to put it to the best possible use. The question, of course, is: Will it?

Any company that treats each of its divisions or units as separate and independent businesses fails to take advantage of its own strength. The traditional profit center concept of management has a fatal defect. It concentrates attention on near-term reported earnings rather than investment potential. This is why many successful diversified companies have been composed of mature businesses and have been notably inconspicuous for their success in incubating new businesses. A company must behave as an investor, not as an operator, if it is to achieve its potential.

Experience curve theory dramatizes how great the potential really is. This theory says that costs are a direct function of accumulated market share. It further says that investment in market share can have extremely high returns during the rapid-growth phases of a product. As long as the growth rate exceeds the cost of capital, then every year in the future is worth more in present value than the current year. Today's losses therefore may be very high return investments, provided those losses protect or increase market share. If market share correlates with cost differential, then it can be translated into investment value.

If this is true, then the logical consequence of competition will be low prices initially on new products. These prices will tend to be so low as to be preemptive. They will also be stable. The result will be negative cash flows for a considerable period until costs decline to below the low initial price. This will be followed by even larger positive cash flows as costs continue their decline and volume continues to increase. This produces the return of investment and the return on that investment.

The diversified company is eminently well suited for this kind of "expense investment." Only the diversified company can match positive and negative cash flows. Only the diversified company can pair off the tax consequences of expense investment. Only the diversified company can accumulate and analyze the detailed information required to make a wise investment involving a sequence of initial negative cash flows.

Everything favors diversified companies: tax laws, capital costs, sources of funds, breadth of business opportunity. Their inherent advantage lies in their ability to manage a set of portfolio tradeoffs. If the flexibility is not used, diversified companies are under a handicap. The individual business has no advantage except uncertain financial backing, which is hardly to be called an advantage! The corporate over-head structure can be a real burden with no offsetting advantage. There are quite a few lackluster diversified companies. It can be quite different if the company is managed as a portfolio.

If a company is to realize its potential, it must have investment and strategy development skills that go well beyond the characteristic needs of the independent business. Some corporations are going to do this. Those that do are quite likely to be the preeminent and dominant firms of the future. They will manage their cash-flow portfolios to con-tinually increase the present value of future cash flows.

RENAISSANCE OF THE PORTFOLIO

ANTHONY W. MILES, 1986

The current wave of corporate restructuring is bringing about radical changes in many companies' business portfolios. For most, this is a positive action, the recognition of a need for focus on areas of competitive strength and greatest opportunity for future growth. For a few it is a retreat to a focus on businesses with secure net cash flow, the aftermath of the Pyrrhic victory of successful takeover defense. In either case, it is compelling witness to the power of the portfolio concept.

This set of ideas was developed in the late sixties, proved immensely popular and powerful during the seventies, and then drifted out of the limelight for a variety of reasons in the late seventies and early eighties. It is time to retrieve these ideas before they are lost to the wastebasket of business fads and to reconsider seriously what they still have to contribute.

What the Portfolio Concept Says

The basic message is very simple. It begins with the fact that most companies participate in a number of different "businesses," even if all fall within one general industry category. These businesses were not created equal, are not equal at any point in time, and will never offer equal opportunities to earn high and sustained returns.

The portfolio concept asserts that one of the primary responsibilities of the chief executive is to make decisive investment choices for the benefit of shareholders. To make choices there must be alternatives. For some companies there are too many, and the challenge is finding a sound rationale for discrimination. For others there are too few, and the challenge for them is creating opportunity. For all there is a need to ensure that every major alternative for a given business has been uncovered and considered before a course of action is chosen.

Companies must choose on the basis of the closely linked combination of sustainable competitive advantage and potential financial contribution to the company. The former yields the high profits that convert to high net cash flow as growth slows and investment requirements moderate. This in turn creates the high returns and high valuations that satisfy shareholders and protect against takeovers. More

Business Performance and Portfolio Position

	Competitive Advantage	Competitive Disadvantage
High Market Growth	Moderate returns High investment Neutral-to-positive cash flow	Low returns High investment Negative net cash flow
Low Market Growth	High returns Moderate investment Positive net cash flow	Low returns Moderate investment Neutral-to-negative cash flow

positively, high returns and high valuation make raising new capital relatively easy and cheap. They make acquisitions possible. The company has superior ability to repeat the process and invest to grow in pursuit of competitive advantage in new businesses.

The portfolio concept stresses the critical need to keep resources fully employed in the areas where they have the highest yield or potential yield. This means focusing technical and human resources where the company can gain and hold an edge over competitors that is valued by customers. It means concentrating physical assets where they can be used to create or support unique or at least scarce capability. And it means using equity capital only where there is no safely cheaper alternative.

Imagine a company following these guidelines, and you have a company that grows, is profitable, earns high returns, has a high valuation, is in full command of its fate, and is very well protected. One of the two basic justifications of potential acquirers—the ability to use existing resources more efficiently or effectively than current management is doing—is all but eliminated.

All enduring and continuously successful corporations follow this pattern, whether they think of it as a portfolio strategy or not.

Real Advantage

Like all great ideas, the portfolio concept is simple—but the application is not. The portfolio concept is a guide to action, a summary of thinking, and not a substitute for detailed analysis and judgment.

First there is the problem of sustainable competitive advantage. The portfolio concept builds on the observation that superior profitability depends first and foremost on competitive advantage and that growth is easiest where the market itself is growing. Often, superior market share carries with it competitive advantage—often, but by no means always. Advantage may be based on superior technology, speed of response, quality, attention to specific customer needs, location—many factors that may or may not translate into overall market share leadership.

What matters is not whether advantage fits some preconception or general rule, but that the company pursues advantages that are truly available to the business, are valued by customers, provide a basis for competitive differentiation, and have lasting power. This almost always requires focus within the marketplace. Thus the search for advantage must be serious, detailed, imaginative, and rigorous. The bigger the company and the further removed the strategist from the business, the more likely it is that opportunity will be overlooked and the greater the risk of oversimplifying what it will take to succeed.

The fact is that some markets yield more opportunities for advantage than others, and some none at all. Some companies invest heavily in pursuit of the mirage of a secure future competitive edge. Nowhere is this more likely to end in disappointment than where there is blind faith in the value of market share or in the rewards of technological superiority. The portfolio concept works only when competitive advantage is real, when all the homework has been done, and when the competitive nature and likely future evolution of the market have been ascertained.

Leveraged buyouts, raiders, and low-labor-cost foreign competition have gone a long way toward taking care of another problem: the disadvantaged business, performing poorly and relatively stable, but with no realistic hope of much improvement in its market, competitive fundamentals, or performance. While these have not disappeared, they have in many cases become freestanding special cases, highly leveraged and managed for cash flow—very much along the lines the portfolio concept indicated. Marketplace forces have brought about an appropriate solution where corporate managements were reluctant to act decisively.

Discovering Growth

Second, there is the issue of growth. The long period of across-the-board expansion through the sixties and into the seventies spoiled us, and we now think of growth as more elusive. The easy conditions of broad market growth have given way to more localized patterns of growth. These often involve substitution—not just product-for-product substitution, but the substitution of one (better) way of doing business for another. Latent customer needs must be uncovered before they become obvious. Creating and exploiting growth opportunities in these conditions calls for more insight, better preparation, and greater risk taking than before. Growth is often where you make it. Growth opportunities often lie dormant within what at first sight appear to be low-growth, "mature" markets. This only heightens the importance of first-class, forward-thinking staff working closely with vigorous and decisive management. Building and sustaining a strong portfolio is more difficult now, but more necessary than ever.

From Strength to Strength

It has been easy to pick at the portfolio concept as being too simplistic or difficult to interpret in action, or to cavil with one aspect or another of the way it has been discussed or displayed. This is to miss the essential point.

All exceptional rewards in business derive from that scarce commodity, competitive advantage. To have the right to stay in business, a company must earn these rewards and then keep doing so. Building new positions of advantage on top of old calls for focus of effort and intensity of application. That is what the portfolio teaches and experience confirms.

Each new turn in the business cycle only strengthens the message.

PREMIUM CONGLOMERATES

DIETER HEUSKEL, 1996

In the 30 years since they first gained broad notoriety, conglomerates have mostly been dismissed as a failed experiment. Focus has become the order of the day.

It's time for a fresh look. As traditional boundaries between businesses erode, simple business definitions are becoming increasingly untenable. Even the most focused companies are finding that they may need to adopt a multibusiness perspective.

Two myths about conglomerates, in particular, need to be revisited. The first is that conglomerates are penalized systematically in the capital markets. In fact, analysis of the recent empirical evidence reveals the following:

- Although some conglomerates sell at a discount, others sell at a premium. On average, they generate returns equivalent to those of the market as a whole.
- Breaking up a successful conglomerate does not create value—and may well destroy it.

The second myth is that business complexity should be minimized at all cost. In fact, the best multibusiness companies—we call them *premium conglomerates*—exploit complexity to enhance and extend their competitive advantage. As complexity explodes in nearly every business, even companies that pride themselves on their focus would do well to emulate them.

Discounting the Conglomerate Discount

The case against conglomerates is compellingly simple. Markets are too specialized, business competition is too complex, and the rate of economic change is too rapid for even the most astute corporate managers to stay on top of a collection of unrelated businesses. And with today's efficient capital markets, it is no longer imperative to ensure internal funding for growth businesses. Better to divide the company into its constituent parts. Managers are better able to focus on the specifics of their individual businesses, and investors get the pure plays they prefer. An increase in shareholder value can often result.

Twenty years ago, this may well have been true, a necessary correction to the excesses of the 1960s and 1970s. But today, there is no apparent correlation between a company's industrial diversity and its performance. From 1985 to 1995, the 40 largest U.S., European, and Australian conglomerates generated total shareholder returns virtually identical to the averages of their respective markets. Half outperformed their markets; half underperformed them. More significantly, the top quartile turned in annual returns almost 5 points above the market averages. Capital markets seem to reward business value creation, whatever the source.

But might the individual businesses of these companies have performed even better on their own? An analysis of 16 recent breakups suggests not necessarily. Ten of the conglomerates in the sample had historically underperformed the market; of these, nine garnered breakup premiums. The six that had historically delivered above-average returns, however, saw the market valuations of their businesses remain level or decline. Breakup seems to create new value only when a conglomerate has consistently underperformed the market.

The conglomerate discount is not automatic. Valuation rests ultimately on underlying business performance. Yes, there are conglomerates that destroy value. But there are also quite a number that consistently create value. Their management practices contribute importantly to their ability to sustain a market premium.

How Conglomerates Create Value

What underlies the deep-seated suspicion of conglomerates? A healthy skepticism about complexity. The more complex the managerial task, the less certain the results. And yet, operating executives know that complexity is increasingly a given in today's global environment. What distinguishes premium conglomerates is their executives' skill in managing this complexity. They excel at three key managerial tasks.

First, premium conglomerates are active, but highly disciplined, business portfolio managers. They make acquisitions only when the competitive logic is compelling, and they don't hesitate to divest businesses that are competitively disadvantaged or a poor fit. General Electric is the classic example. In the early 1980s, GE divested hundreds of operations that had poor prospects for achieving the company's stated goal of being "number one or number two" in its industries. An even more consummate move was the company's 1987 swap with Thomson: GE traded a marginal position in consumer electronics for a key piece of a globally dominant position in medical equipment. Although not every acquisition has been successful, GE's total shareholder return under CEO Jack Welch has been 20.8 percent, a comfortable 6.4 percentage points ahead of the U.S. market average.

Second, premium conglomerates manage portfolios not just of businesses, but also of people and ideas. Companies like ABB engineer the career development of their most promising managers from the corporate center. This ensures that they get a broad range of experience across businesses and functions and that the best talent is assigned to the biggest challenges. Enterprisewide initiatives—to speed product development, to improve quality, or to sharpen asset management—replicate best practices across the company's many businesses and help each to move up the learning curve more quickly than stand-alone competitors.

Finally, perhaps the most distinctive characteristic of premium conglomerates is the way they mobilize and deploy advantaged capabilities to breach competitive barriers and enter new businesses—in effect, making complexity their ally. GE Capital, for example, has invaded sector after sector in financial services. The German conglomerate Veba has parlayed infrastructure from businesses as diverse as nuclear power generation, electricity distribution, gasoline retailing, and real estate to configure a unique entry into the German telecommunications business. And the Korean conglomerate Samsung is drawing on its capabilities in aerodynamic engineering, electronics, heavy manufacturing, and global logistics to drive its foray into automobiles. Premium conglomerates can pop up where they are least expected, and when they do, they are a good bet to upset the competitive status quo.

As they do, other companies are forced to compete in multiple industries as a defensive measure, to secure their claim on the value chain. British Petroleum, for example, has had to turn itself into a world-class retailer to defend its gasoline business from attack by grocery chains in the United Kingdom. It's getting harder to find true single-business companies.

As the boundaries between traditional businesses blur, the distinction between conglomerates and their more focused brethren is blurring as well. To survive and flourish, every company will have to master the complexity-management skills of the premium conglomerates.

Organizational Design

ORGANIZATION STRUCTURE HAS always been a vexing issue for corporate leaders. Models—functional, divisional, SBU, and matrix—seem to come in and out of fashion. Companies find they need to adapt their structures periodically. No design seems to work very well for long.

There is a good reason for this. Every organization scheme makes some things easier and others harder. Each scheme's primary impact is on the organization's communication patterns. Some interactions are hardwired; others are relegated to informal status or allowed to languish, affecting time and accuracy. When the environment changes—and the change is major enough to call for a change in the company's priorities—structure frequently has to change to facilitate the personal connections necessary to effect a change in strategy.

BCG pursues several threads in its thinking about organizational design in this section's *Perspectives*. First, strategy should drive structure. Because of the impact on communication patterns, the optimal design depends crucially on what you are trying to accomplish. Second, certain mechanisms and interactions can be built into an organization to increase its creativity and serve as platforms for growth. Finally, with growth, and especially global growth, comes a high degree of complexity. Organizations need to explore new, sometimes radical, ways of thinking about organizational design if they are to cope.

PROFIT CENTERS AND DECENTRALIZED MANAGEMENT

BRUCE D. HENDERSON, 1968

The idea of profit centers and decentralization often gets in the way of good management if the idea is taken very seriously. Such ideas are often not what they seem.

Many companies that profess decentralization do not really have it. Profit centers are not necessarily so—if overall corporate profit performance is being optimized. Independent profit centers are by definition neither independent nor profit centers if, in fact, there is any significant mutual interaction or synergy between cost centers.

There are several ambiguities involved. They grow out of the underlying assumptions and implications in the concepts of *profit center* and *decentralization:*

1. There is the implication that absolute level of profit is a measure of management's current performance. It may be nothing of the kind. The near-term absolute level of profit may reflect a long series of previous management decisions. It may also represent a conscious decision either to increase heavy "expense investment" for the future or, conversely, to liquidate past "expense investment." All investment and deferred benefits cannot be capitalized.

2. There is the implication that profit can be the measure of divisional performance in a multiunit company. This is seldom the case. If there is any mutual support between divisions, then the resulting benefits are necessarily windfalls to one division or the other, when compared to an independent operation, and are largely beyond the influence of divisional management.

3. There is the implication that each profit center should optimize its own profit when obviously it is the total profit of the corporation that should be optimized. Most unit managers are faced sooner or later with the conflict between improving their own unit's reported performance and improving overall corporate performance. Often there are many circumstances that require the apparent unit performance to be depressed in order to optimize the corporate overall performance.

4. There is the implication that profit centers can be measured and evaluated as if they were separate companies. This is hardly defensible if there is in fact good reason for the separate units to be grouped together.

Profit centers and decentralized management have become almost a hallmark of American business organization. The underlying philosophy is that authority and responsibility should be in parallel. Further, there is the implication that in a complex business the authority, and therefore responsibility, must inevitably be delegated. These principles are valid—but only up to the point that there is a conflict with the principle that overall management should optimize overall performance.

The justification for any central management in a diversified company must always be that it can produce results superior to those that a decentralized organization would produce if left completely alone. By definition, this means that a central management must impose constraints on the direction of decentralized operations.

The best balance between centralization and decentralization must be far more effective than either extreme. At the same time this balance requires a level of management sophistication much more demanding than the simpler modes. The required conditions are easily stated although hard to achieve.

To achieve this balance, the goals and potential of the organization as a whole must be clearly and explicitly understood by the corporate management. This means that the corporation as a whole must have a well-defined and explicit strategy. Those who make decisions of consequence must either understand this overall corporate strategy in all of its complexity or be subject to policy constraints that effectively limit choice to decisions compatible with the overall strategy. When this has been done, then each decision should be delegated to that part of the organization that is in the fullest possession of all the relevant information.

Corporate strategy, corporate policy, and corporate organization are inseparable. They are mutually dependent.

Left alone, each profit center should be expected to maximize its own value system. It is the central authority's responsibility to optimize the combination of profit centers. However, it can do this only by one of two approaches. The first, and obvious one, is to closely supervise the operation and internal policy of the profit center. By definition, this is not decentralization. It also implies a centralization of wisdom. The other alternative is to optimize the system by depressing one profit center's performance in order to achieve an even greater improvement in other profit centers. This is highly desirable and laudable, but it distorts the performance measurement of all the profit centers. The direct use of profitability as a performance measure is immediately undermined. Thus, overall optimization also implies a quite restricted definition of decentralization.

There is a wide range of degrees of freedom possible within the concept of decentralization. Listed here in descending degrees of freedom are some typical levels.

1. Parent company is essentially an investment portfolio custodian (regardless of corporate form).

2. Parent company is in effect a holding company that serves as a board of directors would in setting policy for the individual operations.

3. Parent company in addition provides common financial resources to each operation in accordance with overall corporate policy.

4. Parent company actively participates in strategy development and policy formulation for operating units.

5. Parent company coordinates activity in some key activity or activities—for example, in a common sales organization.

6. Parent company provides detailed policy direction of operations in all major activities.

7. Parent company makes key operating decisions, in addition.

These various parent-division roles require differing degrees of internal communication and of specialization in the decision-making process. This is another way of describing internal organization form.

All practical basic organization forms for complex operations have certain common characteristics:

- Centralized policy direction based on explicit strategy concepts

- Decentralized operation administration based on complex, not simple, operating standards and expectations

- Mechanisms of communication and review that keep both strategy and operating objectives realistically related to each other

- A quality of leadership that achieves consensus on both strategy implementation and operating standards

Profit centers and decentralization are a too-simplified description of this set of organization relationships.

Some form of decentralized operation is essential and always will be necessary for any business of substantial size. This is because there are many reasons that multiproduct organizations are more efficient in the use of their resources than a single-product organization. In fact, virtually all corporations of any consequence sell more than one product. However, as the variety and breadth of product time increases, the degree of relatedness or synergy between products decreases.

It is obvious that management techniques, style, and organization must be modified as products and markets become more numerous, more diverse, and less related. If this is not done, then diversity and size eventually become handicaps instead of advantages. The management organization and policies must be tailored to the individual combination of products, markets, and people.

For each company there is an optimum organization and set of policies that are superior to centralized management, with its inflexibility, bureaucracy, slow response, and insensitivity, and yet superior to fully decentralized profit centers that act independently of their potential for mutual reinforcement.

RICHARD K. LOCHRIDGE, 1984

Every organization can become more intuitive. For this to happen, the leadership of the organization must recognize that intuition operates best when the creative people have a chance to recognize patterns that others cannot see. The ability to see new patterns is greatly enhanced when the collective knowledge and experience of the organization are tapped.

The solution is not to hire people with, one hopes, more intuition, but to use the inherent skills of the organization. This requires consistently maintaining the building blocks of required knowledge in a fashion that allows key people from different functional areas to understand what is evolving elsewhere in the organization.

Organizational processes must be in place to produce a reasonable forecast of the evolution of the market, customers' values, costs, and bases of competitive advantage. These predictions open the way to seeing new patterns, and thus to inventing new options. This is, ultimately, a creative process, but it has no chance of developing a critical momentum unless the building blocks are in place.

If the goal is broad ("Let's be more innovative"), but an individual's perspective is narrow, little insight can develop. The goal and the breadth of perspective must be roughly comparable. This is where management direction and organizational processes are critical in determining the level of organizational intuition.

Creating Organizational Intuition: The Flow

Each person and organizational unit designated to help must play a role in providing the basic data from which the insight or new patterns can be derived. Each can stimulate a broader perspective among colleagues with different biases, databases, or functions. When management sets appropriate intermediate goals and creates effective organizational processes, even those who are ordinarily less than intuitive geniuses can add to the scope and fabric of the pattern. When a critical mass of information is available, intuitive insight will often emerge.

Too many companies do not do an adequate job of maintaining the basic building blocks. Even the required raw data may not exist. If they do, they are rarely shared across functional boundaries. Yet to discover new insights, creative people must share the building blocks of innovation in a way that allows them to see new patterns, challenge old assumptions, and put together new combinations of ideas in a better synthesis.

Communication

This is the great advantage of the successful small entrepreneurship over the large corporation. It inherently has short lines of communication. By necessity, all boundaries mean little. Relationships between people are determined by respect for proven expertise, not rank or status. But the large corporation cannot afford the chaos implied in such an organization. In a firm of several thousand employees, it is physically impossible for everyone to talk regularly to everyone else. Thus, to unleash the intuition of the large corporation, management must go beyond merely identifying the individuals with creative skills and develop ways for them to interact.

Organizational Intuition

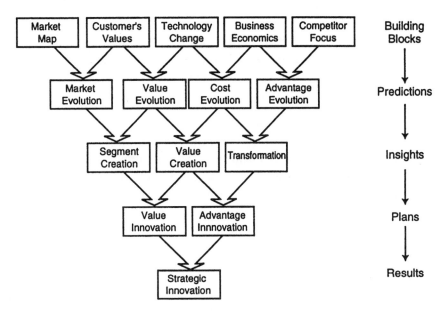

The Five Building Blocks

The intuitive organization encourages teams of people to understand each of the five building blocks and share them across functional boundaries. This can be accomplished organizationally by combining teams of functional experts from neighboring areas to produce valuable intermediate forecasts. When management really invests in a process to produce such predictions, the results themselves can be insightful.

Market Map

The goal of combining the market map and a good description of customer values should be to get a much better idea of how the market will evolve. This is more than a growth forecast. At its core must be a description of segmentation of user groups, the logic that supports the scheme, and a prediction of how the basic forces that determine segment size will influence the growth of each segment over time.

Customer Values

The purpose of combining people who understand customer values and those who know about the potential for technology changes is to forecast how the customers' values will evolve. Users can purchase only what is available. In addition, rarely can a consumer tell an innovator specifically what product or service he or she really wants. For example, the vast majority of the people buying a personal computer today know nothing about the insides of an integrated circuit. Nevertheless, they do have basic needs and value certain attributes. Technologists can estimate what is possible. The basic customer values can be defined. Tools exist to combine these knowledge bases to allow predictions about the evolution of consumers' values.

Technology Change and Business Economics

Combining an understanding of technology and business economics should give a forecast of cost evolution. The potential to relax technical barriers to increase the size of the scale facility, substitution of new materials for old, reduction of the cost of complexity through new manufacturing technologies, and application of electronics can all change the fundamental cost structure of a business and thus the resulting value of investment alternatives.

Competitor Focus

Finally, combining an educated guess about what competitors are doing with a real understanding of the business economics describes how the basis of advantage might evolve. It is the relative advantage versus competition that determines the long-run profitability of a business. Forecasting both changes in relative position and the basic potential of the industry describes both the need for and the value of a change in strategy.

Creating Value through Intuition

Meeting these goals requires not only cross-functional communication, but also cross-functional work. It requires a commitment to putting together the building blocks and making predictions. It can be done reasonably regularly and in an organized (not merely serendipitous) fashion. It may not even need esoteric leaps of creativity.

Combining the predictions about the future with a broad perspective will lead to new strategic insights. This is where the really creative managerial task is demanded. The goal of such an effort should be to produce an inventory of options available to the corporation. Can new segments be created? Is it possible to transform the basis of advantage and the nature of the industry?

Too many companies try to start their innovation efforts with these questions. Without the building blocks and resulting predictions, these questions will remain unanswered and lead to frustration unless exceptional genius is at hand.

Most organizations can unleash an enormous amount of their creative capacity. The fact that too many organizations are not sufficiently innovative means that the creative energies are spent in an inefficient and expensive fashion, relying totally on individual rather than organizational intuition.

Yet one need not fail. The essential insights of Apple Computer, McDonald's, Club Med, Federal Express, and Sony in developing the Walkman are the type one should expect from using the organization's intuition. By combining an understanding of trends across a number of functional areas, each of these companies created new segments, created new value, and transformed an industry.

NETWORK ORGANIZATIONS

TODD L. HIXON, 1989

Today's business problems—shortfalls in quality, innovation, and cost-effectiveness—defy solutions offered by traditional organizational concepts.

These problems will intensify as customers expect ever greater levels of variety and customization. Products are becoming more design-intensive and more service-intensive. Examples range from cars (increased engineering content of four-valve/cylinder engines) to computers (value-added shifting from standard hardware to software) to sweaters (Benetton's infinite variety).

Design and service tasks are best accomplished by small, multidisciplinary teams that are created specifically for the immediate problem, positioned to interact intensely with the customer and each other, and then left alone to do the job. Senior management provides the vision and capability. It can also establish incentives and measure progress. But it can't manage the team process closely, and it shouldn't try. The impatient, independent, and talented person who, for truly creative tasks, outperforms ten well-qualified drones can thrive only in a lightly managed environment.

Such an organization works like a computer network: many autonomous, intelligent work units interacting rapidly with the outside world and each other, and quickly rearranging themselves to solve new problems. The corporate center supervises the network, but it does not pace the work or filter the information moving from one working unit to another. Instead, the center focuses on building the capabilities of the work units, setting overall goals and strategy, and monitoring progress.

The Traditional Organization

Traditional organizational thinking seeks the structure that works best for the company's business and strategy, with resource coordination and decision making coming from the top. In the 1950s and 1960s, for example, many companies followed GE's lead to profit centers, an effective response to increasing company size and product lines. In the 1980s we shifted again to greater functionalization as a way to consolidate staffs and take advantage of scale.

Two assumptions underlie the traditional approach:

- The business strategy determines the organization's structure. Every strategy has its optimal organizational structure, which in turn dictates optimal decision systems, staff composition, and so on. Once discovered and implemented, this structure is expected to function over a number of years.

- Whatever the structure, a management hierarchy must aggregate and screen decisions, funneling the key ones to the senior officers at the top. Hence the typical diagram of an organization is an upside-down tree, or a matrix, which is two trees entangled together.

The Network Organization

Designing and managing a network organization requires overturning the old assumptions:

- You can't reason linearly from strategy to structure and on to systems, staff, and so forth. Instead, the process is iterative: A team is formed to meet a strategic need; it sizes up the situation, develops a specific strategy, and reorganizes itself as necessary. What's more, the structure is temporary. The organization needs to be ready to change its configuration quickly to respond to new needs and circumstances.

- The organization's purpose is not to control from the top; it is to empower a group of people to get a job done. Management occurs through training, incentives, and strongly articulated goals, strategies, and standards.

Network organizations are found most often in businesses that are driven by product development and customer service—electronics and software companies in particular—and often in smaller, younger organizations where traditional boundaries are weaker. Some large-scale models exist: parts of Honda and Panasonic in Japan, 3M in the United States, and, in some ways, GE, which has shown extraordinary flexibility in recent years in reshaping its organization and pushing authority down to frontline managers.

Network organizations have obvious drawbacks: they lack tight controls; they're ill-suited to exploit scale or accomplish massive tasks in large organizations; and they depend on capable and motivated people at the working level. However, companies that cannot use the full network model can appropriate aspects of it, like new-product-development teams.

Some large companies (such as IBM, Digital Equipment, and Dow Chemical), with the need for both innovation and coordination of resources among markets, product lines, and technologies, often use the network concept in modified form. They frequently change the focus of resources and control by reshuffling product groups—shifting power among the parts of the organization—or using ad hoc teams. IBM is quite close to the network concept in the fluidity of its approach—reorganization is the norm, with frequent shifts keeping the organization focused on current problems (such as the recent changes that put strategic decision making closer to the market in the United States).

Western economies are moving toward industries based on product innovation and services. Success will require creative reasoning, quick reflexes, and constant communication with the customer. Managers have to empower their people and live with less control to make this happen. A high-tech CEO recently put it this way: "The less you sign, the more you achieve."

THE MYTH OF THE HORIZONTAL ORGANIZATION

PHILIPPE J. AMOUYAL AND JILL E. BLACK, 1994

One of the messages of reengineering is that companies, once structured as hierarchical pyramids, now need to be "turned on their sides" and restructured as horizontal organizations. The logic for this restructuring flows from the logic for reengineering: if processes, not functions, are the correct way to organize work, then horizontally must be the correct way to organize a company.

It seems obvious. And it is wrong.

There are no great horizontal organizations, nor are there likely to be any. One company has experimented with this new organization, but is now unwinding it. This two-billion-dollar heavy-equipment manufacturer reorganized around its product lines, pulling engineering, marketing, and manufacturing people together into customer-centered units, one for each product line. The payback to the company was immediate—its people, cut loose from old department loyalties, began to work much better together, and customers noticed the difference.

But when the next generation of equipment was needed, there was no one to design it. The best design engineers were busy coming up with incremental new applications that current customers wanted. In addition to breaking up the core engineering group, the reengineering effort had redesigned performance evaluation measures and incentives to reward engineering and marketing people for today's customer satisfaction. For the first time, engineers were getting good bonuses and could relate them to the work they were doing. In this environment, with both customers and employees so happy, the president found it hard to mobilize his organization around the future.

Processes and Disciplines

Horizontal organizations won't survive because they address only half of a company's needs—its processes: managing transactions with the customer from order to delivery, giving better service, developing new products. Today, companies are spending millions on reengineering these processes—and they do need to be fixed. For most companies, breaking old habits and power structures takes a big push. But, ultimately, good enough in horizontal processes is good enough. Like quality in the 1980s, "best practice" processes are table stakes for doing business today. A company can't simply declare victory once it puts its horizontal processes in place.

The reason is simple: great horizontal processes don't make companies great. In telecom transmission equipment, NEC is extremely customer-responsive—with typical Japanese process excellence. But AT&T poured greater effort into creating new technology and is gaining market share against NEC with more truly innovative products. In pharmaceuticals, other competitors have spent more on processes, but it's Glaxo that is envied for its cleverness in defining research priorities and deploying its scientists.

The other half of what companies need is a set of core disciplines: the engineering skill to design state-of-the-art products; the technical expertise to invent out-of-the-box information systems; financial brains, like those at GE Capital, who create the accompanying financial services that differentiate the equipment GE sells. These vertical disciplines replenish the horizontal processes. They provide the professional excellence that elevates a company's processes from best practices to competitive breakthroughs.

In fact, the disciplines are the company's seed corn for its future. While the processes focus on today's customers, the disciplines are inventing the products—and the customers—of tomorrow. You always need people working for the future who aren't absorbed by today's customers. And, despite the brave vocabulary of reengineering, there will always be handoffs—from creators to implementers and from the center to the field.

Horizontal organization isn't the answer because it tries to create what every general manager wants today—the fast-moving, responsive company—through organizational structure. Structure alone cannot do it. In the past, matrix organizations didn't solve the problem. Nor will a horizontal one do so today. The real challenge of building better companies is to intertwine and reinforce the horizontal and vertical dimensions. Achieving this new organization isn't really about structure. It's about infrastructure. Infrastructure is what your people see and feel every day that tells them what really matters. Role models. Location of people. Distribution of rewards. Flow of information. Sense of membership.

Creating the Infrastructure

Companies that build both thriving processes and disciplines do not make it simple for their key people; instead they make it rich. They go beyond structure to infrastructure. They ask their business-unit heads, senior functional people, and key program and process managers to lead the way in integrating the horizontal and vertical dimensions. They follow five ground rules:

- *Build tension into objectives.* Having the industry's fastest customer-delivery lead time will contribute to growth for a couple of years. But beyond that, only innovation will continue the growth. All your key people need to be driven by both objectives.

- *Give senior executives dual roles.* Each functional vice president should either be responsible for one product line's new-product-development process or the health of a business. Our conventional organization charts have made too many key, able people too one-dimensional. Let each senior person wrestle with both dimensions of the organization rather than sit comfortably on just one side of a matrix organization.

- *Emphasize roles along with positions for every manager.* Positions are what you are directly and formally accountable for. Roles cover what you can influence—one steps up to roles.

- *Visibly reward people who contribute in both dimensions.* Don't let rewards be driven wholly by formula incentives. The notion that "you get what you pay for" is one of reengineering's more sterile maxims. It's not that simple. Your best people want to contribute in both dimensions and in uncharted ways. So reward people who step up to new roles for which there are no measures or incentive formulas, and more people will step forward.

- *Remove the one-dimensional barons.* Some want to stay inside their old functional domain. Others get so hooked on the new horizontal world they lose touch with their home base. Both need to get the message they are jeopardizing the company's performance.

American companies are improving their horizontal business performance dramatically. The phone company is getting repairs right the first time. Reengineering is paying dividends by removing obstacles and highlighting interfaces between functions. But it shouldn't try to dominate or eliminate functions. Reengineering is spawning some well-intentioned but simplistic ideas—the horizontal organization, pay people on what you can measure, eliminate all handoffs, and more. If reengineering doesn't recognize what it can and can't do, it will become just another adventure in short-term performance boosting.

THE ACTIVIST CENTER

DENNIS N. RHEAULT AND SIMON P. TRUSSLER, 1995

Is the corporate center dead? An emerging consensus would suggest so. The sentiment goes deeper than the natural impulse—intensified by perennial pressure from Wall Street—to trim bloated bureaucracies. More and more executives are convinced that the traditional functions of the center no longer add value.

Central planning and oversight, the argument goes, make less sense in an era of fast-changing technologies and markets. And information technology and outsourcing have made many centralized support functions unnecessary. Since no one knows the individual businesses as well as the people who run them, better to have a minimalist corporate center that sees to corporate governance, provides a few essential shared services, sets the right objectives, measures, and rewards—and then gets out of the way.

Actually, minimalism may be less the logical consequence of decentralization than a failure of managerial imagination. Some of today's most respected organizations—companies like GE, PepsiCo, and Hewlett-Packard—make strong centers a cornerstone of their managerial practice. These centers are lean, but they aren't minimalist—they're activist.

The Case for Activism

The purpose of the new-style center is to leverage innovation and growth, not to enforce command and control. The very trends that seem to call for a hands-off, minimalist center—fragmenting markets, rapidly changing technologies, faster innovation cycles—probably require the opposite: a corporate center that engages otherwise autonomous business units, stimulating them to transcend the limits of established business-unit boundaries.

Even good managers, running top-performing business units, sometimes let game-changing opportunities pass. They tend, quite naturally, to focus on their own industry and their traditional competitors, missing broader market trends or new competitive threats. An activist center helps ensure that business-unit managers develop and maintain a broad strategic perspective. The center is, after all, the guardian of the company's future. Its job is to encourage, cajole, and sometimes push line managers to look beyond their natural horizons both longer term and across businesses.

In doing so, it contrasts markedly with the old-style center. Rather than imposing a process and an agenda, a few experienced people engage the business units in a dialogue of exploration. At PepsiCo, for example, a small, high-caliber corporate planning staff works with business units to make sure they don't sacrifice long-term strategic thinking for short-term financial goals. And at Hitachi, a central group focuses on the interfaces between business units by identifying new opportunities the business units might miss, thus acting as a catalyst for innovation and organizational evolution.

Even more fundamentally, activist centers are broadening the classic concept of portfolio management. To be sure, these centers take on the traditional—and still necessary—task of allocating cash among the businesses. But they are going much further, applying the same principles to new kinds of resources.

One such resource is the distinctive organizational capabilities that are increasingly central to long-term competitive advantage. An intelligent center can assemble the right portfolio of capabilities and then drive them across the company's businesses. Asea Brown Boveri, for example, has used a small central team to initiate time-based process-improvement programs at all its worldwide companies, as well as to coordinate sharing of the emerging best practices.

Some companies have gone so far as to build an entire business model around the role of aggressively managing the capabilities portfolio. The Newell Corporation, for instance, has developed systems that excel in satisfying the unique and highly demanding requirements for supplying Wal-Mart. Over the past decade, Newell has sustained impressive growth rates by acquiring a series of product-focused companies and then "Newellizing" them by systematically instilling these capabilities.

Another key resource that activist centers manage is the company's portfolio of human talent. Most companies now have the financial measures in place to ensure that business units don't hoard capital, but too few have comparable processes to ensure that business units don't hoard the best people. By actively managing their careers, the center can ensure that the corporation develops leaders with a breadth of experience while at the same time promoting cross-business capabilities transfer.

Building an Activist Center

If activist corporate centers are so important, why do so few companies have them? Many senior executives worry that once they start adding new roles and new people to corporate, they will have taken the first step down a slippery slope and end up losing all the hard-won cost savings of recent years.

That's why the first step in saving corporate is often to destroy it. The process: strip corporate down to the basic governance and compliance functions; take the rest and either streamline it into a shared services arrangement or outsource it; and all the while purge old-style corporate managers. Once bureaucracy and cost are rolled back, companies can rebuild their centers on activist lines.

The next step is to redefine the social contract between the center and the line businesses and to identify the new skills, roles, and career tracks of activist corporate managers. Activism is a tough balancing act. Executives need to know how to support, but also challenge, business unit managers—without undermining either their own credibility or the authority and responsibility of the line.

Getting this balance right requires repopulating the activist center with a small group of the company's most talented individuals. Only accomplished managers with extensive line experience will have the credibility to get senior line executives to buy in and treat the center as a resource rather than as an imposition. Generally, the assignment to corporate is temporary—one stop in a continuous rotation between the center and the business units. And instead of having a fixed brief, these new-style corporate managers focus their attention and energies on a few key priorities at a time. Witness the evolution of GE's strategic planning group, whose composition and focus have shifted repeatedly to support the changing priorities articulated by CEO Jack Welch.

If you are unwilling to routinely cycle a few of your top people into the center, better stick to minimalism. But be prepared to pay the price in timid strategies and underleveraged capabilities and people.

ORGANIZING THE GLOBAL COMPANY

XAVIER MOSQUET AND MARK F. BLAXILL, 1996

Few managers dispute the strategic value of global presence. But despite the paeans to the new global company, managers with experience organizing globally know that it's easier said than done. Globalization means increased complexity. And complexity slows decision making, expands overhead, and multiplies conflicts in the managerial ranks.

Traditional organizational structures—whether designed around functions, products, or geographies, whether centralized or decentralized—can't cope with the complexity that global operations entail. Matrix arrangements, while explicitly designed to manage complexity, too often end up just adding to it. Managers need new ways to think about molding their international organizations, simply and flexibly, to the needs of their customers and the imperatives of their business strategies.

Global leaders are starting to see a glimmer of a solution. They look at their companies through the lens of key global processes. First, they break complexity into manageable pieces by focusing on individual process steps. Then they carefully orchestrate the interactions required at and between steps. The map of these interactions looks like a cylinder. These global cylinders define the strategic and operational logic around which organizational structures and roles, as well as managerial systems and practices, can be built.

An Example of Global Rollout

When the pharmaceutical industry went global in the 1980s, the move exacted a price in slower time-to-market for most pharma companies. New drugs require government authorization. Since requirements vary widely by country, clinical studies done in one are rarely valid in another. The more countries targeted, the more cumbersome and time-consuming new-drug rollout became.

One company, however, refused to accept this seemingly inevitable consequence of global competition. The company tackled the problem by optimizing the design of each step of the new-product rollout process. Because of the scarcity of top researchers and the high value of scale, it centralized research. For new-drug authorization, however, it chose a hybrid of centralization and decentralization, charging local units with conducting clinical trials, but under central guidance and coordination. This allowed the organization to muster its global expertise while meeting local requirements. When it came to marketing, the company chose a purer form of decentralization: Each country defined its own sales approach and positioning, with the responsibility to share plans and experiences. These process decisions are best illustrated visually (see figure).

Taken as a whole, the pharmaceutical company's global drug rollout process is neither centralized nor decentralized. Rather, it is integrated, an assembly of different degrees of centralization and decentralization defined at the right level of detail, the process step. As a result, the company succeeded in taking its time-to-market rates from among the worst in the industry in the 1970s to the very best by the 1990s—despite the increased complexity brought on by globalization.

The Building Blocks: Rings, Stars, and Centers

Our experience suggests that even the most complex global processes can be understood in terms of these three types of cross-border interactions. Think of them as the building blocks for a new kind of global organization.

The ring loosely links a set of local units, functions, or activities. It encourages sharing of information and best practices among country units, while preserving local decision making. In marketing, for exam-

Global Drug Rollout at a Pharmaceutical Company

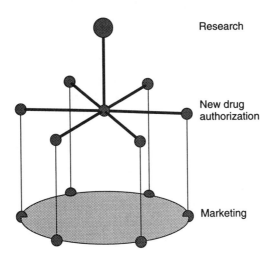

Research

New drug
authorization

Marketing

ple, rings are appropriate where divergent consumer tastes and purchasing behaviors require local empowerment, but where local marketers also need to draw on product innovations, market-study results,
and price positionings from across the company.

The star is more structured and coordinated. Information and decision making flow not around a ring but between decentralized units
and a center (not necessarily headquarters). This pattern works best
where strong coordination is necessary between local operations and a
center responsible for synthesizing information and making tradeoffs.

The center concentrates authority to make decisions and to set
global standards and procedures in a single organizational unit. This
most often makes sense for activities like research, but it can apply
equally wherever one size fits all worldwide, such as global marketing
when customer requirements are relatively uniform across different
regions and markets.

There are both strategic and operational tradeoffs in deciding which
type of interaction is most appropriate for any particular process step.
Centers are simple and scale-efficient—but may not be responsive
enough to pick up important differences in local markets. Rings
encourage local responsiveness and build on economies of learning—
but they also reduce economies of scale and increase the duplication of
practices. Stars combine central coordination and local learning—but
they require a high degree of practice uniformity and multicultural
understanding, and therefore can be difficult and costly to organize.

Integrating Global Processes

Rings, stars, and centers define the horizontal connections among people around the world who are engaged in the same business activity.
Equally important are the vertical interactions necessary to link the different activities of an integrated global business process. Experienced
global companies are finding that these vertical links are far easier to
create when the individuals involved are located in the same region or
even the same country. It is much more difficult to forge links that
cross business activities and geographic locations simultaneously. With
experience, though, companies can master ever more complex forms
of interaction, ultimately building a fully integrated global management capability.

By looking at their global organization in terms of these three cross-
border interactions and the linkages between them, managers find they

A Complex Global Logistics Network

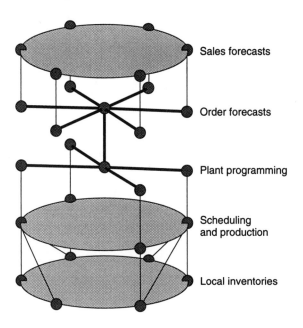

Sales forecasts

Order forecasts

Plant programming

Scheduling
and production

Local inventories

can come to grips with extremely complex business systems. The figure that follows, for example, depicts a global logistics network at one European company that links far-flung plants to worldwide sales subsidiaries.

Cylinder-shaped operating charts like the one shown above determine the practical operating flow of the company and thus provide far more effective support for global organization design than do traditional organizational charts. They also provide a powerful language to communicate the design to a broad international population of managers and teams, giving them a way to visualize their operational roles in the global company.

A truly global company carefully links the different sources of expertise that need to interact around the globe and then creates the roles and infrastructure that will support them. Breaking global complexity down into manageable process steps allows senior executives to combine the leverage of global presence with clear lines of responsibility and fast execution.

Three Cross-Border Interactions

		Decision making	Speed	Economics	Practices
	Ring	Local	Fast	Local scale	Allows differences
	Star	Coordinated	Slower	Local and global scale	Organized for convergence
	Center	Central	Fast	Global scale	Sets the global standard

Leadership and Change

CHANGE IS THE very essence of the business leader's job. Sensing the need, identifying the direction and magnitude of change required, convincing and inspiring the organization, blowing away the obstacles—this is what real leaders do. Most find it excruciatingly difficult.

The *Perspectives* in this section explore two themes. The first is the tension between the conflicting organizational needs for stability and change. On the one hand, for companies of any size, some degree of stability is essential to the effective execution of strategy. On the other hand, competitive environments are notoriously fluid, and organizations must adapt or face extinction. But to do that, they must change the way they operate and, even more fundamentally, their very self-concept. The first four pieces in this section explore how leaders do this.

The second theme is the evolving nature of the relationship between leaders and their organizations. Command and control just doesn't work anymore. Getting change to occur is as urgent as it ever was, but requires greater subtlety. The last three *Perspectives* in this section explore how leaders instill organizational learning and how they orchestrate the interactions necessary to effect change. John Clarkeson's "Jazz vs. Symphony," in particular, is a pioneering classic that has been widely imitated.

WHY CHANGE IS SO DIFFICULT

Bruce D. Henderson, 1968

Success in the past always becomes enshrined in the present by the overvaluation of the policies and attitudes that accompanied that success. As long as the environment and competitive behavior do not change, these beliefs and policies contribute to the stability of the firm.

However, with time these attitudes become embedded in a system of beliefs, traditions, taboos, habits, customs, and inhibitions that constitute the distinctive culture of that firm. Such cultures are as distinctive as the cultural differences between nationalities or the personality differences between individuals. They do not adapt to change very easily.

These characteristics are deep-seated and difficult to change. Frequently, this means that the organization becomes the prisoner of its own past success. Such individual characteristics become so much a part of the firm that any effort to change them is quite likely to be viewed as an attack upon the organization itself.

Examples of these observations are a matter of common experience:

- The sharp and painful adjustments when two comparable organizations merge are the inevitable consequences of the differences in corporate style and culture.

- When a new chief executive is appointed from outside the organization, one of two actions will follow. There will either be a substantial period with little change while he gets to know the organization, or there will be a period of considerable stress and perhaps personnel turnover while a new corporate culture is being evolved.

These problems of change cannot be avoided, however. All organizations, like all organisms, must adapt to changes in their environment or die. All organizations *do* change when put under sufficient pressure. This pressure must either be external to the organization or be the result of very strong leadership.

It is rare for any organization to generate sufficient pressure internally from the ranks to produce significant change in direction. To do so is likely to be regarded as a form of dissatisfaction with the organization's leadership. To change by evolution rather than revolution, the change must not only be tolerated, but actively guided and directed in very explicit terms by the leadership of the firm.

In this process the corporate leadership faces major dilemmas. The organization's investment in the status quo is always a heavy one. This is almost inherent in the definition of a culture. Changes in policy and strategy are inherently threatening, producing a whole series of changes in objectives, values, status values, and hierarchy arrangements. Jobs, rank, and many cherished beliefs are put in jeopardy.

Most of the organization is not in a position to see the needs for policy and organization change until long after the optimum time for action has passed. Corporate culture tends to blind an organization to a need for change until the organization as a whole can accept the reality of the need. But when the need is so obvious that the whole organization can recognize it, competitive advantage in flexibility and speed of response has been lost.

On the other hand, if an effort is made before there is a general awareness of the need, it endangers the very ability to lead. Any fundamental change in corporate policy is almost certain to be regarded by a significant part of the organization as irrational. No matter how sound the change may be, it is at some point rooted in a nonprovable, intuitive concept of the relative values of a complex of factors affecting the future. There will always be a large part of the organization that does not perceive these values in the same way and therefore considers the change unwarranted and a reflection on the leadership's ability to make reasonable decisions.

It is obvious, as well, that major changes in policy have far-reaching consequences that dictate caution and conservatism. The attitude toward change is always conservative or reactionary until both the reasons for the change and the consequences are clearly defined. This is an impossible set of preconditions for most policy changes. Any significant change produces a train of interrelated and often unanticipated corollary changes. Each policy has been keyed to others, and changes in one require a reevaluation of the related policies. Too much readiness to change policies leads to a complete restructuring of the corporate edifice, with all the cost and confusion incident to any major reconstruction.

Not only the organization, but the leadership itself, incurs considerable risk by changing policy. By definition, a policy is applied to decisions in the future. To be valid the policies must be based on assumptions about the conditions and competition in the future. These assumptions in turn are based on other assumptions. At some point, the needed information becomes so problematical and conditional that further fact finding and analysis is unrewarding, and the decision becomes intuitive.

Such decisions on major issues constitute a severe exposure risk. The apparent verities of the past successes must be abandoned for unproven policies based on uncertain data. And to the risk of failure from incorrect choice must be added the risk of failure in leadership because the organization just does not see the need for the change. Even the best-chosen risks may prove to be fatal to the current leadership if the consequences are unprovable in fact.

All the forces of corporate culture are set against change. Yet the rewards can be substantial for those managements who have strong enough leadership to both anticipate the change required and manage the evolution. The competitive advantages of superior strategy will be available only to those managements that can make major shifts in policy *before* the need or the purpose becomes obvious to their organization as a whole or to their competitors.

There are at least three major requirements of management who expect to outperform their competition. The first is to conceive and make explicit a superior strategy. The second is to provide the leadership required to overcome the obstacles to change. The third, and often critical one, is to provide that leadership at a time when the organization as a whole would ordinarily oppose the changes required.

LEADERSHIP

BRUCE D. HENDERSON, 1968

There are three fundamentally different executive functions. The first is preservation of the organization. The second is control of organization response to deviations from expectations. The third is planning future expectations. All of these are made possible by the personal qualities of leadership.

The essence of leadership is the ability to change the organization's conception of ideal performance. The strength of leadership can be measured by the rate at which these ideals are changed. The quality of leadership is reflected by the wisdom used in choosing the new ideals. The initial test of leadership skill is in the choice of the inescapable compromise between speed of change and security of the leader's ability to lead.

Management can be distinguished from leadership. The management function deals with what the organization ought to do. The leadership function deals with motivation of the organization to do that which it ought to do. Normally, the two functions are so interrelated that the differences are not recognized even by the leader-manager himself. However, in very strong manager-leader combinations, the difference may become clearly apparent to the manager-leader because of the obvious compromise required between what good management dictates and what continued leadership will permit.

Both good management and strong leadership require clearly defined goals and objectives. Good management will produce worthy goals, and good leadership will rapidly obtain organization acceptance and motivation toward these goals.

In a business organization, good and strong leaders will do these things:

1. Gain complete and willing acceptance of their leadership.

2. Determine business goals, objectives, and standards of behavior that are as ambitious as the potential abilities of the organization will permit.

3. Introduce and motivate the organization to accept as its own these privately established objectives. The rate of introduction will be the maximum consistent with maintenance of the acceptance of the leadership. This need for acceptance is why the new manager must always go slowly except in emergencies. In emergencies, the boss must not go slowly if he is to maintain leadership.

4. Change the organization relationships internally as necessary to facilitate both the acceptance and accomplishment of the new objectives.

The strengths and weaknesses of different types of managers can be observed with reference to these things.

Some managers are unable to get past the first hurdle to become accepted as leaders of their organizations. They may be managers in title but not leaders. Their organizations fight them on every change.

They are told only that which they ask. Their followers feel "the boss doesn't understand."

Before a leader can lead he must first belong. He, more than anyone else, must live up to the ideals and standards the group has already previously accepted. If he cannot do this, he cannot lead, no matter what his ability or power. For these reasons, leaders are strong or weak only with reference to specific groups. The leader leads only with respect to the group that will accept him first as a member and then as first among them.

Other managers fail even though they are fully and willingly accepted as the leader. They fail because they do not lead anywhere. They conform to the group's norms and standards; in fact, they defend and preserve the status quo. Their leadership can remain secure provided the group standards do not call for the leader to promote or initiate change. With such a manager the leadership survives but the organization eventually dies because of its failure to adapt to a changing world.

Some managers fail even though they are accepted as leaders and actively lead their organizations. They fail because of faulty or inadequate goals and objectives. This is an intellectual failure, not a spiritual one. This is lack of managerial vision, not lack of courage or willingness, and is one of the most difficult of all managerial failures to detect because the strength of leadership hides its own weakness.

Partial failure is still common where leadership is accepted, where goals are wisely chosen, and where leadership is vigorous. The cause is a less-than-optimum choice between rate of progress and leadership security. This failure is not absolute; it is a comparative failure. It is a failure to do as well as it is possible to do. The leader who leads too rapidly loses his leadership; the one who leads too slowly just does not get there as fast. Like driving on a mountain road, the penalty is extreme for loss of control. As in racing, the stress on the driver is very great at maximum speeds. Most leaders just do not take the risks required for maximum results. Many do not attempt anything like maximum performance because of the stress and strain they experience.

Even when a leader has done everything else, he may fall short of the best possible performance by failure to adapt his organization relationships to the current objectives, needs, and resources. This again is a technical handicap in a comparative sense rather than an absolute failure. It is a removable limitation on performance. However, the correct decision is a highly intuitive and subjective decision. The ideal organization, even in a static situation with idealized people, would be difficult enough to formulate; with flesh-and-blood people in a dynamic situation, the optimum organization relationships are virtually unknowable. The inevitable cost of change and the temporary loss in effectiveness must be balanced against the hoped-for benefits. The disturbance in the informal relationships will certainly reduce the leader's acceptance and control, at least temporarily. The hoped-for benefits are based on projected behavior of people, which can never be fully predictable. The benefits will be effective at a time in the future when the situation may be quite different from that now visualized. The net advantage of organization change is most difficult to determine, and the known costs are usually great. Therefore, many leaders cling to the known versus the unknown at the risk of their potential performance.

Being an effective leader and manager has some of the same requirements as being a winning poker player. A knowledge of the odds is indispensable. Ability to intuitively sense others' attitudes is also indispensable. Adequate working capital must first be acquired before any major risks can be taken. Properly choosing balance in calculating risk versus reward is essential.

Good management sees the opportunity and what must be done to grasp it. Good leadership chooses the right timing and speed of implementation while developing an organization that not only can but wants to achieve those objectives.

HOW TO RECOGNIZE THE NEED FOR CHANGE

CARL W. STERN, 1983

Change is a fact of business life. Organizations, like organisms, must adapt or die. Neither course is comfortable. In its operations, an organization evolves a way of thinking about itself, its competitors, and the environment with which it and they must cope. It conceives of itself as playing a game under well-defined rules against a set of easily identifiable opponents, each pursuing well-understood strategies. Since this model has the effect of imposing order on chaos, it first rationalizes and ultimately governs behavior within the organization. The internal culture will tend to resist any challenge to the model or the assumptions underlying it, even when conditions change. Yet adaptation requires that an organization be weaned from outdated conceptions.

The stakes are high. Take, for example, the personal financial services industry. Few days seem to pass in which the *Wall Street Journal* fails to announce a new product, a new competitor, an arrangement among competitors to offer a new package of services, or a merger. How is a bank to view Merrill Lynch's Cash Management Account? How is Merrill Lynch to view Charles Schwab? How is a mutual life insurance company to view a host of new offerings, from ever cheaper term insurance to E.F. Hutton's universal life? How are any of the participants to view the many mergers, consummated or proposed? And how are they to view the widely anticipated changes in the regulatory structure of the industry? It is difficult for the traditional competitor to know how to think about these developments, much less to formulate a response.

Wholesale rethinking of strategy in response to every minor competitive or environmental perturbation robs an organization of its sense of direction and its operational effectiveness. Failure to adapt at critical turning points threatens its viability. Distinguishing the latter from the former is easy after the fact: Failure to adapt leads to deterioration in financial results. By that time, however, it is generally too late to take effective remedial action. Management needs an early warning system that highlights those fundamental threats to which the organization must respond.

Competitive Stability

A useful approach is to characterize the conditions that make for stability, and then to identify potential destabilizing influences. Competitive conditions will tend to be relatively stable in businesses where

- Barriers around the business and between segments are well defined and high
- Relative competitive positions within segments are well established and defensible

While competition is almost by definition never totally stable—there are always skirmishes among competitors, often across segment boundaries—these conditions allow competitors to play the game they know under the established ground rules without fear of intrusion.

Destabilizing Influences

A useful early warning system is one that will identify nascent threats to these conditions for competitive stability. Because the attendant self-examination is painful, disruptive, and therefore generally countercultural, the organization's operating systems rarely prove equal to the task. A combination of vigilance and vision is requisite. It thus falls to top management to be alert to the critical warning signals:

From the marketplace

- Have you lost control over your pricing? Have you recently led a price increase and been unable to make it stick? Have you recently been unable to sustain your customary price premium?
- Have you experienced swings in volume beyond those explainable by cyclical demand fluctuations?
- Is part of your market under pressure from substitute products or services?
- Have you recently lost major accounts? With particular characteristics or needs? To particular competitors? To backward or forward integration?

From the channels

- Have your distributors' margins deteriorated? Have the channels' economics changed in such a way as to threaten their viability?
- Have they had to broaden their lines to defend their competitive position or to supplement their income?
- Have you experienced an abnormal incidence of defection?

From competitors

- Has a traditional competitor been gaining market share? Across the board or through a particular focus? Using what tactics?
- Have new competitors entered? Where do they come from: a complementary industry? overseas? On what part of the market are they focusing, and what tactics are they employing?

From your financials

- Does the historical relationship between volume and profitability no longer hold?
- Have you experienced a cost/price squeeze?

From your organization

- Are your systems no longer capable of answering the questions you deem most relevant? Or do they give you misleading or erroneous signals?

- Do you sense that your organization has lost a measure of its responsiveness? Its morale?
- Have you experienced an unusual defection of key personnel? Is it concentrated on those closest to the marketplace?

From your intuition

- Have you lost confidence in its reliability?
- Have many of your recent intuitive decisions proven wrong?

These signals—some subtle and some obvious—should alert management to the possibility that a threat to competitive stability may be impending.

At minimum, these signals should motivate a diagnosis of the underlying destabilizing influences. A number of areas will bear investigation. On the one hand, the signals may herald a fundamental shift in demand patterns due, for example, to demographic or macroeconomic factors, the emergence of new market segments, or the introduction of substitute products. On the other hand, they may denote a shift in the value-added structure of the business, perhaps as a result of technology affecting the economics of production or delivery.

Such developments generally erode the barriers that have traditionally protected the business and its segment structure. They almost inevitably alter the established balance among competitors. They therefore require a response: often a change in the organization's very basis of competition.

SUSTAINED SUCCESS

ALAN J. ZAKON AND RICHARD K. LOCHRIDGE, 1984

We all need to progress, to achieve, to seek a greater goal. Yet the more successful we are, the harder it is to find the "what next."

Earnings and return on investment are the scorecards of past success. A portfolio of strong and advantaged competitive positions that translate into strong financial performance is the base of current success. But what of the future? What signs are there that success will be repeated?

The Lure of Growth

The most visible sign of future success is market growth. The opportunities are clear, and the only question is whether competitive advantage can be gained—and held. For this reason, managers and shareholders alike seek growing markets. Yet we know that few competitors win, and that pure growth markets are the exception, not the rule, in mature economies.

Sustained success appears easiest, therefore, for companies in large, growing markets. But progress is necessary for all of us, not just those in growth markets. We must build, manage, and gain advantage. Having done so once, we must do it all over again. But this does not necessarily require an all-out assault on new (or unfamiliar high-technology) markets.

A recent study of the 500 fastest-growing private U.S. companies provides dramatic insight. Thirty-one of these companies reached $25 million in revenues by 1982, and all have grown at least 50 percent per year since 1978. Only seven are in high technology. Twenty-four are transforming mature businesses, ranging from shoe manufacturing to agriculture to financial services. They are innovating by approaching old businesses in new ways.

Organize for Success

Sustained success requires most organizations to continually find new opportunities in mature markets. We must find new organizational vehicles that will focus our attention on sustained success, as well as manage what we have today. Unfortunately, it is axiomatic that organization structure is developed to execute current business strategies, not to seek new strategic opportunities.

Corporate strategy is more than the summation of individual business strategies. Corporate strategy must provide for tomorrow's success as well as today's. For this reason the corporate organization is different from each business organization. Corporate organization requires a unifying theme that highlights where the overall company is and what the next strategic challenge will be. It must recognize the management needs of each business unit, the skills required for success in it, and the need for transitions.

Successful business units pass through four phases in their development toward maturity. Each phase is most fundamentally different from the others in orientation.

PHASE	GOAL
Creation	Finding the opportunity
Growth	Making it real
Advantage	Gaining competitive position
Efficiency	Tying it down

Each of these phases—and orientations—requires a different set of management skills, imperatives, and focus. Success within one phase is necessary for survival, but does not guarantee transition to the next.

Sustained success requires managing the transitions between phases. Competitors who do not see the transitions fall by the wayside. This is, in part, a question of skills and attention. It is also a question of orientation, goals, and values, as reflected in organization.

Low-calorie beer was a brilliant insight in the creation phase, but did not succeed until Miller added the skills and attention needed for growth. Xerox built a worldwide business, but Ricoh found a cost-effective strategy to attack a segment with efficiency.

Creation of opportunity rests on entrepreneurial skills—and people. Successful businesses are founded by entrepreneurs, grown by marketers, made great by strategists, and fine-tuned by administrators. The complex of orientations, goals, and success skills becomes the organizational values. The more powerful the values in each orientation phase, the more difficult the transition. In part, this is "the way we do things" in the culture.

In a more concrete sense, corporate culture is the information collected and acted upon for each orientation, the quantitative measure of achievement for each goal, the skills rewarded in money and promotion for each phase, as well as "the way we do things" for each value.

	PHASE			
	Creation	*Growth*	*Advantage*	*Efficiency*
Orientation	World	Market	Competition	Internal
Goal	Find the opportunity	Make it real	Gain competitive position	Tie it down
Skills	Inventor	Marketer	Strategist	Administrator
Measures	New business	Growth	Relative position	Return on investment
Transition skills	→	Building →	Strategy →	Operations

Orientation Phases and Transition Skills

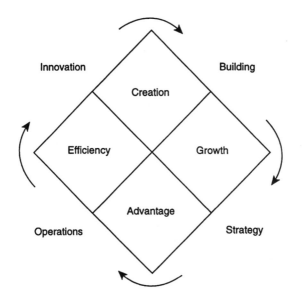

Manage Transitions

Of all the ideas presented, only a few are built into businesses. This explains why successful entrepreneurs are so highly rewarded and praised. But business can be grown into bankruptcy unless competitive advantage is gained and maintained. This explains why so many businesses fail. The transition skill required from growth to advantage is strategy, and the change from building to strategy is difficult for most organizations.

Once advantage is captured, the next transition is often much easier—perhaps too easy. Organization structure moves from loose to increasingly hierarchical and rigid. The internalization of "the way we do things" becomes even stronger.

Action plans become rules of thumb.

Rules of thumb become beliefs.

Beliefs become norms.

Each business—and the corporation—becomes larger as ideas become businesses and businesses grow and mature. Transitions then become not only harder, but more risky. Efficiency has a way of depressing innovation. The fourth transition skill is innovation.

The Adaptive Organization

Managing an adaptive organization is far more than managing a business within each phase. Managing within a phase is structured by clear orientation, goals, success skills, and measurements of success. Managing adaptation is attending to the transitions from phase to phase.

Managing adaptation requires understanding that all four phases must exist simultaneously in a vital corporation. Whenever the orientation, goals, skills, and measurements of any one phase become the dominant corporate values, change will cease to occur. Thus we see the great tension between efficiency and innovation in many companies today. Innovations come too often from outside the company, even in our strongest businesses. Perhaps they especially come from outside in our strongest businesses.

Great businesses should come from great corporations. Large companies can and will innovate. All it requires is

- Managing transitions as well as businesses

- Making the culture tangible to see what it is, what it should be, and what to change

- Internalizing the fact that vitality depends on finding and acting on opportunities in all of our businesses, even if the ideas come from the outside

- A willingness to compete with ourselves, for if we don't, someone else will

Change is never easy, but we need not make it harder by locking ourselves into the success pattern of one phase. We all want to be professionals and do things right and better. At the same time we must remind ourselves that management means vision as well as professionalism. While we manage today's business, we must see the next phase clearly and build a road map for transition.

This is sustained success.

STRATEGY AND LEARNING

Seymour Tilles, 1985

In a fast-changing industry, learning and strategy are so tightly linked that they are virtually synonymous. Effective strategy cannot be determined unless the senior executive group understands in detail the changes taking place in the competitive system and their implications for future competitive advantage.

The most difficult aspects of learning in connection with strategy are:

- Letting go of obsolete concepts
- Creating the relationships between people that make learning feasible
- Appreciating rates of change
- Developing a systems perspective

Letting Go of Obsolete Concepts

Old concepts are very sticky. It is hard to let go of them, which effectively inhibits new learning.

Will Rogers is reported to have said, "It ain't what you don't know that hurts—it's what you know that ain't so." That summarizes well a common deterrent to adaptation: a set of beliefs that is no longer appropriate to the company's reality.

All companies operate with a set of assumptions about how the business works. It is this set of assumptions, typically the result of long years of experience in the industry, that determines corporate behavior. These beliefs, once rooted, are persistent, and they lead to manifestations of the classic symptoms of prejudice: rejection of data not consistent with prior beliefs and a strong reluctance to experiment. As a result, previously successful strategies have a high probability of being pursued long after they have ceased to be appropriate. For example:

- As the proportion of standard cars in the U.S. market continued to decline, the U.S. automotive industry resisted a major thrust toward small cars because, "The American public likes a large car."
- Howard Johnson created a successful formula for a highway-oriented family restaurant that was not changed until long after

the demographics and the travel patterns of U.S. families indicated that it was no longer appropriate. As a result, it has been totally eclipsed by more aggressive and innovative competitors.

• With rapid growth in world trade over the past 40 years, many U.S. companies have been seriously disadvantaged by their inability to shift soon enough from a domestic system to a worldwide system. Particularly glaring examples are the major rust bowl industries, including steel, auto parts, and machine tools.

• Even the formidable IBM has been late in responding to the transition from centralized data processing to an office environment characterized by networking and compatible equipment. The greater the past success, the greater the challenge of potential change.

The basic step in promoting corporate adaptation is to recognize that the old belief system is no longer working and that a new one is required. For this to occur, senior executives need to be encouraged to make the old belief system explicit, so that its continued utility can be appraised.

Our experience suggests that when the old beliefs are replaced with new ones, effective adaptive behavior quickly follows.

Creating the Relationships That Make Learning Feasible

Whether learning is feasible within a company is critically sensitive to the character of existing relationships between people. Effective organizational learning is necessarily a joint activity. It can take place only if those who normally work together can contemplate a joint exploratory activity. Necessarily, this will include:

• The relationship between the chief executive and his immediate subordinates

• The relationship between peer senior executives

• The relationship between executive groups and potential sources of support

The relationship between the chief executive and his subordinates: If real executive learning is to take place, the chief executive must set the pace.

There is a Gresham's law of executive behavior that causes the urgent to drive out the important. Without a strong executive example to lend some urgency to the learning effort, it will inevitably be crowded out of executive calendars. We have never been part of a major learning effort that was not personally sponsored by the chief executive or by a division manager within his own division.

Some time ago, the chief executive of one of our client companies, an old organization in a mature industry, said to his six key subordinates: "We are jointly going to spend one-third of our time creating a corporate strategy. You have three months to make the arrangements necessary to allow you to do this."

Within a year, the group had created a major new business that remains an important part of the company's overall position.

The relationship between peers: If effective strategy is to be developed, it must encompass the whole firm. Consequently, an important challenge is to produce cross-functional learning, so that each function can improve not only its own activity, but also the way it interacts with others.

It is important to understand not only how to do better from the perspective of each function, but also how that connects to the relevant system: the company as a whole. The key to overall company performance is the relationship between peers. When there is tension between peers, systematic learning is not feasible.

The relationship between executive groups and sources of support: As important as the role of the chief executive in legitimizing the learning process is the task of providing staff services to this process.

This is commonly the role of external resources. It would be possible for the strategic planning function to be an important agent in the process. In many companies, however, it has disqualified itself, either by being simply a compiler of results or by being concerned primarily with issues outside the current operations, such as acquisition.

Appreciating Rates of Change

One of the most severe tests of learning is whether something is so well understood that rates of change can be predicted.

In a recent interview, Jack Welch, chairman of General Electric, observed: "I make the argument that 80 to 90 percent of the things that fail are not because people don't execute or implement—it's because they don't read how fast our competition is moving or how fast the market is changing."*

* "At G.E., More Planning Means Less Planning," *The Washington Post*, 30 Sept. 1984, p. B8.

One of the most powerful devices for helping senior executives understand rates of change is to require them to develop an explicit forecast of their industry as a basis for assessing their company's future performance. We would expect this forecast to be wrong initially, given the way industries change. We would also expect, however, that effective companies would spend a significant amount of time looking for and trying to understand what was missed, what strategies would be required to deal with the uncertainties, and what might be considered to make future forecasts more reliable. We would expect ineffective companies to make the same errors repeatedly, without deriving any learning benefit from their expensive experience.

As change has accelerated, forecasting has become more difficult, but also more and more important.

Developing a Systems Perspective

Strategy is inherently a systemic issue. To deal with it effectively, people responsible for major components of the system have to learn how their activities mesh with those of others in the system to create an overall direction. Unless this perspective is learned, it will be difficult to create consistent behavior. Few things are as disruptive to the long-term interests of a large company as a strong function narrowly pursuing its own interest.

One of the most powerful ways to promote systems learning is to require people to become knowledgeable about external events before they develop a joint strategic response. Among the more important external events to be used for this purpose are competitive initiatives and other changes in the evolution of the competitive system.

As part of this activity, it is important that senior management support an analytical effort that has two basic purposes. One is to develop, pool, and integrate information about competitors' actions, capabilities, and intentions. We are struck by how seldom this is done adequately. The second is to model the evolution of the competitive system.

For example, after a recent discussion with a major U.S. company that had completed an analysis of what was happening within its industry in Japan, the observation we heard was, "We knew most of that information, in the sense that someone within our company had observed most of the individual activities described. But we had not put it together to form the picture displayed, nor had we considered its implications."

Conclusion

Learning is a major requirement for corporate survival. Executive turnover is a fact of life—and sometimes a fact of death. The combination of a rapidly changing external world and substantial internal mobility makes learning a necessarily high priority.

How this priority is pursued is greatly influenced by the chief executive, who determines both the time committed to learning and the agenda. It is also strongly influenced by the willingness of senior managers to open existing practices to challenge and to support the CEO's effort to carefully examine sacred cows.

A prerequisite for learning is to continue to develop comprehensive data that are externally relevant and to see that these data are shared across organizational boundaries. This requires group activity, which can be effective only if there is leadership to make it effective and a time commitment to make it possible, and if there are support services to make it efficient.

Executive learning is hard. Among the major difficulties are letting go of obsolete concepts, developing the relationships that make learning possible, and creating a systems perspective. Such learning is essential, however. When companies stop learning, they begin to pursue relentlessly what used to be appropriate behavior. How long they then survive is a function of how rapidly their industries change.

LET MIDDLE MANAGERS MANAGE

JEANIE DUCK, 1991

In the annals of corporate reorganization, the eighties might well go down as the decade when CEOs rediscovered their workers. Walking the plant floor and the front lines, CEOs found that employees knew a lot about how the business worked and had suggestions worth following. This revelation, together with a competitive environment that demands quality, flexibility, and customer satisfaction, has paved the way for such concepts as the delayered organization, flattened hierarchies, empowered employees, and self-managed work groups.

The results are now coming in from these brave new reorganization programs, and they are mixed. After months of drafting vision statements and rearranging organizational boxes, many companies have bogged down in the muddy terrain that separates theory from implementation, change on paper from change in reality. What went wrong? In their eagerness to unlock the creativity of the worker, some companies neglected a most valuable and necessary player in any change process—the middle manager.

The Management Vacuum

Stationed between the executives who shape the new vision and the employees who are to carry it out, middle managers are in the ideal position to bridge the gap between vision and implementation. With their years of experience and knowledge about the business, they are the people who can show newly empowered teams what to do and how to work effectively.

Japanese companies are noted for building on the experience and knowledge of their middle managers, but American companies have often undervalued them. Now they may be confusing them as well. Told they should relinquish their former roles of directing and enforcing, some managers are at a loss to know what they should be doing instead.

Empowerment can be abandonment when employees are given responsibility without guidance or training. A vice president who suddenly shows up one day and tells his plant manager that he will have sign-off authority for $1 million instead of the $5,000 he formerly had isn't empowering his employee, he's setting him up to fail.

Many companies are now struggling with the consequences of moving too quickly from authoritarian management to little or no management. Given new power and responsibility but little guidance and instruction, employees can become confused and demoralized, programs can get slowed down, and the skeptics of change seem justified.

Managers Are Essential

Of course, we prefer to think that employees will happily rise to meet any new challenge, and that given the opportunity, they will exhibit the necessary initiative and ability. This can happen. But it is not realistic or fair to expect people to acquire the experience, skills, and information they need overnight. Nor should they be expected to show unbounded enthusiasm for something they haven't done before and that looks like more work and responsibility with little likelihood of success.

Here's an example from a Fortune 100 company that shows the value a strong middle manager can add. This middle manager had run up against a problem common to companies undergoing organizational change: her people were taking too long to establish viable cross-functional teams. She suspected that their often-voiced skepticism about the new process was a contributing factor.

The usual approach to this problem would be to call the group together for a series of pep talks on the new vision, its goals, and its purpose and to remind them that it's up to them to make it happen. Instead, the manager drew up a list of detailed activities and requirements (number and length of group meetings, who would attend, a list of prioritized problems for each group to address, the required deliverables, etc.) and insisted each team accomplish its assignment by a deadline and report back. She also arranged a training program for people who lacked skills for facilitating cross-functional teams and agreed to meet with any team whenever asked. What's more, she made it clear that she was available to help.

Forced to perform the required activities, the group learned that the change did, in fact, lead to impressive improvements. By determining what activities were necessary to get teams working cross-functionally and requiring that they perform them in spite of their skepticism, the manager gave them the experience of success, which led to a change in attitude.

Reactivate the Middle Manager

Ask yourself the following questions to determine whether you are getting the full value from your middle managers:

- Do my managers have a clear vision of how our business works as a whole, not just in their functions? Have they ever met a customer? Do they know the business from the outside in?

- Do they understand that their role is not only to communicate the company vision, but also to determine which processes and activities will make it a success? Do they know how to focus people on processes and the appropriate activities? Do they know how to coordinate these processes horizontally and vertically?

- Are my middle managers spread too thinly? Have I given them the adequate time, training, and resources needed to succeed?

- In the attempt to empower the workers, have I undermined the managers? Do my managers have to direct the workers in performing the necessary activities?

- Do my managers feel that they are part of the solution, not part of the problem?

Eager as we are to unleash the initiative and creativity of our workforce, we must remember that employee empowerment is a goal to work toward. The transformation from authoritarian to participative management cannot be accomplished in a single leap, and it should not bypass the middle managers. Rather, it must evolve over time and with help from all levels of the organization. No one can help to speed this evolution along more than middle managers. Employee empowerment may mean fewer managers, but the role those managers play will be even more crucial to the company's success.

JAZZ VS. SYMPHONY

JOHN S. CLARKESON, 1990

Is there a leadership crisis? Are we really lacking executives to lead our organizations into the twenty-first century? Or are the specifications for the job changing: Should we reexamine what kinds of leaders our organizations need?

The critical function in today's organization is the creative function. As change accelerates, organizations that are not continuously re-creating their reason for existence will not survive for very long.

Whether a business is driven by the need to increase variety, to segment the market more finely, to cope with shortening life cycles, to harness the possibilities of new process technologies, or to reposition against new competitors, the key task is to lead the organization to create products, processes, and services that have not existed before.

Routine work can eventually be broken down into individual, repetitive, and ultimately unchallenging tasks. Creative work requires harnessing the knowledge and thinking abilities of many people with different and highly specialized skills—in other words, professionals.

Most of our organizations today derive from a model whose original purpose was to control creativity. The Ford assembly line's virtue was that each man did one job the same way every time, without distractions, interactions, or self-expression. Today's organization follows a similar blueprint in maintaining walls between its specialized functions: marketing, manufacturing, engineering, finance.

This suits many professionals just fine. Professionals of all types share a number of preferences: commitment to their specialty, insistence on autonomy and the right to choose their work methods, and resistance to direction and evaluation by anyone other than their professional peers. Our modern organizations often encourage specialists to pursue the goals of their specialties at the expense of the other functions, the firm, and the customer.

As a result, the biggest leadership challenge in business today may be leading specialized professionals from various functions to achieve the overall aims of the firm in a rapidly changing environment.

What kind of leaders are able to do this? Where might we look for examples?

In the world of classical music, the symphony is regarded by many as its most complex creation, requiring the integration of a large assembly of highly talented individuals for its performance. It has been suggested that the CEOs of the future may resemble the great conductors.

There is one major flaw in this analogy: no one gives a CEO the music he should play. But American music suggests another possible answer.

Duke Ellington was not an unusually gifted individual or musical theorist. It is disputed how well he could read musical notation. But measured by his output of original compositions, he may be the dominant figure in twentieth-century music.

How is his prodigious creativity to be explained? From people who worked with him, it appears he learned how to forge the divergent personalities of his jazz group into a single, highly creative instrument.

Members of his band have described how he learned to create on the run: he would offer up a scrap of an idea, suggest in general what he wanted, and then rely on his players to take cues from each other and to fill in their parts as they thought best.

His players were good but not without equal. He knew their quirks, their gifts, their problems, and he encouraged them to learn to do things they didn't think they could do. Some players came and went, but many stayed for years. They developed through their membership in the group, and they learned from each other. Most of all, their capacity for innovation grew as they built on their cumulative experience.

Finally, by performing live in the close atmosphere of a jazz club, audience reaction was immediately visible to all, and refinement of new ideas came fast. On piano, Ellington was in the middle of the process, and communication was instantaneous. The results were astonishing.

The winning organization of the future will look more like a collection of jazz ensembles than a symphony orchestra. Functional barriers will be reduced. Different specialties will work in more permanent teams around specific customer opportunities. Customer contact will be continuous. Information will be current, rich, and available to all.

Leaders will be in the flow, not remote. Teamwork and cooperation will increase at the expense of individual competition. Cooperative support will moderate anxiety and encourage risk taking. Talented people will be attracted by the ability to see and influence the whole process, to learn from other knowledgeable people, and by the opportunity to create and grow.

The leaders who emerge from this environment will not look exactly like the old models. They will not necessarily excel at any one specialty. They will not have all the ideas. They will not be able to rely on exclusive decision-making authority, on the overwhelming force of personality, or on a monopoly of information.

Leadership will flow to those whose vision can inspire the members of the team to put their best abilities at the service of the team. These leaders will create rather than demand loyalty; the best people will want to work with them. They will communicate effectively with a variety of people and use the conflict among diverse points of view to reach new insights. They will exert influence by the values they choose to reinforce. They will make leaders of their team members.

There are no set pieces anymore. The distinctions between composer/conductor/performer are eroding. The new leaders are all around us.

PART FOUR

Business Thinking

BRUCE HENDERSON DEDICATED his life to learning and ideas. The preface cites Jay Forrester's observation that "virtually everything interesting in business lies in fourth-order effects and beyond." Bruce pushed beyond fourth-order effects as a common practice, and he expected his colleagues to do the same. Intellectual curiosity was one of the main characteristics he looked for in people he sought to attract to The Boston Consulting Group. Thinking insightfully and defending conclusions were rites of passage—and often intimidating ones—for new consultants. One recounts that on his first day of work at BCG, Bruce trapped him in the corridor with the question, "How would you price a new jet fighter aircraft?"

The intellectual energy Bruce brought to BCG has driven high standards for analysis and higher aspirations to creativity. Both are reflected in this group of *Perspectives*. These essays do not posit concrete maxims on strategy. Rather they muse on the essential nature of strategy and competition—very simply, business thinking.

BUSINESS THINKING

BRUCE D. HENDERSON, 1977

Business thinking starts with an intuitive choice of assumptions. Its progress as analysis is intertwined with intuition. The final choice is always intuitive. If that were not true, all problems of almost any kind would be solved by mathematicians with nonquantitative data.

The final choice in all business decision is, of course, intuitive. It must be. Otherwise it is not a decision, just a conclusion, a printout.

The tradeoff of subjective, nonquantifiable values is by definition a subjective and intuitive choice. Intuition can be awesome in its value at times. It is known as good judgment in everyday affairs. Intuition is in fact the subconscious integration of all the experiences, conditioning, and knowledge of a lifetime, including the emotional and cultural biases of that lifetime.

But intuition alone is never enough. Alone, it can be disastrously wrong. Analysis, too, can be disastrously wrong. Analysis depends on keeping the required data to manageable proportions. It also means keeping the nonquantifiable data to a minimum. Thus analysis by its very nature requires initial oversimplification and intuitive choice of starting assumptions with exclusion of certain data. All of these choices are intuitive. A mistake in any one can be fatal to the analysis.

Any complex problem has a near infinite combination of facts and relationships. Business in particular is affected by everything, including the past, the nonlogical, and the unknowable. This complexity is compounded by multiple objectives to serve multiple constituencies, many of whose objectives must be traded off. Problem solving with such complexity requires an orderly, systematic approach in order to even hope to optimize the final decision.

When the results of analysis and intuition coincide, there is little gained except confidence. When the analysis reaches conclusions that are counterintuitive, then more rigorous analysis and reexamination of underlying assumptions are always called for. The expansion of the frame of reference and the increased rigor of analysis may be fruitful.

But in nearly all problem solving there is a universe of alternative choices, most of which must be discarded without more than cursory attention. To do otherwise is to incur costs beyond the value of any solution and defer decision to beyond the time horizon. A frame of reference is needed to screen the intuitive selection of assumptions, relevance of data, methodology, and implicit value judgments. That frame of reference is the *concept.*

Conceptual thinking is the skeleton or the framework on which all the other choices are sorted out. A concept is by its nature an oversimplification. Yet its fundamental relationships are so powerful and important that they will tend to override all except the most extreme exceptions. Such exceptions are usually obvious in their importance. A concept defines a system of interactions in terms of the relative values that produce stable equilibrium of the system. Consequently, a concept defines the initial assumptions, the data required, and the relationships between the data inputs. In this way it permits analysis of the consequences of change in input data.

Concepts are simple in statement but complex in practice. Outputs are almost always part of the input by means of feedback. The feedback itself is consequently a subsystem interconnected with other subsystems.

Theoretically, such conceptual business systems can be solved by a series of simultaneous equations. In practice, computer simulation is the only practical way to deal with the characteristic multiple inputs, feedback loops, and higher-order effects in a reasonable time at reasonable cost with all the underlying assumptions made explicit. Pure mathematics becomes far too ponderous.

Concepts are developed in hard science and business alike from an approximation of the scientific method. They start with a generalization of an observed pattern of experience. They are stated first as a hypothesis, then postulated as a theory, then defined as a decision rule. They are validated by their ability to predict. Such decision rules are often crystallized as policies. Rarely does a business concept permit definitive proof enough to be called a law, except facetiously.

Intuition disguised as status, seniority, and rank is the underlying normative mode of all business decisions. It could not be otherwise. Too many choices must be made too often. Data are expensive to collect and often of uncertain quality or relevance. Analysis is laborious and often far too expensive even though imprecise or superficial.

Yet two kinds of decisions justify rigorous and painstaking analysis guided by intuition derived from accumulated experience. The irrevocable commitment of major reserves of resources deserves such treatment. So do the major policies that guide and control the implementation of such commitments.

All rigorous analysis is inherently an iterative process. It starts with an intuitive choice and ends with an intuitive decision. The first definition of a problem is inescapably intuitive. It must be in order to be recognized as a problem at all. The final decision is also intuitive. It must be or there is no choice and therefore no need for decision.

Between those two points of beginning and ending, the rigorous process must take place. The sequence is analysis, problem redefinition, reanalysis, and then even more rigorous problem redefinition, and so on, until the law of diminishing returns dictates a halt—intuitively.

The methodology and sequence of business thinking can be stated or at least approximated.

- State the problem as clearly and fully as possible.

- Search for and identify the basic concepts that relate to the perceived critical elements.

- Define the data inputs this conceptual reference will require. Check off and identify any major factors that are not implicitly included in the conceptual base.

- Redefine the problem and broaden the concept as necessary to include any such required inputs.

- Gather the data and analyze the problem.

- Find out to which data inputs the analysis is sensitive. Reexamine the range of options with respect to those factors and the resulting range of outputs.

- Based on the insights developed by the analysis, redefine the problem and repeat the process.

- Reiterate until there is a consensus that the possible incremental improvement in insight is no longer worth the incremental cost. That consensus will be intuitive. It must be. There is no way to know the value of the unknown.

It is a matter of observation that much of the value of a rigorous and objective examination of a problem will be found in one of three areas:

- First, the previously accepted underlying assumptions may prove to be invalid or inadequate as the problem definition is changed.

- Second, the interaction between component functions may have been neglected, resulting in suboptimization by function.

- Third, a previously unknown or unaccepted or misunderstood conceptual framework may be postulated that both permits prediction of the consequence of change and partially explains these consequences.

It is also a matter of common observation that the wisest of intuitive judgments come after full exploration and consensus on the nature of the problem by peers of nearly equal but diverse experience.

Finally, it is also a matter of general experience that implementation of the optimum decision will prove difficult if that discussion and consensus have not been continued long enough to make the relationship between the overall objective and the specific action seem clear to all who must interpret and implement the required policies. Otherwise, the intuition of those who do the implementation will be used to redefine the policies that emerged from analysis. This is one reason planned organization change is so difficult and random drift is so common.

Here are some fundamental procedural suggestions. Define the problem and hypothesize the approach to a solution intuitively before wasting time on data collection and analysis. Do the first analysis lightly. Then and only then redefine the problem more rigorously and reanalyze in depth. (Don't go to the library and read all the books before you know what you want to learn.) Use mixed project research teams composed of some people with finely honed intuitions from experience and others with highly developed analytical skills but too little experience to know what cannot be done. Perhaps in this way you can achieve the best of both analysis and intuition in combination and offset the weaknesses of both.

BRINKMANSHIP IN BUSINESS

BRUCE D. HENDERSON, 1968

A businessman often convinces himself that he is completely logical in his behavior when in fact the critical factor is his emotional bias compared to the emotional bias of his opposition. Unfortunately, some businessmen and students take the attitude that competition is some kind of impersonal, objective, colorless affair, with a company competing against the field as a golfer does in medal play. A better case can be made that business competition is a battle royal in which there are many contenders, each of whom must be dealt with individually. Victory, if achieved, is more often won in the mind of a competitor than in the economic arena.

I shall emphasize two points. The first is that the management of a company must persuade each competitor to voluntarily stop short of his maximum effort to acquire customers and profits. The second point is that persuasion depends on emotional and intuitive factors rather than on analysis or deduction.

The negotiator's skill lies in being as arbitrary as necessary to obtain the best possible compromise without actually destroying the basis for voluntary mutual cooperation or self-restraint. There are some commonsense rules for success in such an endeavor:

1. Be sure that your rival is fully aware of what he can gain if he cooperates and what it will cost him if he does not.

2. Avoid any action that will arouse his emotions, since it is essential that he behave in a logical, reasonable fashion.

3. Convince your opponent that you are emotionally dedicated to your position and are completely convinced that it is reasonable.

It is worth emphasizing that your competitor is under the maximum handicap if he acts in a completely rational, objective, and logical fashion. For then he will cooperate as long as he thinks he benefits at all. In fact, if he is completely logical, he will not forgo the profit of cooperation as long as there is any net benefit.

It may strike most businessmen as strange to talk about cooperation with competitors. But it is hard to visualize a situation in which it would be worthwhile to pursue competition to the utter destruction of a competitor. In every case there is a greater advantage to reducing the competition on the condition that the competitor does likewise. Such mutual restraint is cooperation, whether recognized as such or not.

Without cooperation on the part of competitors, there can be no stability. We see this most clearly in international relationships during times of peace. There are constant encroachments and aggressive acts. Without mutual self-restraint, these acts would rapidly escalate into all-out war. Constant confrontations occur. And the eventual consequence is always either voluntarily imposed self-restraint or all-out mutual destruction. Thus international diplomacy has only one purpose: to stabilize cooperation between independent nations on the most favorable basis possible. Diplomacy can be described as the art of being stubborn, arbitrary, and unreasonable without arousing emotional responses.

Businessmen should notice the similarity of their economic competition to the peacetime behavior of nations. The object in both cases is to achieve a voluntary, cooperative restraint on the aggressiveness of competitors. Complete elimination of competition is almost inconceivable. The goal of the hottest economic war is an agreement for coexistence, not annihilation. The competition and mutual encroachment do not stop; they go on forever. But they do so under some measure of mutual restraint.

A breakdown in negotiations is inevitable if both parties persist in arbitrary positions that are incompatible. Yet we have identified major areas in business where some degree of arbitrary behavior is essential for protecting a company's self-interest.

In effect, a type of brinkmanship is necessary. The term was coined to describe cold war international diplomacy, but it describes a normal pattern in business, too.

In a confrontation between parties who are part competitors and part cooperators, the decision as to what to accept is essentially emotional or arbitrary. The decision as to what is attainable is essentially an evaluation of the other party's degree of intransigence. The purpose is to convince him that you are arbitrary and emotionally committed while trying to discover what he would really accept in settlement. The competitor known to be coldly logical is at a great disadvantage. Logically, he can afford to compromise until there is no advantage left in cooperation. If, instead, he is emotional, irrational, and arbitrary, he has a great advantage.

The heart of business strategy for a company is the creation of attitudes on the part of its competitors that will cause them either to restrain themselves or to act in a fashion that management deems advantageous. In diplomacy and military strategy the key to success is very much the same.

The most easily recognized way of enforcing cooperation is to exhibit obvious willingness to use irresistible or overwhelming force. This requires little strategic skill, but there is the problem of producing conviction in the competing organization that the force will be used without actually resorting to it (which is expensive and inconvenient).

In industry, however, the available force is usually not overwhelming, although one company may be able to inflict major punishment on another. If each party can inflict such punishment on the other, we have the classic case. If there is open conflict in such a case, then both parties lose. In the event of cooperation, both parties are better off, but not necessarily equally so—particularly if one is trying to change the status quo.

When each party can punish the other, the prospects of agreement depend on three things:

1. Their respective willingness to accept the risk of punishment

2. Their beliefs about each other's willingness to accept the risk of punishment

3. Their degree of rationality in behavior

If these conclusions are correct, what can we deduce about how advantages are gained and lost in business competition?

First, management's lack of willingness to accept the risk of punishment is almost certain to produce either the punishment or progressively more onerous conditions for cooperation—provided the competition recognized the attitude.

Second, beliefs about a competitor's future behavior or response are all that determine competitive cooperation. In other words, it is the judgment not of actual capability but of probable use of capability that counts.

Third, the less rational or less predictable the behavior of a competitor appears to be, the greater the advantage he possesses in establishing a favorable competitive balance. This advantage is limited only by his need to avoid forcing his competitors into an untenable position or by creating an emotional antagonism that will lead them to be unreasonable and irrational (as he is).

If I were asked to distill the conditions and forces described into advice for the businessman-strategist, I would suggest five rules:

1. You must know as accurately as possible just what your competition has at stake in his contact with you. It is not what you gain or lose, but what he gains or loses, that sets the limit on his ability to compromise with you.

2. The less the competition knows about your stakes, the less advantage he has. Without a reference point, he does not even know whether you are being unreasonable.

3. It is absolutely essential to know the character, attitudes, motives, and habitual behavior of a competitor if you wish to have a negotiating advantage.

4. The more arbitrary your demands are, the better your relative competitive position—provided you do not arouse an emotional reaction.

5. The less arbitrary you can seem to be, the more arbitrary you can in fact act.

These rules make up the art of business brinkmanship. They will guide a businessman to winning a strategic victory in the minds of competitors. Once he has won it there, he can convert it into a competitive victory in terms of sales volume, costs, and profits.

BUSINESS CHESS

Rudyard L. Istvan, 1984

Profound parallels exist between business and chess. Both are complex forms of competition. Both have been studied for centuries, and both depend on strategy.

Chess is a simplified, stylized representation of ancient conflict. Two forces of 16 pieces, each in six types representing different rules of maneuver and engagement, are arrayed in perfect view of each other on an eight-by-eight playing field. The game lasts at most a few hours.

Yet even for this simplified representation of competition, the most powerful computer is unable to devise a winning strategy on the basis of analysis alone. Rather, sophisticated chess computers depend on rules of thumb and experience-based policies and procedures to develop strategies and direct tactics.

These rules to simplify a complex world are the parallels to the mental maps successful managers develop to determine a corporation's strategy and tactics. Like chess programs, these maps become implicit decision rules based on experience. Learning organizations build success on success as they revise and update their maps. Others continue to follow old maps and gradually become ineffective. Making maps explicit and continually reflective of reality separates grand masters from computer programs and successful businesses from bureaucracies.

The immense sophistication of business compared to chess makes us even more dependent on our experience and less aware of how much our maps guide behavior. Business is an infinitely more complex form of competition. The number of players is almost always more than two. The variety of pieces and the extent of the playing field are limitless. Nothing is ever fully in view. The rules of business maneuver and engagement can be changed by any competitor at any time. And for corporations, the competition never ends.

Despite their dramatic differences in complexity, chess and business share two essentials:

• They are systems of competition.

• The competition involves indirect consequences.

Basic competitive lessons are more readily understood in chess. Yet they are paralleled in business.

Strategy over Tactics: The Japanese Gambit

In chess, a good strategist excels over a good tactician. Good individual moves do not add up to good play. The strategist sees and manipulates patterns and positions. Certain offensive and defensive chess sequences have become so familiar and predictable that knowledge of appropriate responses is mandatory for skilled players. Truly innovative responses to the Queen's gambit or the Sicilian defense have a high probability of failure, no matter how well played.

In business, the Japanese gambit has become equally familiar. Take a complex product, but one for which the technology is fairly mature. Begin with simple goods catering principally to domestic or Southeast Asian markets. Build very high volumes to drive costs down and get quality up. Then attack the North American market at the lower end with these low costs. Roll up the market as domestic manufacturers execute a segment retreat to higher-margined, lower-volume specialties suitable only for their market. Add high-end complexity only at superior total volume and cost. Finally, mop up Europe with the full line of higher-quality, lower-cost goods.

The Japanese gambit became a familiar pattern in transistor radios and televisions. The pattern is being repeated in autos, machine tools, trucks, farm implements, engines, and forklifts. Yet some domestic competitors appear to be executing segment retreats as if the gambit had not been recognized. The best defense against the gambit is strategic offense, not tactical retreat. One response is confrontation in as many markets as possible to choke the volume growth that facilitates the roll-up. A second is to form alliances of complementary strengths. In the automobile industry, Ford seems to be doing the former with the world car and GM the latter with Toyota in California. Both may be more strategic responses to the Japanese gambit than segment retreat.

Competitive Evolution

The strategic value of chess pieces changes during the course of the game. On a crowded early-game board the knight, although limited in range to three squares, is essential because it can skip over pieces to drop behind enemy lines. At that time, the rook, able to strike anywhere on the board along its rank and file, is virtually useless because it has no ability to exercise its inherent range. Later in the game, their utilities are reversed. Pieces fall in battle, enhancing the rook's ability to strike while placing much action out of the knight's range.

The strategic value of various economic competitive advantages also changes as a business evolves. Early on, production experience and cost position may be essential. Later, as markets mature and basic needs are satisfied, differentiated segments can emerge. Marketing may become more important than production. Henry Ford's unassailable cost position with the volume-based Model T strategy was devastated by General Motors during the 1920s with a marketing-oriented strategy of model variation and style change.

Win, Lose, or Draw

Many chess games do not result in a win or a loss, but rather in a stalemated draw. This occurs when neither side has sufficient forces left to checkmate the opposition. Inexperienced players frequently fail to recognize these conditions. They continue pointlessly to maneuver. Masters foresee an impending stalemate and either change strategy or agree to stop play.

Impending stalemate can be recognized in business. If a product is relatively undifferentiated and costs are essential, and if the market is large, with many capacity units at maximum scale and with comparable technology, then the industry will have a significant flat section on its supply curve. Stalemate threatens when growth slows. Portions of the forest products, chemicals, metals, and financial-services industries failed to recognize impending stalemate. They continued to invest in unchanged strategies long after such investment was pointless.

Strategy and Complexity

Direct lessons from chess are applicable in business. More applicable still is the intellectual process by which the game can be mastered. This process describes how an organization plays the business game—and how its performance can be improved.

Many attempts to understand chess have been made by computer scientists and artificial-intelligence researchers. If a computer could play chess well, then perhaps it was intelligent. All early attempts failed miserably.

The problem is permutations. Given rules and positions, it is easy to calculate all possible next moves and select the best. There are always fewer than 1,024 possibilities. It is more than just difficult to do this for the move after next, for that requires calculating all possible responses to the position that results from the best of all possible opposing reactions to one's own best of all possible moves—where the next move may not be clearly best until later, and where the opponent may not choose its best move!

Nevertheless, there are computer programs that play passable chess. Such programs depend on two devices to circumvent the multiplying combinational permutations required to devise a winning strategy. These devices are equally useful in the formulation of business strategies.

Pattern Recognition

One device is recognizing patterns. This is the art of making useful abstractions. Rather than analyzing square by square and piece by piece, a pattern of play becomes the unit of analysis. Strategies rather than tactics are evaluated.

Failure to seek patterns in business results in either analysis paralysis or firefighting. The forest becomes lost in the trees. Patterns filter extraneous information, reduce complexity, focus on the essential. Only key patterns of competitive behavior are evaluated. Chess gambits are patterns of moves. Stalemate is a pattern of low growth in a large commodity market with multiple units of similar cost and capacity and high operating leverage.

Rules of Thumb

The other device is guidelines, rules of thumb. Rules of thumb are guiding principles that, while never strictly true because oversimplified, point reliably to the probable direction of action. Experience builds rules by remembered results of trial and error.

All good chess programs depend on rules of thumb to simplify calculations. Some moves are not examined because they almost never pay. Very possibly, the brilliantly innovative winning move will be excluded by such a process. But the frustrations of novice players matched against the simplest chess programs demonstrate their power.

Most of the major ideas in business strategy are conceptual rules of thumb about economic competition. The experience curve, the growth-share matrix, average costing, and the environments matrix are all rules of thumb. They help to pattern competitive behavior. They point toward the relevant and away from the extraneous, and they suggest probable courses of action. They simplify, but cannot substitute for, the thought process.

Learning

In chess, the ability to learn and adapt still gives grand masters an edge over computer rules. Rules are fixed. Even modern "learning" programs merely readjust the probabilities attached to a predetermined set of rules as their experience accumulates. They cannot rewrite their basic logic.

Most organizations behave like such chess programs. They become bureaucratized. Their decision processes become fixed and difficult to revise.

A learning organization can both refine its pattern recognition and revise its rules of thumb as business competition evolves. The failure of most major businesses does not involve bad initial play; at one time they grew and prospered. Rather, it is a failure to learn and adapt as the business changes.

The effort to create successful chess programs parallels the effort of top management to form successful business organizations. Strategic success requires:

- *Appropriate pattern recognition.* The organization must seek out all relevant information but not be overwhelmed by trivial detail.

- *Appropriate rules of thumb.* Decision rules must reflect competitive reality at several levels of complexity. Too simple, and decisions will be erroneous; too elaborate, and they will be made late or never.

- *Learning.* No intelligence networks, reporting systems, filters, or decision rules can be appropriate always, everywhere. Learning when rules do not apply, and when exceptions justify new ones, is the essence of adaptive strategy.

Business is infinitely more complex than chess. It is played continuously, in earnest, for real and significant consequences. Good strategies, flexible responses, and recognition of end games are valuable lessons. Pattern recognition, rules of thumb, and learning are needed to cope with the infinite diversity and indirect consequences of business decisions. The grand masters of business may never truly master it. But they do win consistently over the competition.

WHAT IS "JAPANESE" ABOUT THE KAISHA?*

JAMES C. ABEGGLEN AND GEORGE STALK, JR., 1985

When the kaisha are looked at as social organizations there is likely to be an emphasis on their uniqueness and on the difficulties of transferring methods from Japanese social organizations to social organizations in other cultures with different histories. But the analysis need not and should not stop at this point. The fact is that Japan's kaisha are economic organizations as well as social organizations, and nothing in Japan's dash for affluence has allowed its economy to repeal the basic laws of economics, or change the basis and nature of economic competition.

When the kaisha are analyzed as economic organizations, the questions of lessons to be learned and transferability of methods receive quite different answers. There is a great deal to be learned, and much that can be transferred. The kaisha as competitors are not products of "the mysterious East," but are economic organizations responding rationally to opportunities and problems. In the process, the best of the kaisha have developed approaches to dealing with competitive problems that can be used to advantage in any competitive system.

The approach Japanese manufacturing firms are taking to increasing productivity and reducing costs in the manufacture of a wide range of products is a good example of developments that Western firms are able to, and urgently need to, adopt. It took Toyota some twenty years to develop its manufacturing system. It is possible that the system could

* Excerpted from James C. Abegglen and George Stalk, Jr., *Kaisha, The Japanese Corporation.* Copyright © 1985 by Basic Books, Inc. Reprinted by permission of Basic Books, a division of HarperCollins Publishers, Inc.

only have been developed in the context of Japanese labor-management relations, building on a competent and dedicated labor force. Yet the system is not Japan-specific—it is the result of applying rigorous economics and engineering to the factory system to optimize the volume, quality, and variety of output.

At present, the Japanese approach to manufacturing is yielding cost advantages in the range of 30 percent over Western competitors. The advantage is unbearable, competitively, and will destroy important Western firms if they fail to respond. The response of Western firms should not be constrained by culture. There is nothing in their system of manufacturing that is peculiar to Japan, or to Japanese companies. It can be adopted abroad, as the example of Omark Industries well illustrates. A medium-sized Portland, Oregon, company, and the world's leading producer of saw chain, Omark perceived the competitive advantages of Japanese manufacturing methods and pioneered their introduction into U.S. factories. The system can be considered a Japanese invention, but like most inventions, can be adopted elsewhere if adequate study and efforts are made. A failure to adopt the Japanese flexible manufacturing system is likely to ensure competitive failure of Western companies in many industries.

Just as there are important lessons to be learned in the area of manufacturing methods, so, too, many Western firms can study Japanese financial methods for a competitive advantage. It is not news to Western firms that dividend policy powerfully affects the firm's ability to fund growth at relatively low costs of capital. A number of fast-growing U.S. companies pay little or no dividends. Japanese levels of dividend payments are possible in the West without unduly damaging share price levels. The mystery is why so few Western companies take advantage of that fact, when so many Japanese companies do.

Complaints by Western firms that their boards of directors and shareholders will not tolerate higher levels of earning retention and that thereby the Western firm is at a disadvantage against its Japanese competitor are simply not credible. If a change is needed, present shareholders should be warned so that widows and orphans in search of dividend income can be given the opportunity to change their portfolios. The market as a whole, however, is quite likely to prefer growth and capital gains to dividends, and is likely to welcome a coherent and determined growth strategy based on earnings reinvestment. Western complaints of Japanese advantage are misplaced; the Japanese lesson needs the attention.

It is similar with debt levels. The cost and growth advantages of debt are familiar, and indeed it is because they are well known that Japanese firms are attacked for unfairly using high levels of leverage in asset acquisition. Yet the same Western companies that complain are using levels of debt well below those commonly available to Western companies. If even these levels are below those available to the Japanese competitor, perhaps the Western competitor needs to reexamine its banking relations and move to a greater degree of bank dependence and involvement in its affairs so as to achieve higher levels of borrowings. Japanese financial practices provide a powerful competitive advantage, but it is an advantage available to Western firms as well.

In terms of technology, the lesson to be learned from the kaisha is clear. While there is little that a company in the West can do to improve the level of education or output of engineers in its society, it can improve its position through consistent and sustained hiring policies and increased opportunities for its engineering staff. More important, there is a great deal the Western company can do to ensure that it is searching the world, and Japan in particular, for new products and processes. The kaisha have been beneficiaries of a massive transfer of technology, a transfer made possible by constant assessment of potential world sources of technology.

Japan is now generally recognized as a major source of new technology in many of its industries. Yet very few foreign firms possess the capability of searching for and acquiring the results of Japan's research efforts. Few foreign firms are prepared even to acknowledge the value of acquired technology. Most technology evaluation is in the hands of technicians with a "not-invented-here" bias, rather than business executives who are seeking competitive opportunities. The lesson from the kaisha is that these attitudes are costly and inefficient, that technological arrogance is an expensive luxury, and that technological complacency is an unwarranted weakness.

The single overriding characteristic of the kaisha is their unrelenting focus on competitive position. They constantly search for growth, driven by the economics of relatively high fixed costs and the dynamics of their system of labor relations. The result is a preoccupation with market share and competitive position in contrast to the Western firm's return-on-investment objective. Leading market share will provide high margins in time, which in turn makes possible investment in still another growth area, and still another drive for leading share. The Western firm's preoccupation with current profits can be a devastating weakness when competing with a market-share-preoccupied competitor. That competitor takes a leading share, and in time the profit position reverses.

Consistent with their corporate objective of increasing market share, the kaisha do their planning in competitive-system terms, with a focus on relative competitive position and prospects. This is in contrast to the planning of a great many Western firms, whose plans are often prepared and implemented as though the firm operated in isolation. The single greatest weakness in most U.S. corporate planning is the absence of the "what if" question in their competitive analysis. That is, little or no attention is paid to competitive reactions to changes in capacity, distribution methods, pricing, and the like, or to the possibility that competitors may see very different patterns and opportunities in different parts of the business. This is an omission that the kaisha are most unlikely to make, as they work in competitive-system terms.

One highly visible consequence is that the kaisha are positioned in the home markets of Western competitors who are not positioned in the home market of their Japanese competitors. Such positioning has a real price in terms of current earnings. However, it has a very high earnings payout in terms of long-term competitive position. Too many Western competitors have ceded the emerging "high ground" that fast-growing Asia is to the kaisha.

Perhaps, then, the single most important lesson to be learned from the study of the kaisha is in terms of corporate objectives and corporate planning. For a great many products and companies, the competitive arena has become the world market. World share is the measure of corporate stability and success. The kaisha's preoccupation with competitive position has equipped them well for planning for and dealing with worldwide competition.

PROBING

JONATHAN L. ISAACS, 1985

The single most important word in strategy formulation is *why*.

Asking *why* is the basic act of probing. Searching for root causes takes strategy formulation away from the unconscious repetition of past patterns and mimicry of competitors. Asking why leads to new insights and innovations that sometimes yield important competitive advantages.

Asking why repeatedly is a source of continuous self-renewal, but the act of inquiry itself is an art. It can evoke strong reactions from the questioned. It is only rarely welcomed. It is sometimes met with defensiveness and hostility, on the one hand, or, on the other, the patronizing patience reserved by the knowledgeable for the uninformed.

To ask why—and why not—about basics is to violate the social convention that expertise is to be respected, not challenged. Functional organizations in mature industries have a particular problem in this regard. One risks a lot to challenge the lord in his fiefdom.

Questioning the basics—the assumptions that "knowledgeable" people don't question—is disruptive. Probing slows things down, but often to good effect. It can yield revolutionary new thoughts in quite unexpected places.

Few new thoughts have been as revolutionary as the so-called Japanese manufacturing technique. Toyota was a leader in its development, and over more than 20 years slowly learned to turn upside down the most basic assumptions about how manufacturing must be conceived and organized. Central to this rethinking was tireless probing. In his book on the Toyota production system, Taiichi Ohno, vice president of manufacturing for Toyota, cites the practice of "the five whys." He gives an example of how asking "why" five times (or more) led him through all the explanations to find the most important root cause.

CAN YOU REPEAT "WHY" FIVE TIMES?*

It's easy to say, but difficult to practice.

Suppose a machine stopped functioning.

* Source: *Toyota Seisan Hoshiki—Datsu-Kibo no Keiyei o Mezashite* (*Toyota Production System—Aiming at an Off-Scale Management*) by Taiichi Ohno, published by Diamond Inc., Tokyo. May 25, 1978.

1. *"Why did the machine stop functioning?"*

"There was an overload, and the fuse blew."

2. *"Why was there an overload?"*

"It was because lubrication of the bearing was not sufficient."

3. *"Why was the lubrication not sufficient?"*

"Because the lubrication pump was not pumping sufficiently."

4. *"Why was it not pumping sufficiently?"*

"The shaft of the pump was worn, and it was rattling."

5. *"Why was the shaft worn out?"*

"There was no strainer attached, and this caused metal scrap to get in."

To have stopped anywhere along the way would have ended the search before the root cause was found. To probe to the limits is to simplify the problem to its essentials and solve one problem rather than five.

To pursue such probing takes a special, strongly motivated person, unless one makes it the norm for the organization. Asking why five times is easy to say, but hard to do. It challenges people's knowledge and even self-respect. It can call into question their diligence and the basis of their expertise. It requires fresh thinking on all sides. Yet it's so basic to learning, to seeing new things from the familiar. In the early nineteenth century, doctors routinely went, without washing, from autopsies to the treatment of patients—with disastrous results. Ignaz Semmelweis is the man who first hypothesized the basic relationship and proposed and tested a change to clean hands—yet in his own time he had to struggle with his peers because he questioned the accepted practice.

Probing Takes Us beyond Data Analysis

Good strategy depends critically on knowing the root causes. Finding them is often a task beyond quantitative analysis. One must look to broader frames of reference and bring basic judgment and common sense to bear. Probing—asking why—is the often intuitive search for the logic that heavy data analysis can miss or bury.

Asking why is a qualitative act. It is different from quantitative analysis, but the one gains power from the other. It propels analysis forward by raising new questions to be subjected to rigorous analysis. It takes us beyond the numbers to new answers, new solutions, and new opportunities. Quantitative analysis should not become both the means and the end.

Asking why can raise the questions that are fundamental, but not necessarily answerable through rigorous analysis itself. These are the basic questions of leadership and common sense. They are the search for "the point." For example:

- Why do we continue in this business?
- Why should anyone buy this product?
- What will prevent competitors from matching us? What will we do then?
- Why are we making so much money? Why won't it eventually come to an end? What must we do now to prepare for or moderate that change?

These sorts of probes search for the bedrock reasons for value and advantages to test how enduring they may be. They ask whether the shape and character of the business and its strategy make sense.

Asking why five times is easy in concept, but harder in practice. It can be very rewarding. Why not do it?

CREATIVE ANALYSIS

ANTHONY W. MILES, 1987

We think of successful entrepreneurs—those who have not only started a business, but steered it successfully through the shoals of expansion—as people primarily gifted with remarkable enterprise and get-up-and-go. Surprisingly, though, classic entrepreneurs are as characterized by a high order of creative analytical ability as they are by dynamism.

Entrepreneurs have tremendous drive and energy. They are endlessly creative and imaginative about their business and its opportunities. They have strong people skills, and they know their operations inside and out. They know their competitors so well they can anticipate, outguess, and outsmart them consistently. They at once respond to and lead their customers, with whom they spend a lot of time. And they are constantly analyzing and reanalyzing the business—although their intense familiarity with it, and their depth of experience, are such that much of this goes on inside their heads or on the backs of envelopes.

They would probably be surprised to be told they were superb analysts. Yet without a tremendous command of the details and of the relationships within the details, and an unusual if not unique insight into the meaning of the details, they would not have been so successful for so long.

The power of creative analysis usually is not made much of when the virtues of successful entrepreneurship are being extolled. It is masked by terms like *savvy* or *street-smart* or *feel for the business*. It is, however, central. If a primary goal for companies in our time is to recapture as far as possible the instincts and abilities of the entrepreneur on a larger scale—and it should be—then developing powerful creative analytical skills must be close to the top of the agenda.

Analysis slid into some disfavor in much of the business world a few years ago. "Analysis paralysis" was a catchy tag used to describe obsessive and pedestrian staff work, the indiscriminate regurgitation of information by mainframes, and the use of a ready delaying tactic by bureaucracies reluctant to face and make decisions. There had been a period in which too many managers saw numbers as all of reality, rather than as an illumination of reality.

The reaction was to stress immediate experience, face-to-face motivation, direct involvement in operations, and time in the field with customers—no question a necessary and beneficial shift. But as often seems to be the case, this risks becoming its own overexploited panacea. Numbers may make nothing happen, but action for its own sake can quickly become perilous. Many senior executives have been saying for some time that things have gone too far, that the reaction to excessive abstraction has become an excuse in their organizations for not thinking very thoroughly at all. Analysis—efficient, directed, incisive—is definitely back in fashion.

What distinguishes this analysis is that it feeds directly off an imaginative interpretation of experience and feeds directly back into more effective action. Like the most fruitful scientific research (as great scientists describe the experience), it requires excellent notions of what might be revealed before the analysis begins, expects and quickly recognizes better ideas while it is proceeding, foresees the profound practical consequences of what is being revealed as this happens, and is enthusiastic about exploiting the possibilities.

This is the creative analytical process of the outstanding entrepreneur. It is the right and left sides of the brain in harness, thinker and doer in one. In a large organization, it comes with close-knit teams of first-class thinkers and first-class doers.

Both groups are in short supply.

THE SEDUCTION OF REDUCTIONIST THINKING

JEANIE DUCK, 1992

There's hardly a company today that isn't grappling with the difficulty of change. The problem isn't so much figuring out what to change—everyone knows that business has to become faster and better—it's how to get from here to there. Unfortunately, the approach to managing change that seems most reasonable and least arduous also turns out to be wrong.

For example, one general manager of a $500 million business unit took the seemingly rational approach and came up empty. He summed up his experience this way: "We tackled the change process the same way we would approach any other project: divide it up into specific tasks to be executed by the appropriate functional heads and put it together at the end. We monitored the various pieces as we went along, and it seemed everything was pretty much on target. But as we got closer to the goal, everything started to unravel. We were worse off than when we had started and everyone was demoralized."

What went wrong? The problem, as is often the case, was the seduction of reductionist thinking.

Reductionist thinking teaches managers how to respond to complex problems: break them down into simple parts and then attack them separately. It's a method that works fine for solving problems of algebra; it even worked in the early days of industrialization, as Adam Smith demonstrated with his pin factory and Frederick Winslow Taylor illustrated with his pig-iron workers. But it doesn't work very well in complex organizations where the whole really is greater than the sum of its parts.

A reductionist approach reduces a change process to a nice, neat checklist of tasks. But it doesn't account for how the separate pieces fit together or how they should go on fitting together in the future. It mistakenly treats change as a series of isolated episodic events—not as the continuously evolving process that change really is. Too many managers approach the change process as if it were a series of stepping-stones to negotiate across a rushing river. If they can only get across without slipping, they tell themselves, they'll be home free. In fact, change is more like the river—it keeps coming and it doesn't stop. The only answer that will work is to jump in and learn to swim.

So if the reductionist approach doesn't work for managing the change process, why do so many organizations persist in following it? What makes it so seductive? There are a number of reasons. First, it appears to do away with the ambiguity and complexity that are implicit in change. Managers can reassure themselves: "If everyone will just concentrate on improving his or her own piece of the problem, we'll have 100 percent improvement." Second, it allows managers to spread responsibility around, thereby creating the sense that a lot of organizational effort is going into the process. And third, since the checklist does contain items that will actually help, legitimate improvements do occur—although they're often not profound or long-lasting.

But the strongest appeal of the reductionist approach is that it plays into an all-too-common response to change: skepticism. It provides a rationale for failure, an easy out. If results don't materialize, it's because someone failed to execute his or her part of the formula: "Corporate wouldn't let us guarantee jobs and that was one of the required steps." If it's someone else's fault, you're off the hook. But if the fault is in the formula, or even more profoundly, in the whole approach to change, then you've got to go back to the drawing board.

In that naive belief in the simplicity and surety of a formula, the change process runs aground. People become wedded to their separate tasks and ignore the overall goal. When change is continuous and complex, like the river instead of the stones across it, managers need to focus on the dynamics of the system, not the checklist. That means making sure not just that tasks get done, but when and how they get done and how the performance affects everything else in the system. In a large company the process is too extensive for one person to keep track of and too complex to be delegated in pieces. It calls for the full attention of a dedicated cross-functional team. It requires fast feedback loops that permit the team to monitor what's working and what's not. And when something isn't working, the team has to have the flexibility and imagination to make the necessary adjustments, rather than adhering blindly to a checklist or a "foolproof" formula.

Here's how a major high-tech equipment manufacturer describes learning this lesson:

A few years ago when we reorganized to streamline our interface with customers, each vice president was in charge of the changes in his area. We had come up with a radical new design to drive synergies, but each VP listened only to his part of the organization and then narrowed it to suit his management purposes. By the time implementation was done, the changes weren't radical and the necessary synergies couldn't occur. The VPs lost touch with each other and the compelling rationale of the original idea.

We learned that our piece-parts formula didn't work. In fact, we were dealing with a dynamic system and we had to manage the system. We knew that making just one person responsible for the whole thing would limit the buy-in of others, while a large team would be unwieldy and spread ownership too thin. The answer for us was to create a small "breakthrough" team consisting of the heads of our different functions: marketing, sales, R&D, and manufacturing.

Along with establishing the breakthrough team, this CEO also created incentives that encouraged a radical change in the team members' points of view. They not only looked down the stovepipes of their own separate functions, they also worked together across functions. With their new horizontal perspective, the managers could see what had previously been hidden: a no-man's land between functions where the change process got derailed. The team was able to spot problems in communication, learning, and performance between and within functions and make the necessary adjustments to keep the process moving in a productive and constructive direction.

In most large companies, change is a complex, constantly evolving process that requires constantly evolving solutions. It's natural to want to simplify a complex problem in order to solve it—that is the seduction of reductionist thinking. But when the simplification turns the dynamic problem into a static one, you no longer have an accurate picture of the problem—and therefore your solution can't possibly work. A checklist, after all, is only a simple solution for a simple problem.

The right approach is to accept the complexity of change and to manage accordingly. A dedicated and empowered breakthrough team can manage the company's momentum as it enters the swirling waters of change and ensure that it is moving with the current, not just treading water.

PART FIVE

Social Commentary

AMONG THE MANY *Perspectives* that Bruce Henderson wrote are a set that consider the motivations and effects of various U.S. social and economic policies. All of these were written in the 1970s and address public policy and the harsh economic realities of the time.

Inefficiency drove Bruce crazy, as much in the public sphere as in the corporation. He believed that rules analogous to those making for efficient and successful businesses could be applied to macroeconomic issues—and that by pointing out the opportunities to do so, he could contribute to the betterment of society. A classic was his 1973 piece on U.S. energy policies and their likely impact on supply, which turned out, sadly, to be prophetic. The most direct application of his business theories was to antitrust policy, which he believed to be deeply anticompetitive, and he extended this line of thinking to tax and trade policies. He wrote prolifically and originally on inflation, bringing fresh insight to its causes and consequences.

Over the years, Bruce wrote more than 20 *Perspectives* that can be categorized as social commentary. Their contents are highly personal—

they reflect Bruce's character and beliefs, and not necessarily the views of The Boston Consulting Group. We have chosen one on each of his favorite topics for inclusion here. In addition, there is a more recent piece on health care policy, a reflection of BCG's intention to continue to make our voice heard on policy issues when we feel we have something useful to contribute.

FAILURE TO COMPETE

BRUCE D. HENDERSON, 1973

The dominant producer in every business should increase his market share steadily. Failure to do so is prima facie evidence of failure to compete.

Cost and market share are inversely related. The highest market share should produce the lowest cost as a result of the experience curve effect. At least part of that superior cost should be passed on to the customer in lower prices or better quality. That in turn should lead to faster growth of the leading competitor.

Failure to gain market share even with superior costs is failure to compete. This failure is also a failure to achieve even lower costs.

Competitors' market shares should be unstable. Low-cost competitors should displace higher-cost competitors. Customers should share the benefits of lower cost with those suppliers who make it possible. Any failure to gain market share even with lower cost is self-evident restraint of trade.

Displacement of high-cost competitors by lower prices benefits the customer. It leads to benign monopoly. No monopoly can be justly accused of exercising monopoly powers if it does not raise prices more than the extent of inflation.

Failure of an industry to concentrate is failure to compete and a failure of the national economy to optimize productivity and reduce inflation.

Public policy note: See your lawyer before gaining market share if you are a leader. What is best for the customer and the country is not necessarily legal.

BRUCE D. HENDERSON, 1973

Natural Gas

Set a ceiling price on natural gas. This discourages exploration and increases use. Keep the prices down in spite of inflation. This amplifies the effect and guarantees a shortage eventually.

Coal

Ban the use of coal with sulfur content. This sharply restricts the supply. Sharply restrict strip mining for cosmetic reasons. This further restricts the supply. Then suddenly impose drastic new safety rules which will substantially cut output from existing mines. Freeze prices so no one can offset cost increase from reduced output or justify further investment.

Atomic Power

Delay construction a matter of years by uncertainty about licensing requirements. Delay operation at full power after construction. Delay start of construction by environmentalist suits.

Oil

With natural gas, coal, and atomic power all severely restricted, that leaves only petroleum. First, grossly increase automotive consumption of gasoline by requiring drastic reductions in engine efficiency because of pollution-related modifications. That alone will ensure a severe shortage of energy. Then ban the use of oil containing sulfur. This severely reduces refining capacity. Put into effect new pollution objectives that make refineries far more expensive. At the same time, introduce great uncertainty into the requirements that must be met. That will virtually stop refinery construction or expansion. Eliminate practically all new refinery sites because of environmental legal delaying tactics. Further curtail refinery investment by making supplies of crude oil very uncertain. Block the use of Alaska North Slope oil by arguments on the cosmetic effects in uninhabited and unreachable regions. Stop the use or search for oil offshore in California because of potential leaks. Slow all offshore operations for environmental reasons. For good measure, hold down the price of gasoline to half that in Europe. This encourages large cars.

To be sure that all of the above is misunderstood by the general public, bring a lawsuit that charges all the largest energy companies with being noncompetitive and therefore causing the energy shortage.

The preceding scenario has actually occurred in the United States. Each and every action described here has been the result of public policy. Each act had laudable objectives. In the aggregate, these actions will prove to be very punishing to the general public for years to come.

Such program management by a private business would justify charges of gross mismanagement. The whole task of management is optimization of value delivered from the resources available. False weighting of values or misallocation of resources are equal failures.

All the ultimate objectives can, in due course, be achieved by coordination, by scheduling, by value/cost optimization, and by resource-allocation priorities. That, however, is what management is.

The object of management is optimization of benefits from the use of the available resources. The objectives of public policy also require management to achieve optimum results. Impulsive, extremist, poorly timed, and uncoordinated actions produce inevitable frustration, waste, and cures that are worse than the disease.

Whom do we blame when mismanagement in public policy is imposed by the Congress and amplified by the judiciary? This kind of mismanagement is occurring at all levels of our government in all areas of public policy.

INFLATION AND INVESTMENT RETURN

Bruce D. Henderson, 1974

Financial growth as a result of inflation requires the same financial funding as physical growth. That is why profit margins must widen in proportion to inflation or business will concentrate in the low-cost producer.

Inadequate profit eventually results in shrinkage of capacity as retained earnings become an inadequate source of funds. The alternatives are decreased dividends, increased debt, or reduced sustainable growth.

All assets of a company except its land must eventually be replaced at inflated levels. This includes working capital as well as depreciable assets. The rollover of fixed assets is delayed by the life of the asset, but the effect is the same on trend. Either debt or net worth must be increased as an offset to inflation.

The eventual effect of increased inflation on business is therefore predictable if profit margins are kept constant.

The first most likely consequence is an increase in the ratio of debt to shareholder net worth. This occurred on a massive scale in the United States between 1966 and 1974. Following such occurrence, dividends must be cut or margins increased or debt/equity ratios continually increased.

Marginal companies with high debt and no dividends begin to fall behind. They cannot finance the growth in assets forced by inflation. Their relative growth starts to decrease. Over time their relative costs become less favorable. Eventually the marginal companies are squeezed out.

The implications for public policy are obvious but unpopular. "Encourage high prices and discourage dividends." By doing so, the government will increase its cash income from corporate profits. The increase in retained earnings will be deflationary, both short term and long term.

For business, the policy implications are equally obvious. Each and every strategic business unit should compound its own assets at a rate in excess of the inflation rate plus industry physical growth. If the promise of the future is less than this, then the business must be controlled to generate cash, rather than managed for profit. It is a cash trap. Delay in liquidation is a compounding loss.

For the investor, the warning is clear. Historic growth rates and competitive relationships are misleading. A comparative evaluation can be made by subtracting the actual inflation rate from the actual reported earnings as a percentage of net worth.

Higher inflation will slow real growth. It will increase effective tax take compared to shareholders' receipts. It will shake out marginal competitors and concentrate business. Yet with all of its undesirable side effects, increased inflation can have consequences that are beneficial to the economy and the consumer as well. For this to happen, business must eliminate its cash traps and stop investing in them. The pressure to do so will be great. Leading profitable companies must fully utilize their potential debt capacity to further increase their competitive advantage. Leverage, for them, can be used to offset inflation as well as increase profit, even at high interest rates.

Inflation can force many successful companies to do what they should have done for their own benefit and their customers' benefit under normal competition.

CONFLICTING TAX OBJECTIVES

BRUCE D. HENDERSON, 1975

Taxes raise money to finance government spending. That is obvious. Taxes also redistribute income and control the creation of wealth. This may be the more important consequence.

The universal worldwide drive toward leveling of personal consumption by use of taxes has created layer on layer of taxes on income and wealth as well as on the basic flow of commerce itself.

Such tax practices do raise revenue and they do reduce the after-tax income of those who are the most productive. But such policies may substantially curtail productivity and leave the average man much worse off than he needs to be.

It is possible to encourage capital formation, capital investment, and the creation of wealth and to increase productivity by the direction of tax policy. It is possible to redistribute the power to consume and at the same time to limit that power as much as desired. Someone must own all the wealth of every nation. Ownership of productive wealth confers no real benefit except future security until it provides an opportunity to consume. A progressive income tax for individuals can be restrictive enough to put any desired limit on the ability to consume, if that tax is based on consumption instead of income itself.

Capital can be left untaxed and protected as long as it is productively employed. To do this, several changes in tax policy would be very healthy.

- Corporations should not be taxed at all. They are only surrogates for individuals, not the ultimate consumer. Tax the consumer, not the producer.

- If corporations are to be taxed at all, then tax the dividends, not the paper profits of reported earnings and the capital still employed productively in the business.

- If dividends are to be taxed (instead of income), then eliminate the double taxation and make the corporate income tax on dividends a direct tax credit for the recipient of the dividend.

- Eliminate capital gains taxes. Instead, credit all net investment as a direct decrease in ordinary taxable income. Likewise, tax all net disinvestment as a direct increase in ordinary taxable income.

- Eliminate direct estate taxes and death duties. Instead, make all benefits received as legacies or gifts ordinary income in the year actually realized and disinvested.

These rather unorthodox proposals need not reduce tax receipts at all. The progressive personal income tax can be increased as necessary to equate tax revenues.

Those who provide capital must defer consumption to make the capital formation possible. Those who use capital must have a return above the cost of capital to justify its use. Many tax laws are extremely destructive to both capital formation and capital use.

- Any tax that reduces the return on capital to the supplier of capital reduces the supply of capital and increases its cost.

- Any tax that reduces the return on capital reduces the demand for capital and raises the effective cost of production of products and services.

Taxes that reduce both supply and demand for capital while raising the cost of capital are truly self-defeating and punishing beyond measure to the general public. This is not necessary.

High productivity requires high capital investment. Anything that produces a wider differential between the payoff to the supplier of capital and the return to the user of capital inhibits the formation of capital as well as its use. Taxes should be levied when, and only when, individuals disinvest in order to consume. Capital still at work should not be taxed at all. Our taxes could be made both to increase average income and to level actual consumption by individuals.

BRUCE D. HENDERSON, 1978

Dumping should be encouraged. It is a gift from the nation that provides the products. Dumping reduces inflation for the buyer. It permits the same money to buy more. But dumping is never intended to be a gift. It is, in fact, a realistic and often superior business strategy.

No one ever invested in added capacity in order to sell more output below cost. Therefore, dumping occurs only when the buyer gets a lower price and the seller makes more profit on the same transaction.

Dumping may be the sale of temporary excess capacity at marginal cost. Such overcapacity can exist only temporarily except in dying industries. Consequently, supplies will inherently be intermittent. Available quantities will inevitably be limited. Such spot sales can be made only in markets where prices are not permitted to respond to the normal forces of supply and demand for some reason.

Dumping can continue forever and be profitable to the seller if the seller is the lowest-cost producer. It is immaterial and irrelevant that the selling price in some markets may be lower than it is in the country of origin. The lowest-cost producer's prices should be set to meet and better the local competition. Similar segmentation pricing is the basis for competition in the whole universe of business, from fashion goods to airline fares to automotive options.

Dumping can be a deliberate investment to buy market share and reduce future costs. It should be done wherever it will accomplish that purpose sufficiently well. Such investments in the future are the basis for lower prices in the future as well as the present. Every product, every business, and every industry requires ever increasing investment until its growth slows. Rare indeed is the business that generates more cash internally than its reinvestment rate as long as financial growth continues. Investment in higher market share and lower cost may be a prerequisite for future competitive capability. The consumer is always the beneficiary. That competitor who misjudges the return on the investment in penetration pricing subsidizes the consumer with his own losses.

The principal victims of dumping are those competitors who attempt to stabilize price levels instead of responding to marketplace supply and demand. Such artificially stabilized prices avoid the extremes in highs and lows inherent in market-sensitive commodities. However, stabilized prices lead to cyclical shortages and periodic allocations. They require prices high enough to support and protect the inefficient competitors. On average, they make both prices and costs higher then they otherwise would be. Such pricing policies by any industry are a major handicap, perhaps a fatal handicap, to effective competition in products with international markets.

The appropriate response to dumping is to respond in kind. Sell at marginal cost into the markets of competitors who are dumping into your markets. The dumping will stop! If other things are equal, the low-cost competitor will survive and prosper regardless of the country of origin. However, this kind of competition requires national government support in equalizing any barriers to trade. Effective competition of this kind also requires a recognition and acceptance of the inherent price volatility of a free marketplace.

The world must be a free marketplace without artificial barriers if we are to achieve our potential for productivity. The alternatives are not attractive. Increasing government regulation and intervention into the marketplace has always led to nationalization of the industry in the past. Perhaps that is inevitable. But nationalized industries seem to lead to major degradation of productivity based on the record of most past experience.

The existence of dumping as a political issue is a measure of the barriers to world trade and the extent to which government regulation and intervention prevent effective competition.

ADVERSARIES OR PARTNERS?

BRUCE D. HENDERSON, 1983

The labor wars must end. Hostile confrontation between members of the same organization is a barbaric legacy of a past that we should put behind us. It is a fundamental defect in Western productivity. A company divided against itself cannot compete.

The Japanese are teaching the West a humiliating object lesson. One by one the Japanese have entered industries in which the United States has led the world. Now Japan is becoming the new world leader in these industries. It is doing this without significant resources or advantages except the ability of its people to cooperate. The time is overdue for the West to reexamine its fundamental assumptions about business cooperation and competition. The starting point should be cooperation, coordination, and teamwork within the firm.

Philosophy is not a substitute for action. The action must come after rethinking:

- The labor/management hostility

- The logic of labor monopolies, industrywide bargaining, and the social sanctity of labor negotiation by threat, strike, and interfamily war

- The lifetime role and mutual commitment of employers and employees in an increasingly specialized society

- The role of the face-to-face group and its function in our society

The debilitating "English disease" of labor strife is the bitter fruit of the Industrial Revolution. In the beginning the need for production equipment and machinery required factories. But factories broke down the intimate and personal communication of the farm families, the tradesmen, and the artisan guilds. The factory substituted the faceless indifference and jostle of a crowded city. The small groups that formed within the factory banded together to control the hostile, prisonlike environment within which they struggled. The factory itself became the enemy.

The upper Clyde River near Glasgow was once the greatest shipbuilding complex in the world. Eventually, small groups of organized craft unions found that by respecting one another's picket lines each in turn could hold for ransom every ship under construction. Cooperation led to suicidal destruction.

In Japan, cooperation led to the opposite result. The production of the ship became the common cause, rather than the welfare of the small group at the expense of the common purpose. Each worker, to the limit of his ability, did whatever was needed most at a given time. Japan became the world's dominant shipbuilder.

During World War II, the British rose to the heights of courage, heroism, and cooperation. Against impossible odds, they fought, survived, and won against the enemy. But with the return of peace, the cooperation ended and the English disease slowly reduced the United Kingdom from the greatest of the industrial powers to the most stagnant.

Perhaps Japan was favored by skipping the Industrial Revolution and going almost directly from feudal baronies to a modern industrial society. For Japan the process from world isolation to world leader took less than a hundred years.

Constraints on Productivity

Deep in the heart of our self-inflicted constraint on productivity is the myth that we must decrease our individual productivity in order to create additional jobs so more people can share an unchanged total net output. Every society should take care of its own to the best of its abilities, regardless of the capabilities of its individual members. But anything in a culture that suppresses the productivity of any individual or limits achievement of any individual's potential is destructive of the common good.

Where industrywide labor-bargaining monopolies are supported by law, competition between corporations based on productivity is suppressed. The whole industry suffers. Where competition is worldwide, as it is in steel and automobiles, the whole industry withers whenever labor acts as a monopolist. Competitively, the result is that such an industry cannot supply value equivalent to that of foreigners.

Parasitic work practices that kill the host are not uncommon. Railroad work rules required a fireman for an engine with no fire. Railroad work rules limited the mileage of a train crew per day no matter how fast or steadily the train ran. These practices were major contributors to the decline and decay of the railroads. Strikes by such public services hold the entire economy for ransom regardless of the damage done to innocent third parties.

Corporations have prospered and grown to towering heights of achievement, then sunk into obscurity and been forgotten. All of them started with small groups with extensive face-to-face exchange and consensus on goals and values. All prospered as extended families with shared objectives and a common cause. All failed when they became pitted against themselves internally instead of coordinating and cooperating to achieve common purposes.

Whatever the services of organized labor have been in the past, its role as an adversary is self-defeating. Its future role must be that of communicator. Whatever the perceived role of management has been in the past, its future role must be as internal coordinator and external interface. All employees of a corporation, like the crew and passengers of a ship, have a common destination.

The Social Commitment

The payments and benefits of a company to its employees are typically many times greater than those to its shareholders. For that reason, employees are the true beneficiaries of a corporation's prosperity. But the changes in benefits to employees that are practical, or possible, are trivial unless matched by a change in productivity per employee when compared to the company's competition.

The ever greater specialization inherently required for increased productivity means that labor skills are not ordinarily transferable or fungible without very high cost. The labor market becomes increasingly thin and inefficient. The relationship eventually represents mutual dependency.

The long-term services of any organization's employees represent a substantial investment by both the individual employee and the organization. The knowledge, skills, background, organizational fit, and teamwork interactions are often not transferable to another organization. Even if they are transferable in some measure, they have far less value. These capabilities represent a major investment on the part of both the organization and the employee.

That investment is the true basis for the Japanese commitment to lifetime employment. That commitment must represent a social contract. The obligation of the employee to the firm can be no stronger than the obligation of the firm to the employee. For it to be effective, it must be part of the firm's culture, not public law.

The Japanese have set a standard of achievement and internal integrity others cannot match unless they rise above their past cultures and make common cause. Non-Japanese can outperform their competitors by learning from the Japanese just as the Japanese learned from Westerners. The Japanese did not copy Western practices. Instead they learned from us, adapted our practices to their own culture, and then began to outperform us. We can do the same, perhaps even better.

A whole new culture must be built in Western business if it is to realize its potential. True cooperation is based on mutual commitment. True commitment is based on mutual purpose, mutual evaluation, and mutual trust. For that to be possible, the corporate purposes and the implicit responsibilities of each member of the organization must constantly be reaffirmed. For that to happen, management must be more than coordinator; it must be leadership. In the future this probably means that:

- Industrial organizations will move steadily toward smaller and smaller separate factories of 500 or fewer employees with work teams of 10 to 25 members.

- Labor unions will become primarily company unions in those companies that survive.

- Work rules will become a relic of the past. Instead, each member of the team will do whatever is most valuable.

- Permanent employment will come after an extended courtship that leads to long-term mutual commitment and responsibility to the members in an extended family.

- Productivity will become a measure of corporate citizenship and status.

- Corporate stature will be measured by the corporation's ability to provide personal security to its employees, outperform its competitors, and support the norms of its society and culture while repaying its moral obligation to those who make its existence possible.

These things can all be done. They are a matter of will, morality, energy, and culture. Those who can and do will be the survivors. Failure to achieve them in real time is to invite mutually assured destruction.

THE PROMISE OF DISEASE MANAGEMENT*

JOSHUA GRAY AND PETER LAWYER, 1995

Disease management is an approach to patient care that coordinates resources across the entire health care delivery system and throughout the life cycle of a disease. Traditional approaches focus mainly on discrete medical episodes, attempting to minimize the expense of individual cost components, including hospitalization, physician services, and pharmaceuticals. Disease management takes a more systemic approach, focusing on the patient with a disease as the relevant unit of management, with an emphasis on quality as well as cost. Early experience sug-

---

* Excerpted from "The Promise of Disease Management," a booklet published by The Boston Consulting Group in 1995.

gests that disease management can lead to demonstrably better outcomes, as measured by clinical results, patient satisfaction, and cost.

The Elements of Disease Management

The three primary elements of disease management are:

- A *knowledge base* that quantifies the economic structure of the disease and describes care guidelines (what care should be provided,
  by whom, and in what setting) for discrete patient segments

- A *delivery system* of health care professionals and organizations,
  closely coordinating to provide care throughout the course of a
  disease, breaking down traditional boundaries between medical
  specialties and institutions

- A *continuous improvement process* that measures clinical behavior,
  refines treatment standards, and improves the quality of care provided

From a competitive perspective, disease management creates system
value and allows the company successfully coordinating the care—the
disease manager—to capture a share of the value created.

Many industry players have high expectations for disease management. They believe that focusing on patients grouped by their common
medical conditions will control costs, improve clinical outcomes, and
create system value. Can disease management live up to these objectives? Can organizations generate profits and improve their competitive
position by pursuing disease management? As with any new direction,
the potential benefits will sometimes be exaggerated. Early evidence
clearly reveals, however, that the approach shows great promise for
reduced costs and better health care.

A Comparison with the Traditional Approach

When health care professionals first hear of disease management, typical reactions are, "How is that different from other health care techniques?" or "We already do that." Its unique qualities become clearer
when disease management is compared with component management—the primary traditional approach to managing health care
costs.

In component management, the individual health care transaction—
a doctor's visit or a procedure—is viewed as the relevant unit of cost.
The treatment cycle's various transactions and component categories

are analyzed to establish statistical norms for unit cost and frequency in a population or a provider's practice. Incentives and penalties encourage compliance with the norms, thereby reducing some of the extreme practices, such as nonessential operations, excessive tests, and too many pharmaceuticals. The unit cost of each component is then driven as low as possible through aggressive contracting, utilization management, case management, and other cost control techniques.

Component management provided one of the first tools to address the relentless growth of health care costs. Its limitations, however, became evident in the late 1980s, as component management successes were relatively meager and medical costs continued to outpace inflation. Component management's process and limitations are summarized in the figure on the next page.

The distinction between disease management and component management is critical from a competitive perspective. Component management can be a powerful approach in the first phase of cost and quality management. For example, using mostly component management techniques, some physician groups in Southern California have driven down hospital utilization dramatically. Successful systems have used a combination of utilization profiling and powerful financial incentives, especially capitation. Clearly, many health systems can become more efficient using these conventional techniques, but they can only progress so far.

The road map for component management is well articulated, and a significant portion of the value it can create has already been captured by progressive organizations. Building competitive advantage in the future will require a more fundamental redesign of care than is possible with a component-based approach.

Several industry and technology trends have helped identify disease management as the way to move beyond component management. Total quality management (TQM), originally developed in manufacturing settings, increasingly is being applied with great benefit to health care. The realization that key business processes can be mapped and measured, best practices identified, and variation reduced has provided major insights in the emergence of disease management. Improved measurement techniques and more flexible information technology systems have helped physicians and health managers make substantial contributions to outcomes research. In addition, the emergence of integrated delivery vehicles, such as physician-hospital organizations, has provided an appropriate structure and incentives to encourage disease management. Finally, increasing cost pressure on payers and public frustration with the health care system have increased organizational willingness to try new approaches.

Disease Management Advantages

In disease management, the unit of analysis is a patient with a disease, not an individual transaction. The most important segments are groups of patients with the same disease. This perspective gives disease management several advantages over component management.

1. Disease management provides a clean-sheet, systemic view of health care management that can fundamentally change practitioners' perspectives. Component management is incremental. It assumes that the overall structure of health care is directionally correct, but the mix of individual components of care may need adjustment.

2. Disease management approaches unit cost and use of products and services according to clinical need and systemwide economic impact, while component management attempts to decrease cost and use without regard to underlying clinical drivers. Component

Traditional Cost Control Efforts Focused on Components

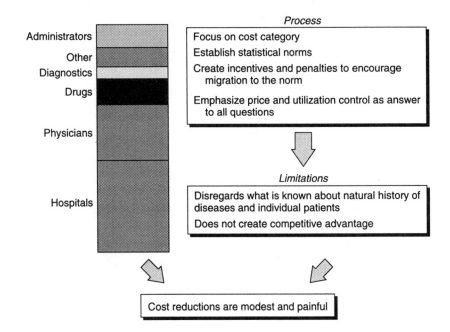

managers, for example, may take aim at the aggregate cost of drugs and specialist consultations for all asthma patients. Contrast that with a disease manager, who may initially invest in higher drug and specialist cost for a severely ill segment of asthmatics in order to reduce downstream emergency room and hospital costs.

3. Disease managers work closely with physicians to develop more creative and effective solutions with a higher level of buy-in. Component management typically employs a confrontational approach, policing physician and hospital care.

4. Disease management emphasizes the optimal deployment of resources, ensuring that patients receive the care they need, in the most appropriate setting, from the right physician or practitioner. It does so with continuous self-correction. A disease management approach may implement a specialized diabetes program to monitor brittle patients and educate them so they can self-manage elements of their treatment, such as diet and insulin injections. Component management typically does not address the issue of how an overall health system should be designed and managed, nor is it a learning system.

Disease management, summarized in the figure on the next page, goes deeper and forces more fundamental rethinking than component management, with potentially more enduring results. Traditional tools, such as case management and utilization review, may still be used, but in the context of an overall system approach designed to address the unique economic, clinical, and resource requirements of specific diseases. The tools are not ends in themselves; they are merely building blocks in an overall disease management strategy.

Strategic Roles

For organizations deciding to pursue disease management, there are several strategic options. A health care organization can generate tremendous value if it can effectively coordinate and deploy a group of providers around a specific disease, or if it can help other health care players to do so. The approach to disease management taken by a pharmaceutical company will necessarily vary from that taken by an HMO or a hospital, and even competitors within the same sector will find different success formulas over the coming years. No single approach to disease management is inherently superior.

Next Generation of Managed Care: Organize Care Management by Disease

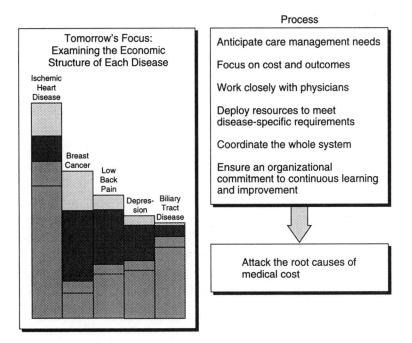

Process

Anticipate care management needs

Focus on cost and outcomes

Work closely with physicians

Deploy resources to meet disease-specific requirements

Coordinate the whole system

Ensure an organizational commitment to continuous learning and improvement

Attack the root causes of medical cost

Broadly speaking, we see three roles for organizations focusing on disease management:

- *Integrated disease manager:* Provides care across the spectrum of diseases.

- *Carve-out disease manager:* Assumes responsibility for providing a range of services for a specific disease.

- *Enabling disease manager:* Provides critical services, products, or information to integrated and carve-out disease managers.

The integrated and carve-out managers typically deal directly with payers, providing full service for either the full range or a limited number of diseases. The enabling manager plays a supporting role, as shown in the figure on the next page, perhaps offering disease guidelines or information technology services to the full-service organizations.

Choosing the best role is a critical strategic challenge that must reflect a realistic assessment of each organization's capabilities. We expect successful players to emerge in each of the three groups outlined above, with many partnerships and hybrids coalescing along the way. The choice of role has significant ramifications for the type of part-ners required and who makes up the competitive set. Depending on the path chosen, some companies may well find themselves competing against customers, suppliers, or other emerging competitors.

Redefining Health Care Success

Many of today's leading health care companies are embracing disease management. They are investing heavily to build the capabilities and infrastructure required to compete in this evolving area. We believe dis-ease management will be a potent approach to building competitive advantage, but not all companies will succeed. Although it is hard to argue with the concepts underpinning disease management, its appli-cation presents an enormous challenge. For those that succeed, how-ever, the reward will be a sustainable competitive advantage built on superior outcomes. Disease management will widen the gap between industry leaders and laggards, and accelerate industry consolidation.

Excelling in disease management often requires a broader array of capabilities than individual organizations can marshal. Consequently, we believe that much of the activity in disease management over the

Strategic Roles of Disease Management

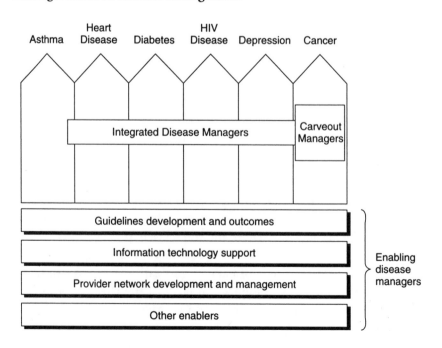

next several years will focus on partnering arrangements. The potential partners with unique expertise or structural position will be courted first, offering early movers a substantial advantage if they choose correctly and implement effectively.

The challenge of assessing prospective partners, negotiating arrangements, and ultimately integrating elements of the health care delivery system is likely to consume tremendous management time and attention. Although partnerships will clearly be part of the solution for many players, we expect many companies to overestimate the value their partners bring to the table and to underestimate the resources required to capture the ultimate opportunity.

Disease management implementation presents a major communications challenge. The customers for disease management services will have a great deal to gain, but they will not necessarily understand the concept, nor will they automatically attribute improvements to disease management. Disease managers must forge links with patients and payers. The disease management approach must be made user-friendly and understandable. This becomes especially important when patient education and behavioral commitment are central to successful treatment. By drawing patients into the process, a disease manager not only motivates them to become informed and rational consumers of care, but also creates a competitive advantage by building a consumer franchise.

The stakes are high. Many organizations attempting disease management will fail because of insufficient analytical insight or a lack of financial, informational, or managerial resources to bring their insights to market. Those that succeed will be positioned to assume market leadership in the increasingly integrated health care industry of the future.

Index